INTERMEDIATE MOISTURE FOODS

An industry–university co-operation Symposium organised
under the auspices of the National College of Food Technology,
University of Reading

THE SYMPOSIUM COMMITTEE

GORDON G. BIRCH, B.Sc., Ph.D., F.R.I.C., M.R.S.H., F.C.S.
Reader at National College of Food Technology, Reading University,
Weybridge, Surrey.

R. DAVIES, B.Sc., S.M., Ph.D.
Senior Lecturer at National College of Food Technology, Reading
University, Weybridge, Surrey.

J. A. FORD, B.A. (Oxon.)
Secretary at National College of Food Technology, Reading University,
Weybridge, Surrey.

G. W. GOULD, B.Sc., M.Sc., Ph.D.
Unilever Research, Colworth/Welwyn Laboratory, Unilever Ltd, Colworth
House, Sharnbrook, Bedford.

K. J. PARKER, M.A., D.Phil. (Oxon.)
General Manager, Tate & Lyle Ltd, Group Research and Development,
Philip Lyle Memorial Research Laboratory, Reading University, PO Box
68, Reading, Berks.

A. J. REYNOLDS, B.Sc., M.I.Biol.
National College of Food Technology, Reading University, Weybridge,
Surrey.

E. J. ROLFE, B.Sc., M.Chem.A., F.R.I.C., F.I.F.S.T.
Principal, National College of Food Technology, Reading University,
Weybridge, Surrey.

Mrs B. A. SHORE
National College of Food Technology, Reading University, Weybridge,
Surrey.

R. H. TILBURY, B.Sc., Ph.D.
Tate & Lyle Ltd, Philip Lyle Memorial Research Laboratory, Reading
University, PO Box 68, Reading, Berks.

INTERMEDIATE MOISTURE FOODS

Edited by

R. DAVIES, G. G. BIRCH
and K. J. PARKER

APPLIED SCIENCE PUBLISHERS LTD

LONDON

APPLIED SCIENCE PUBLISHERS LTD
RIPPLE ROAD, BARKING, ESSEX, ENGLAND

ISBN: 0 85334 702 6

WITH 54 TABLES AND 56 ILLUSTRATIONS

© APPLIED SCIENCE PUBLISHERS LTD 1976

Printed in Great Britain by Galliard (Printers) Ltd Great Yarmouth

List of Contributors

J. Y. ALLISON
Department of Food Science and Nutrition, University of Strathclyde, 131 Albion Street, Glasgow G1 1SD, Scotland.

D. BARKER
Applied Research Department, Pedigree Petfoods Ltd, Melton Mowbray, Leicestershire LE13 1BB, England.

I. E. BURROWS
Applied Research Department, Pedigree Petfoods Ltd, Melton Mowbray, Leicestershire LE13 1BB, England.

H. A. A. CLAPPERTON
Department of Food Science and Nutrition, University of Strathclyde, 131 Albion Street, Glasgow G1 1SD, Scotland.

J. E. L. CORRY
The Metropolitan Police Forensic Science Laboratory, 109 Lambeth Road, London SE1 7LP, England.

R. DAVIES
National College of Food Technology, St George's Avenue, Weybridge, Surrey KT13 0DE, England.

R. DUCKWORTH
Department of Food Science and Nutrition, University of Strathclyde, 131 Albion Street, Glasgow G1 1SD, Scotland.

v

G. W. GOULD
Unilever Research, Colworth/Welwyn Laboratory, Unilever Ltd, Colworth House, Sharnbrook, Bedford, MK44 1LQ, England.

T. M. HARDMAN
Department of Chemistry, The University, Whiteknights, Reading RG6 2AD, England.

B. JARVIS
Microbiology Section, Leatherhead Food R.A., Randalls Road, Leatherhead, Surrey KT22 7RY, England.

M. KAREL
Department of Nutrition and Food Science, Massachusetts Institute of Technology, Cambridge, Massachusetts 02139, USA.

L. LEISTNER
Institut für Bakteriologie und Histologie, Bundesanstalt für Fleischforschung, 8650 Kulmbach, West Germany.

J. C. MEASURES
Unilever Research, Colworth/Welwyn Laboratory, Unilever Ltd, Colworth House, Sharnbrook, Bedford MK44 1LQ, England.

D. A. A. MOSSEL
Department of Food Microbiology, Faculty of Veterinary Medicine, The University, Leidsweg 65A, Utrecht, The Netherlands.

R. PAWSEY
National College of Food Technology, St George's Avenue, Weybridge, Surrey KT13 0DE, England.

D. S. REID
Unilever Research, Colworth/Welwyn Laboratory, Unilever Ltd, Colworth House, Sharnbrook, Bedford MK44 1LQ, England.

T. A. ROBERTS
Agricultural Research Council, Meat Research Institute, Langford, Bristol BS18 7DY, England.

J. N. ROBSON
Food Division, Marks and Spencer, Michael House, Baker Street, London W1A 1DN, England.

W. RÖDEL
Institut für Bakteriologie und Histologie, Bundesanstalt für Fleischforschung, 8650 Kulmbach, West Germany.

E. J. ROLFE
National College of Food Technology, St George's Avenue, Weybridge, Surrey KT13 0DE, England.

D. A. L. SEILER
Flour Milling and Baking Research Association, Chorleywood, Herts, England.

A. J. SINSKEY
Department of Nutrition and Food Science, Massachusetts Institute of Technology, Cambridge, Massachusetts 02139, USA.

J. L. SMART
Agricultural Research Council, Meat Research Institute, Langford, Bristol BS18 7DY, England.

A. SUGGETT
Unilever Research, Colworth/Welwyn Laboratory, Unilever Ltd, Colworth House, Sharnbrook, Bedford MK44 1LQ, England.

R. TILBURY
Tate & Lyle Ltd, Group Research and Development, Philip Lyle Memorial Research Laboratory, University of Reading, Reading RG6 2BX, England.

J. C. WILLIAMS
Tate & Lyle Ltd, Group Research and Development, Philip Lyle Memorial Research Laboratory, University of Reading, Reading RG6 2BX, England.

Contents

Session II (Chairman: Professor D. A. A. Mossel)

1

A Place for Intermediate Moisture Foods

E. J. ROLFE

*National College of Food Technology,
Weybridge, Surrey*

Urban populations are heavily dependent on processed and preserved foods, nutritious foods that are stable during storage—often for long periods—and can be safely distributed to reach the consumer in good condition. The rapid expansion of the frozen food industry can be explained in such terms, but its success is dependent on a sophisticated system of cold stores and a refrigerated distribution chain.

Dehydrated foods may be stored and distributed using ordinary warehouse and distribution facilities. In addition the abstraction of water from the food reduces weight and bulk and thus offers substantial logistical advantages over other methods of preservation. Dehydration thus has the potential of providing an ideal method of food preservation. However, foodstuffs are usually of complex composition and are often cellular in structure. Unfortunately therefore they do not behave like, for example, sugar or gelatine in a completely reversible manner towards the abstraction and addition of water. Pieces of raw vegetable without any pretreatment and dried in a current of warm air yield a product which refuses to rehydrate into a structure resembling the original material, and when heated in boiling water does not achieve the familiar texture of the cooked vegetable, but remains tough and chewy. This defect is overcome to a large degree by blanching (*i.e.* scalding) the vegetable in hot water or steam before drying. Blanching vastly improves the quality of the dehydrated food by inactivating the enzymes and thus improving the stability of the dried product during storage, and in addition the dehydrated food then rehydrates and cooks to resemble the cooked fresh vegetable.

1

Because of the advantages of debulking and easy storage, great interest was shown towards dehydrated foods by governments during and after the Second World War, and extensive research was supported by them. Many people will remember the Dried Egg Powder and National Dried Milk of those times; products which were inferior to the fresh but very welcome in the absence of alternatives. The Services were asking for dehydrated foods which would remain palatable and nutritious after storage for several years in temperate climates or after storage for about two years under tropical conditions. After such protracted storage periods, dehydrated foods from which sufficient water had been removed to ensure stability against microbial spoilage were observed to have deteriorated due to slow chemical changes occurring between constituents of the food. These deteriorative changes were lumped together under the name 'non-enzymic browning'. However, not only was the product discoloured, but in addition off-flavours developed, the extent of rehydration and reconstitution in water progressively decreased with consequent adverse effects on texture, and there was a loss in nutritive value. Non-enzymic browning was inhibited by many means, removal of sugar—an active component of the browning reaction—from the foodstuff, addition of sulphite and drying to even lower moisture contents. Drying to lower moisture contents unfortunately not only inhibited the non-enzymic browning reactions, but replaced it by another problem, the increased susceptibility of the dried food to oxidation. Under such conditions, during storage carotene in the foodstuff oxidises to β-ionone, so that dried carrots develop an odour of violets, foods containing fats become rancid, even when the fat content is low as in, for example, potato.

Abstraction of water from foods to these low levels removed much of the bound water and in some instances, led to irreversible structural changes in the molecular components and hence caused to a greater or lesser degree textural changes in the product. Foods rich in native proteins were most susceptible to damage, *e.g.* raw meat and fish. It was in the dehydration of foods of animal origin that I spent many years of research and invented the Accelerated Freeze Drying process which minimises texture change to such foods. The products reconstitute almost instantaneously in water, but many suffer from the defect of fragility and require careful packing.

Now instead of seeking stable products through extensive removal of water, interest is being focused on the development of stable products with the removal of the minimum amount of water to prevent microbial spoilage. The bound water will be retained within the food so that structural changes affecting texture will be much reduced or eliminated, and the addition of humectants will permit relatively high moisture levels thus providing 'ready to eat' foods. Considerable stability may also be achieved by removal of lesser amounts of water from the food supplemented by suitable adjustment of pH, addition of antimycotic agents, etc.

The existence of a considerable interest and incentive to research this class of foods—intermediate moisture foods—is evidenced by the attendance at this symposium. This is not a new class of foods, familiar examples are cheese and jam, but with imagination it could provide a wide range of new and interesting foods. The confectioner has excelled in the development of foods with new flavours and textures, marshmallow, nougat, fudge, toffee, chocolate, etc., the list is almost limitless. Perhaps intermediate moisture foods will result in a new proliferation of foods with novel textures, making use of the research in progress on food texture, structure and flavour. The development of dehydration depended on researchers drawn from many disciplines and the study and progress in the development of intermediate moisture foods is similarly dependent. The contributors to this symposium represent relevant disciplines and have applied their knowledge to the study of specific aspects of the subject. Collectively they will present a general picture of the fundamental considerations, together with applications and an appraisal of the present state of the art.

It is a pleasure to have them with us at this Symposium, and a warm welcome is extended to them, and to all participants, particularly those who have travelled far and come from overseas to be here.

2

Technology and Application of New Intermediate Moisture Foods

MARCUS KAREL

*Department of Nutrition and Food Science,
Massachusetts Institute of Technology,
Cambridge, Massachusetts, USA*

ABSTRACT

Intermediate Moisture Foods (IMF) are among the oldest preserved foods of man, but recently there occurred a revival of interest in them. Modern IMF are based on: (1) lowering of water activity through addition of humectants, (2) addition of mycostatic and bacteriostatic agents and (3) incorporation of additional chemicals to improve stability and organoleptic properties. Wide scale application of new IMF for human consumption will require solution of several technical and marketing problems. The experiences of the pet food industry which utilises these foods widely and of the US and USSR space programmes in which some IMF were used may prove useful in solving these problems.

Several current research areas are of importance to future development of IMF, and are reviewed.

(1) Principles for formulation of IMF. *Lowering of water activity through addition of solutes will be facilitated by the development of equations and other techniques which predict water activity resulting from compounding a given composition.*

(2) Search for new humectants and their synergistic combinations. *Presently available humectants are limited in utility by defects in organoleptic properties or by a lack of assured safety. Research is under way to overcome these drawbacks.*

4

(3) Application of antimicrobial additives. *Current research is developing a basis of utilisation of such additives in an effective and safe manner.*

(4) Development of methods for production of IMF. *One of the major approaches to production of IMF is based on the diffusion of humectants into plant- or animal-derived tissues, or into other food structures, such as cheese. Osmotic drying is another related technique in which there is a simultaneous removal of water and incorporation of solutes. Current research is providing a basis for understanding of the diffusional processes occurring in foods during these operations, and this understanding will lead to improved methods for osmotic processing.*

(5) Elucidation of mechanisms and kinetics *of chemical, physical and biological deterioration in storage will allow the improvement of storage stability of IMF, and research in this area is of particular importance to the commercial success of these foods.*

CURRENT STATUS OF INTERMEDIATE MOISTURE FOODS

One of the oldest methods of food preservation is based on lowering of water activity to a level at which growth of micro-organisms is prevented, or greatly reduced. Many of the earliest preserved foods of man were sun-dried to achieve the necessary reduction in water content, or were made by mixing ingredients lowering the water activity, such as salt or sugar, with other food components.

In more modern times, dehydration became an important food preservation technology, and the science and engineering upon which this unit operation is based have undergone a remarkable development. Principles of heat and mass transfer involved in dehydration have been studied on a very sophisticated level, and the chemistry and microbiology of dehydrated foods have been the subject of numerous research studies.[1,2] The scientific basis of formulation of foods through mixing of ingredients to achieve a water activity permitting safe storage is, however, only now being developed.

In the 1960s, a number of developments have led to a renaissance of technology for production of foods with an intermediate moisture content, which have been often referred to as intermediate moisture foods (IMF).[3-5] The modern IMF is a direct descendant of the traditional IMF.

Some examples of traditional intermediate moisture foods are: products which have been dried with no addition of humectants (prunes, apricots, dates, figs, etc.); products to which sugar has been added (candied fruits, soft candies, marshmallows, jams, jelly, honey, pie fillings and syrups); products which have been dried with added salt and sugars (country ham, pemmican); and bakery products such as fruit cakes and certain pie fillings. These traditional foods have moisture contents between 10 and 40% (on a 'wet basis') and range in water activity from 0·65 to 0·9. Table 1 shows the water activity of some of the traditional IMF.

TABLE 1

Water activity of selected traditional IMF

Food	Water activity	Reference
Liverwurst	0·96	6
Salami	0·82–0·85	6
'Landjäger' sausage	0·79	6
Dried fruits	0·72–0·80	7
Jams and jellies	0·82–0·94	7
Honey	0·75	7
Fillings of commercial pastries	0·65–0·71	Author's measurements

The modern IMF experienced the most dramatic growth in the pet food industry. Within very few years, the production of IMF for pets reached the 100 million dollar level in 1969. In 1974, IMF pet foods captured over 40% of the pet food market. IMF for human consumption have potential logistical advantages and these led to programmes to develop new IMF technology sponsored by commercial interests as well as by the US Department of Defense, and the US National Aeronautics and Space Administration. These programmes have resulted in the development of modern IMF production techniques which may be classified as follows:

(1) 'Moist-infusion' in which solid food pieces are soaked and/or cooked in an appropriate solution to result in a final product having the desired water activity (a_w) level.

(2) 'Dry-infusion' in which solid food pieces are first dehydrated, following which they are infused by soaking in a solution containing the desired osmotic agents.

(3) 'Blending' in which the components are weighed, blended, cooked and extruded or otherwise combined to result in a finished product of the desired a_w. Various processing variations are included to produce improved products.

These processing steps include means for: (1) a_w adjustment in the finished product by either dehydration or evaporation, (2) microbiological stabilisation by heating or use of chemical additives, (3) enzymatic deterioration inhibition by blanching, (4) prevention of physical and chemical deterioration by addition of antioxidants, chelators, emulsifiers or stabilisers and (5) inclusion of appropriate nutrients.

IMF have recently been developed along the following technological principles: (1) lowering of water activity by addition of polyhydric alcohols, sugars and/or salt; (2) retardation of microbial growth by addition of antimicrobial and primarily antimycotic agents such as propylene glycol and sorbic acid and (3) improvement of organoleptic properties such as texture and flavour through physical or chemical treatments.

Some recently developed IMF are shown in Table 2.

The Defense Department and the National Aeronautics and Space Administration of the USA have supported development of IMF for military and space rations. Swift's Company produced under US Air Force Contract a number of IMF by the 'dry-infusion' method.[10]

TABLE 2

Characteristics of some recently developed IMF systems

	IMF Catfish[8]	IMF Coconut milk[9]	IMF Cheese[5]
a_w	0·8	0·75–0·8	0·82
Water (%)	26·6	30–35	~25
pH	6·4	7	5·2
Additives	K-sorbate	0·1% sorbic acid	K-sorbate
	P.G.		P.G.
	Sorbitol		NaCl
	Sucrose		
	NaCl		

P.G. = Propylene glycol.

Some IMF which have been made by the 'dry-infusion' method include bite-size, ready-to-eat cubes of: roast beef, roast pork, barbecue beef, barbecue chicken, chicken à la king, beef stew, corned beef, chili with beans, sausage and ham. These products were prepared by freeze-dehydration of the solid ingredients followed by their blending in a low speed mixer and subsequent infusion. The formula for one of these products is shown in Table 3. Each product

TABLE 3

Formula of ready-to-eat intermediate moisture roast beef cubes[10]

Ingredients	% by weight
Beef, cooked, ground, freeze-dried	51·00
Water, distilled	12·00
Water as steam	4·941 5
Glycerol	6·00
Pregelatinised starch	5·00
Gelatin (100 Bloom)	5·00
Non-dairy coffee whitener	3·50
Sorbitol, dry	3·00
Soup and gravy base, beef flavour	2·50
Sucrose	2·00
Salt	2·00
Hydrolysed vegetable protein, beef	2·00
Onions, dehydrated	0·50
Monosodium glutamate	0·25
Sorbic acid	0·20
Ascorbic acid	0·045
Black pepper	0·040
Ribotide	0·020
Citric acid	0·003 5
Total	100·000 0

required specialised infusion techniques in regard to sequence of addition and method of addition of ingredients. In general, it was found that 5–10 % glycerol, about 5 % gelatin and about 3 % sorbitol in the infusion solution and 7–12 % fat in the dry product provided excellent physical binding properties. This formulation also resulted in an acceptable texture and minimum need for sugar with resultant reduction in browning on storage at 38°C. The resulting moisture

TABLE 4

Analysis of example intermediate moisture foods

Cubes	Water content (%)	Average percent salt	pH	Water activity
Roast beef	22·2	3·0	5·75	0·79
Barbecue beef	16·2	2·7	5·05	0·66
Roast pork	22·4	3·6	5·70	0·74
Barbecue chicken	19·7	4·0	5·20	0·70
Chicken à la King	14·9	3·6	5·90	0·61
Beef stew	17·3	3·7	5·80	0·65
Corned beef	16·2	5·4	5·85	0·62
Chili with beans	13·9	2·6	5·65	0·79
Sausage	24·2	4·5	4·90	0·78
Ham	19·9	4·5	5·90	0·72

content and water activities of these products are summarised in Table 4.

The 'blending' technique represents the principal method of production of the economically successful intermediate moisture pet foods. A typical intermediate moisture pet food will contain: chopped meat by-products 30–40%, cereal 30–40%, sucrose 15–20%, plus 1–2% of each of such ingredients as: dicalcium phosphate, dried non-fat milk solids, propylene glycol, tallow, mono- and diglyceride, salt and nutritional supplements. Potassium sorbate is usually added to inhibit yeast and moulds. Colours and flavours are also commonly used. The fresh or frozen meat products may be pasteurised separately or together with sugar, propylene glycol or potassium sorbate prior to addition of the remaining ingredients. An alternative method is to blend all ingredients at one time and pasteurise. The product may be extruded in the form of chunks. A typical ingredient formula for a common intermediate moisture animal food is shown in Table 5.

Intermediate moisture foods played a role in the US and USSR manned space flights. Among the foods used in the US space flights in the APOLLO and Skylab programmes were a number of IMF items. IMF included in APOLLO flights are listed in Table 6.[11]

Special IMF items were developed for consumption on the moon.[3] Historically, the most innovative food systems have been those developed for explorers. The advances made by food systems for

TABLE 5

*A typical formula for 'texturised' soft-moist
(intermediate moisture) pet food[a]*

Ingredients	Percentage
Meat and/or meat by-product	30–70
Sodium caseinate	7·5–25
Sugar	15–30
Propylene glycol	2–10
Starch	0·5–10
Nutritional supplements	1–5
Flavour and colour	as desired

[a] From US Patent 3,380,832 (1968).

manned space flight are no exception to this tradition. The first solid
food ever to be consumed by man while walking on the moon was an
intermediate moisture food. This item was a gelatin–fruit–sugar bar
fitted inside the pressure suit so it could be consumed without the
need for manipulation by hand. The bar was designed to provide a
source of energy while minimising any tendency toward increasing
thirst. Several varieties of fruit bars were used including strawberry,
apricot, cherry and lemon.

TABLE 6

*Intermediate moisture foods included in US space
flights' food supply*

Food	Apollo flight(s)
Bacon squares	7–16
Date fruit cake bites	7–16
Gingerbread bites	7–16
Pineapple fruit cake bites	7–16
Cinnamon bread cubes	7–16
Brownies	7–16
Dried fruit bars	11–16
Pear IMF	17
Peach IMF	17
Apricot IMF	17
Cherry bar	17
Cereal bar	17

TABLE 7

Apollo 17 fruit cake ingredients[a]

	% by weight
Flour, wheat, soft	7·3
Flour, soy	7·3
Sugar	19·0
Shortening	7·8
Eggs, whole, fresh	6·96
Salt	0·4
Baking powder	0·4
Water	2·2
Cherries, candied	10·4
Pineapple, candied	8·6
Pecans, shelled	13·8
Raisins, bleached	15·6
Clove powder	0·06
Nutmeg	0·06
Cinnamon	0·12
	100·00

[a] Developed by US Army Natick Laboratories.

The most popular IMF space foods have been jellied fruit candy, pecans, peaches, pears, apricots, fruit cake, bacon bites and nutrient-defined food sticks. The intermediate moisture fruit cake consumed on the moon on Apollo 17 was designed by fortification to be nutritionally complete. It is planned to use an item like this for the emergency food supply aboard the forthcoming Space Shuttle flights. The principal ingredients in this food are shown in Table 7. The Skylab space programme food system also had a shelf-stable intermediate moisture food including a specially developed IMF bread. This product has a 2-year shelf-life and is of excellent quality. The Soviet space rations also contained a number of IMF. Particularly noteworthy is the variety of IMF breads and pastries included in their flight rations.

CURRENT RESEARCH AREAS IN IMF

Development of Principles for Formulation of IMF

One of the principles of IMF is the depression of water activity by incorporation of water soluble substances. Ideally, the activity of water is equal to the mole fraction of water in the solution: (Raoult's Law)

$$a_w = x_w \tag{1}$$

where x_w is the mole fraction of water in the solution. (In determining x_w the total number of kinetic units in solution is counted. One mole of NaCl for instance, counts as 2 moles of kinetic units (Na^+ and Cl^-).)

In real systems there are substantial deviations from ideality. These deviations are due to the following factors.

(a) Not all water in food is capable of acting as solvent. Water bound on specific sites (monolayer water) does not act as solvent and additional portions of the total water may also be unavailable as solvent.

(b) Not all of the solute is in actual solution (some may, for instance, be bound to other insoluble food components, as in the case of salts bound to proteins).

(c) Interactions between solute molecules may cause deviations from ideality.

The determination of how much of the total water present in food acts as a solvent for a particular set of solutes is often difficult. One of the methods used for that purpose involves mixing of a water-soluble solute with the food, assuming perfect dilution, and the determination of concentration of the solute in a portion of the water withdrawn from the food for analysis. A variant of this method is to determine the concentration of the solute directly in the food, provided that other food components do not interfere with determination of solute concentration in the aqueous phase. The method has the inherent problem of uncertainty of complete mixing and of complete availability of the added solute.

In systems containing starch, alcohol and water, Duprat and Guilbot[12] found that ethanol-dissolving water appears first when the most active sites of starch are saturated, and that above this level the fraction of water acting as solvent depends only on water activity and is independent of ethanol concentration.

In the study of non-solvent water in other systems it was observed that the amount of water available as solvent depended not only on the water activity but also on the type of solute. Walstra[13] found that at any given water activity less water was available as solvent for large than for small solute molecules. Duckworth[14] and Duckworth and Kelly[15] used NMR techniques to show that in polymer–solute–water systems, the minimum *water activity* at which solvent action was first apparent depended on the solute, but not on the polymer. The *amount* of water not available as solvent, however, depended on the polymers present.

Since the water activity of food solutions deviates strongly from the ideal relationship given in eqn. (1) a number of more complicated equations were developed to achieve the prediction. These were reviewed recently by Bone *et al.*,[16] Karel[17] and Labuza.[5] A recently developed equation assuming independent behaviour of different solutes in a complex solution was published by Ross:[18]

$$a_f = (a_i)(a_1)(a_2) \ldots (a_n) \qquad (2)$$

where a_f = final water activity of a food to which various solutes were added; a_i = initial water activity of a food; $a_1 \ldots a_n$ = water activity of a solution containing a given solute at a concentration which could exist if all the water in the food were available to dissolve this solute only.

It was observed that this equation is very useful if the values of the individual activities $a_1 \ldots a_n$ are known experimentally or through use of theoretical approximations. In the case of mixtures of insoluble and soluble components graphical techniques are often useful.[5]

Search for New Humectants and Humectant Combinations

The water activity level at which microbial activity is effectively inhibited is affected by a number of other factors, including nature of the solutes, pH, presence of chemical inhibitors and the nature of the flora. Nevertheless, it is generally accepted that growth of most bacteria will cease below $a_w = 0.9$; and that below a water activity of around 0.80 only xerophilic moulds, halophilic bacteria and osmophilic yeasts represent a potential danger.[19] In the presence of antimycotic agents, such as sorbate, a water activity of around 0.8 represents a safe level for IMF, and if bacteriostatic agents are included or the pH lowered, a level of 0.85 and even higher is often satisfactory.

The water contents of foods and of potential food components at activities of 0.7–0.9 are shown in Table 8. Sodium chloride and other

TABLE 8

Moisture content of selected materials at room temperature

	Moisture content % (dry basis)		
	$a_w = 0.7$	$a_w = 0.8$	$a_w = 0.9$
Peas	9·65	16·0	30·7
Casein	15·0	19	26
Potato starch	15	20	28
Coconut skim milk	28	56	95
Glycerol	64	108	215
Sorbitol	46	67	135
Sucrose	38	56	77
Polyethylene glycol 400	38	60	120
Corn starch	16·5	19·7	26·7
10 D.E. hydrolysate	15·2	22·6	40
42 D.E. hydrolysate	25·8	37	80
NaCl	—	332	605

salts, glycerol and sugars allow the highest moisture contents at these activities. This is to be expected since their molecular weights are low and their solubility high. Unfortunately all of these compounds present taste problems when used in high concentrations.

Actually, per unit of hydrophilic groups, polymers are often more effective than lower molecular weight compounds, as is shown in Table 9. The problem with polymeric compounds lies in the high viscosity of their solutions. Table 10 presents the viscosity of several humectants at specified activities.

Several research approaches are being taken in an effort to overcome the problem of achieving adequate depression of water activity

TABLE 9

Polyethylene glycol[20]

M.W.	Molality	a_w (Raoult's law)	$a_w{}^a$	a_w (experimental)
200	4·25	0·925	0·925	0·915
300	4·25	0·925	0·896	0·895
400	4·25	0·925	0·866	0·870
600	4·25	0·925	0·811	0·838
1 000	4·25	0·925	0·721	0·680

[a] Assuming depression of water activity to follow Raoult's law and assuming P.G. with M.W. = 200 to represent a kinetic unit.

without adverse effects on flavour, viscosity and appearance. Loncin[21] reported that several humectants show a strong deviation from ideal behaviour in the desired direction, that is produce more depression of a_w than expected. Of these, sodium lactate shows particularly remarkable behaviour and is further particularly effective in synergistic combinations with sodium chloride. In our laboratory[17] we confirmed the particular effectiveness of sodium

TABLE 10
Viscosity v. water activity

	$a_w = 0.7$	Viscosity (cP) 0.8	0.9
Glycerol	12	5	2
Sorbitol	300	10	2
Sucrose	Solid	Solid	Solid
Starch	Solid	Solid	Solid
20 D.E. syrup	Solid	5000	150
Coconut skim milk with coconut water[9]	20 000	2 500	n.a.
NaCl	—	~2	~1.5

lactate, but we have noted that it is not synergistic with sugars and glycerol, and its effectiveness in lowering a_w is impaired by addition of citric acid. Loncin[21] has also suggested that mixtures of insoluble solids with solutes may offer synergistic effects in depressing a_w. Order of mixing effects were studied by Labuza[5] who found that these effects were not significant, but Bone *et al.*[16] and Loncin[21] did find some changes in water activity due to the order of mixing.

The search for humectants other than polymers (which are generally too viscous), glycerol (off-flavour problems) sugars (too sweet for some applications) and salts (too salty), is being undertaken by several groups.

Researchers at the Western Regional Laboratory of the USDA in Berkeley studied the composition and water activity of natural plant juices hoping to determine if some naturally occurring substances or combinations offer an especially effective means of depressing water activity.[22] In their study french-cut snap beans were used as the matrix for observing the effects of additive treatment on water content at a fixed water activity. 250 g of bean pieces were cooked in 100 ml of each test solution, allowed to equilibrate with the solution in a refrigerator and then dried to a water activity of 0·6–0·7. A solution was judged to be effective if it raised the water content significantly above that of the beans themselves, at the specified water activity. Tapioca starch, algin, lactic acid, glycerol and glycerol oligomers were active as humectants, as were some plant extracts, but none of the compounds investigated to date offers unique advantages.[22] It is possible, however, that combinations of a large variety of humectants may be useful since the potential off-flavour problems may be reduced if each individual component is used at a concentration below its off-flavour threshold, but the total concentration of solutes is high enough to depress water activity to the desired levels. This approach, however, must be used with great care, since potentiation of off-flavour and of other undesirable effects cannot be excluded in mixtures. In the same study it was observed that a mild lactic acid fermentation had additional desirable effects beyond increasing water content. In particular the texture of the IMF vegetables was improved significantly.

A number of diols and diol esters have been tried in intermediate moisture systems. Dymsza[23] recently obtained a patent for compositions containing diols, and Frankenfeld et al.[24] hold patents for compositions containing diols and diol derivatives. As humectants these compounds are less effective than glycerol, but several of them are very effective inhibitors of microbial action.[24,25] Their potential application will require further studies on minimising off-flavour, and will also require approval of regulatory agencies.

Another approach is to use the traditional ingredients including insoluble polymers (starch, cellulose, proteins) and to plasticise the resulting IMF by the addition of surface active agents or of semisolid fats. The foods are thereby softened to a degree allowing consumption without the need for rehydration prior to use. The use of fats in plasticising low moisture foods is, of course, an old technology of particular importance in candy formulation. The use of surfactants to soften food is well known in the baking industry, and has been applied to 'soft-moist' pet foods.[26]

Antimicrobial Food Additives

Since the depression of water activity to a level below 0·8 without impairing organoleptic properties is often very difficult, antimicrobial food additives imparting protection against microbial growth in the range of water activities of 0·8–0·9 are an important ingredient of IMF. Recent surveys of preservatives suitable in IMF were prepared by Haas *et al.*[7] and by Labuza.[5]

Haas *et al.*[7] surveyed a number of micro-organisms occurring in IMF and chose three organisms as suitable indicators. They were: *Aspergillus glaucus*, *Aspergillus niger* and a staphylococcus. On the basis of tests with these organisms they established certain combinations of pH, water activities and preservative concentrations which offer adequate protection.

Labuza[5] surveyed a number of preservatives and water activity conditions and came to the following conclusions.

(1) Most mould inhibitors are not effective by themselves against *Staphylococcus aureus*, especially at a_w 0·86–0·90 and pH 5·6.
(2) Acidification to pH 5·2 improves the effectiveness of mould and *S. aureus* inhibitors. At this pH most common mould inhibitors also inhibit *S. aureus*.
(3) Pimaricin can be used to prevent mould growth in systems where staphylococcal growth is being studied.
(4) In a complex food system containing both moulds and staphylococcal species, very few inhibitor systems show complete inhibition at high a_w.
(5) Overall a combination of propylene glycol at 4–6% with either potassium sorbate or calcium propionate (0·1–0·3%) would seem to be totally effective as a microbial inhibitor system at pH 5–6.

In tests on IMF Labuza[5] found that at pH 5·6 a number of preservatives assured absence of mould growth (Table 11).

Frankenfeld *et al.*[24,25] found that esters of aliphatic diols in combination with humectants such as glycerol or butanediol give effective protection against moulds and bacteria. Some of the compositions found effective in intermediate moisture food models are shown in Table 12. As mentioned previously, however, the introduction of new food additives requires extensive testing of safety and may be often uneconomical even if the safety tests are satisfactory. If a thorough understanding of mechanisms of action of antimicrobial additives were developed along with a thorough knowledge of their interactions with human cells and organs, a rationale for preservative development would be easier to achieve,

Marcus Karel

TABLE 11
Time of mould appearance on Hennican (pH 5·6)[5]

Inhibitor	% Level (w/w)	Day of appearance
Methyl paraben	0·2	19
	0·4	none[a]
Propyl paraben	0·03	19
	0·05	19
Methyl/propyl paraben	0·02	19
	0·05	19
Sodium benzoate	0·05	19
	0·10	27
Calcium propionate	0·20	none[a]
	0·30	none[a]
Potassium sorbate	0·10	none[a]
	0·30	none[a]
Propylene glycol	7·0	none[a]
	10·0	none[a]
1,3-Butylene glycol	5·0	none[a]
	10·0	none[a]
Glycerol	1·5	32
	6·0	39
Polyethylene glycol 600	3·0	32
	10·0	33
Sorbitol	4·3	32
	14·3	51
Control	0	19

[a] No mould growth by day 51.

and prospects for a renaissance of chemical preservation of foods would be much better. Efforts in this direction are in progress, and a recent paper by Freese *et al.*[27] presents an analysis of the mechanisms of action of lipophilic acids as antimicrobial food additives. In this conference Dr Sinskey will report on his recent research on mechanisms of antimicrobial activity of humectants.

Osmotic Treatment as a Method for Production of IMF

Dehydration of foods by immersion in liquids with a water activity lower than that of the food forms the essence of osmotic drying. Solutions of sugars or of salt are usually employed, giving rise to two simultaneous counter-current flows: solute diffuses from solution into food; and water diffuses out of the food into the

TABLE 12

Effectiveness of selected additives in preventing growth of micro-organisms after several weeks storage at 37°C[24] (+ = growth)

Additive	Medium	
	Apple flakes water content = 66% pH = 4·4	Chicken baby food containing 25% glycerol water = 62%, pH = 6·5
No additive	+	+
20% glycerol	+	not tested
10% butanediol	–	–
0·3% potassium sorbate	–	+
0·3% 1,3 heptanediol	–	–
0·5% 1,3 octanediol-1-monopropionate	–	–
0·3% 1,3 butanediol-1-mono-octanoate	–	not tested

solution. Unfortunately, the processes are complex and no correlations between effective diffusivities and process conditions have been published. Most studies report only penetration under selected conditions, with no attempt made to analyse the mass transfer in terms of engineering properties.

An interesting mass transfer situation arises in osmotic dehydration of fruit pieces by immersion in concentrated sugar solution. Diffusivity of sugars is much lower than that of water, making it possible to design processes which result in substantial water removal with only marginal sugar pickup. Slow processes, on the other hand, approach equilibrium for both sugar and water resulting in production of 'candied' sugar-rich fruits. One would expect also that disruption of structural barriers within the fruit pieces would increase diffusivities of both water and of sugar, but would tend to allow a faster approach to equilibrium, and thus favour 'candying' as opposed to dehydration. Indeed, an improved candying process incorporating presoftening of the fruit with enzymes produced by the mould *Aspergillus niger* was recently patented.[28]

We have been conducting research on osmotic treatment of fruits as a pretreatment for freeze drying.[29] Many of the principles developed in these studies apply to production of IMF as well.

Fruits which were to be osmotically treated were soaked in an aqueous solution of 60% osmotic agent (either sucrose or malto-dextrin), 0·52% ascorbic acid and 0·14% malic acid. (The malto-dextrin used was Maltrin-15, a 15 D.E. material from Grain Processing Co., Muscatine, Iowa.) The fruit slices were contacted with the osmosis solution in two ways (circulation or vacuum infusion) to be described below. Following the osmotic treatment, the fruit is rinsed for 30 s to remove osmosis solution adhering to the fruit surface. This prevents stickiness after dehydration.

Two systems were evaluated for use in contacting the fruit slices with the osmosis solution. These have been labelled the circulation method and the vacuum infusion method.

The system for circulation consists of a conical, bottom draining polyethylene tank (either 1 or 4 litres capacity) and a centrifugal pump. The osmotic solution was drawn from the bottom of the tank and recirculated to the top, above the level of the fruit. The fruit pieces were held continuously submerged in the solution by a porous polyethylene plate. The relative amount of fruit and solution were such that the solution concentration would not change appreciably during the process.

The system for vacuum infusion was composed of a 2 litre Erlenmeyer flask with side tubulature connected to a vacuum pump. Fruit slices were placed through the flask neck which was then sealed with a fitting which connected, through a shut-off valve, to a tank containing the osmotic solution. The flask was evacuated through the side arm and when the desired vacuum was achieved, the tank shut-off valve was opened and the solution allowed to contact the fruit. In some cases the vacuum pump continued to operate following the contacting, while in others it was turned off just prior to opening the valve. No difference in behaviour was noted.

Evaluation of the kinetics of water loss and sucrose uptake by apple slices indicate both some important differences and similarities of the two procedures. In particular, the rate of water loss does not appear to depend on the presence or absence of vacuum during initial contact of the sucrose solution with the apples. In contrast, with the circulation system very little sugar is taken up by the slice (*i.e.* little is retained following a 20 s water rinse), while with the vacuum impregnation system sugar uptake results have been more variable. A typical set of curves for water loss and sugar weight gain are given in Fig. 1.

Kinetic studies with the circulation system shown in Fig. 1 indicate

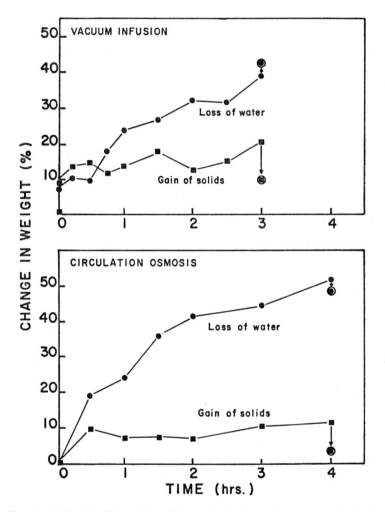

FIG. 1.   Gain of solids and loss of water during osmotic treatment of sliced apples. Initial solids content of sliced apples was 12·8 % in circulation osmosis, and 12·9 % in vacuum infusion.

a rapid loss of water for a period of 2 h, followed by a rapid, but decreasing rate of loss for the period 2–6 h. Results showed that, with this system, rinsed apple slices of about 30% solids could be prepared in 4–6 h of treatment. At this time, about 25% of the *solids* was added sugar.

It has been noted that for piece sizes utilised in these studies (between 5 and 10 mm minimum thickness) the initial rates of water loss were relatively insensitive to rates of circulation in the apparatus,

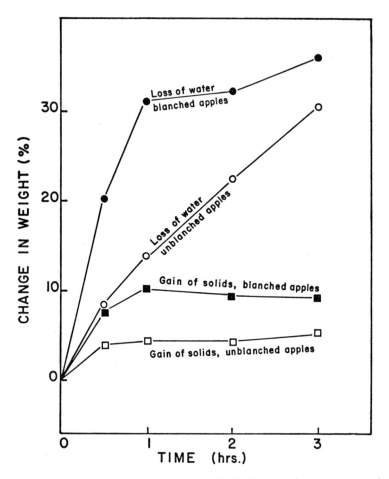

FIG. 2.   Water loss and carbohydrate uptake during osmotic pretreatment of blanched and unblanched apple slices.

though at the intermediate times (1–5 h) the circulation system does give some improved water loss.

One study related to the effect of steam blanching of apple slices on the kinetics of water loss and sugar uptake during the osmotic pretreatment of apple slices (Fig. 2). It was noted that the blanched samples lost water more rapidly in the initial phases of the pretreatment, though the ultimate water loss was not sizably different from the unblanched slices. The amount of sugar taken up by the slices was about twice as great for the blanched as the unblanched (corrected for differences in water loss). The uptake was very rapid in both cases, reaching the ultimate level with 0·5 h of treatment, at which point it remained constant. Organoleptic tests which were conducted on these products showed no significant difference between blanched or unblanched apples.

Table 13 shows the solids content of a number of fruits which have been osmotically treated.

TABLE 13

Increase in solids concentration due to osmotic pretreatment

Fruit	Solids concentration (%)	
	Before osmosis	After osmosis
Strawberries	9·4	23·0
Honeydew melon	9·6	33·6
Cantaloupe melon	9·6	28·0
Peaches	10·7	29·4
Pears	14·3	28·0
Pineapple	12·1	27·9
Apples	12·8	29·9

In order to design an optimum process for production of IMF by osmosis it will be necessary to understand diffusional processes which occur in food systems. Some progress has been made in this direction.

Non-ionic solutes diffuse in water-swollen gels, in polymeric membranes and in non-cellular food systems at rates which can be explained by a process of simple diffusion in aqueous solution taking into account local viscosity increases and tortuosity factors present in foods and in crosslinked or aggregated gels. Table 14 shows some of the diffusion coefficients reported in the literature for non-ionic solutes and food-related systems.[30,31] In very concentrated sugar solutions diffusion coefficients decrease substantially due to local viscosity.[32,33]

Diffusion of ionic compounds is more complicated. Salting is an old process for preservation of foods by the IMF principle, but research into the scientific basis of it is recent. Del Valle[34] studied diffusion of NaCl in fish muscle and found it to be concentration dependent. The diffusion coefficient (D) at 25°C was in the range of $0.95–1.45 \times 10^{-5}$ cm^2 s^{-1}, and at 5°C was around 0.6 cm^2 s^{-1}.

TABLE 14

Values of diffusion coefficient (D) *reported for non-ionic solutes in food-related aqueous systems at room temperature*[33, 31]

Diffusing solutes	System	D (cm^2/s) $\times 10^6$
Polyhydric alcohols	Water-swollen cellulose gels	1·6–3·9
Sucrose	Water-swollen cellulose gels	1·2–2·6
Raffinose	Water-swollen cellulose gels	0·9–1·2
Polyethylene oxide 1000	Water-swollen cellulose gels	0·4–0·9
Polyethylene oxide 4000	Water-swollen cellulose gels	0·08–0·14
Polyhydric alcohols	Water	~9
Polyethylene oxide 1000	Water	~2·4

Among more recent fundamental studies on diffusion of ions in foods are those of Geurts et al.[35] who studied salt penetration in cheese, and those of Paulus[36] who studied ion uptake in potatoes.

During the process of salting studied by Guerts et al.[35] water moves out of cheese while salt moves into it. The diffusion coefficient for salt was found to be as low as 1/5 of the value for salt in water. Guerts et al.[35] proposed that the lower value may be explained by the following factors.

(1) Errors due to insufficient consideration of changes in diffusion geometry due to simultaneous outflow of water.
(2) Errors due to unavailability of a part of total water for dissolution of salt.
(3) Local viscosity increases.
(4) Obstructions to diffusion due to tortuosity of pores.

Paulus[36] used radioactive ions to study transport in potato tissue and found the phenomena involved to be complex. In his experiments the osmotic pressure of the tissue was higher than that of the surrounding solution. Under these conditions there was, in addition to diffusive transport of ion, an osmotic flux of water. Also, the ions underwent extensive binding to potato components, and these binding reactions decreased the rate of flux. Paulus was able to calculate the diffusion coefficients for several ions in potato and these ranged from 5×10^{-8} cm^2 s^{-1} for cerium to 5×10^{-6} for caesium.

In a more practical study Urie and Shahbenderian[37] studied desalting of pickled gherkins and found that the process was controlled by simple diffusion with a diffusion coefficient of about 1.5×10^{-5} cm^2 s^{-1}.

Stability of IMF

Storage stability of intermediate moisture foods is a complicated subject. It is one of the major problems remaining to be solved before IMF for human consumption becomes a commercial reality.[3]

A review of this problem has been recently published[38] and the major conclusions reported in it remain valid. Once stabilisation against microbial attack is achieved the major deterioration reactions are non-enzymatic browning and lipid peroxidation. Oxidation can be effectively controlled in most systems through the use of conventional antioxidants (BHA and BHT). Non-enzymatic browning, on the other hand, is difficult to control because the maximum rates of browning coincide with the typical IMF water activities (0·65–0·9). In a recent study Labuza[5] found that high concentrations of polyhydric alcohols such as glycerol or propylene glycol inhibit the browning reaction. Similar observations were made by our associates in animal rations containing 1,3-butanediol.

The application of these laboratory findings to commercial practice remains to be proven.

CONCLUSION

The commercial potential for intermediate moisture foods (IMF) is large. These foods offer a combination of shelf stability, convenience, ease of nutrient content adjustment and safety. The rapid penetration of the pet food market by IMF clearly proves the practical potential for these foods. The convenience, safety, acceptability and nutrition provided by IM pet foods have been major factors in their success.

This relatively rapid application of controlled food systems in animal husbandry has been made possible largely because economics often completely dictate the food selection on the basis of relatively simplistic objectives compared to human nutrition. In contrast, foods for human consumption are evaluated on the basis of far more complex requirements. This is coupled with food preferences, prejudices, fads and taboos. Food intended for human consumption must be highly acceptable organoleptically as well as being in compliance with prevailing fads and being judged safe for a 'long-term' consumption. To date, however, modern IMF has been slow to become a significant factor in human food systems primarily because of poor organoleptic acceptability.

Specialised food systems such as space feeding and clinical nutrition demonstrate that the drawbacks in IMF for human consumption can be overcome by intensive application of technology. These drawbacks, nevertheless, still largely remain in regards to the mass marketing of IMF for human consumption. The chief areas in which research and development are required are:

(1) Development of new formulations containing humectants of high organoleptic acceptability.
(2) Development of new antimicrobial agents suitable for inclusion in IMF.
(3) Control of storage-induced organoleptic changes, in particular those due to non-enzymatic browning.
(4) Development of economic processes for large scale production of IMF.

Progress in the above areas will not be easy to achieve. One of the major obstacles is the need to prove the absolute safety of any new chemical additive to be utilised. The concept of Intermediate Moisture Foods is particularly dependent on utilisation of additives and safety considerations, and consumer concerns are of special importance in their marketing. It is therefore not surprising that the only initial marketing success was with two atypical groups of consumers: (1) animals and (2) a select, well-informed and non-timid group of human consumers—the astronauts.

REFERENCES

1. Spicer, A. (Ed.) (1974). *Advances in Preconcentration and Dehydration of Foods*, Applied Science Publ. Ltd, London.
2. Karel, M. (1974). 'Fundamentals of dehydration processes', in: *Advances in Preconcentration and Dehydration of Foods*, ed. A. Spicer, Applied Science Publ. Ltd, London, pp. 45–94.
3. Heidelbaugh, N. D. and Karel, M. (1975). 'Intermediate moisture food technology', in: *Freeze Drying and Advanced Food Technology*, ed. S. A. Goldblith, L. Rey and W. W. Rothmayer, Academic Press, London, pp. 619–41.
4. Karel, M. (1973). *CRC Critical Revs. Fd. Technol.*, **3**, p. 329.
5. Labuza, T. P. (1975). *Storage Stability and Improvement of Intermediate Moisture Foods*, Final Report on Contract NAS9-12560 Phase III with the National Aeronautics and Space Administration, Houston. Published by University of Minnesota, St Paul, Minn., 55108 (August 1975).
6. Schmidhofer, Th. and Egli, H. R. (1972). *Alimenta*, **5**, p. 169.
7. Haas, G. J., Bennett, D., Herman, E. B. and Collette, D. (1975). *Food Product Dev.*, **9**(3), p. 86.
8. Collins, J. L. and Yu, A. K. (1975). *J. Food Sci.*, **40**, p. 858.
9. Hagenmaier, R. D., Cater, C. M. and Mattil, K. F. (1975). *J. Food Sci.*, **40**, p. 717.
10. Pavey, R. L. and Schack, W. R. (1969). *Formulation of Intermediate Moisture Bite-size Food Cubes*, U.S.A.F. School of Aerospace Medicine Technical Report on Contract F41609-67-C-0054.
11. Smith, M. C., Heidelbaugh, N. D., Rambaut, P. C., Rapp, R. M., Wheeler, H. O., Huber, C. S. and Bourland, C. T. (1975). In: *Biomedical Results of Apollo*, ed. J. F. Parker, publication NASA SP-368, by NASA, Washington, D.C.
12. Duprat, F. and Guilbot, A. (1975). 'Solvent versus non-solvent water in starch-alcohol-water systems', in: *Water Relations of Foods*, ed. R. A. Duckworth, Academic Press, London, pp. 173–82.
13. Walstra, P. (1973). *Kolloid Z.*, **251**, p. 603.
14. Duckworth, R. B. (1972). *Proc. Inst. Fd. Sci. Technol.*, **5**, p. 60.
15. Duckworth, R. B. and Kelly, C. E. (1973). *J. Fd. Technol.*, **8**, p. 105.
16. Bone, D. P., Shannon, E. L. and Ross, K. D. (1975). 'The lowering of water activity by order of mixing in concentrated solutions', in: *Water Relations of Foods*, ed. R. B. Duckworth, Academic Press, London, pp. 613–26.
17. Karel, M. (1975). 'Physico-chemical modification of the state of water in foods', in: *Water Relations of Foods*, ed. R. B. Duckworth, Academic Press, London, pp. 435–63.
18. Ross, K. D. (1975). *Food Technol.*, **29**(3), p. 26.
19. Mossel, D. A. A. (1975). 'Water and microorganisms in foods—a synthesis', in: *Water Relations of Foods*, ed. R. B. Duckworth, Academic Press, London, pp. 347–61.

20. Bone, D. P. (1969). *Food Product Dev.*, 3(5), p. 81.
21. Loncin, M. (1975). 'Basic principles of moisture equilibria', in: *Freeze Drying and Advanced Food Technology*, ed. S. A. Goldblith, L. Rey and W. W. Rothmayer, Academic Press, London, p. 599.
22. Farkas, D. F. (1976). Western Regional Laboratory, U.S.D.A., Berkeley. Private communication.
23. Dymsza, H. A. (1975). US Patent 3,904,774.
24. Frankenfeld, J. W., Karel, M. and Labuza, T. P. (1973). US Patent 3,732,112.
25. Frankenfeld, J. W., Karel, M., Labuza, T. P. and Sinskey, A. J. (1974). US Patent 3,806,615.
26. Oborah, E. V. and Mohrman, R. K. (1974). US Patent 3,852,483.
27. Freese, E., Sheu, C. W. and Galliers, E. (1973). *Nature*, **241**, p. 321.
28. Mochizuki, K., Isobe, K. and Sawada, Y. (1971). US Patent 3,615,687.
29. Karel, M. and Flink, J. M. (1975). *Mechanisms of Deterioration of Nutrients*, Phase III. M.I.T. Report on Contract Research Project No. 9-12485 with the Manned Spacecraft Center, NASA. Cambridge, Mass., USA.
30. Brown, W. and Chitumbo, K. (1975a). *J. Chem. Soc. (Faraday Trans. I)*, **71**, p. 1.
31. Brown, W. and Chitumbo, K. (1975b). *J. Chem. Soc. (Faraday Trans. I)*, **71**, p. 12.
32. Quinn, J. A. and Blair, L. M. (1967). *Nature*, **214**, p. 907.
33. Chandrasekaran, S. K. and King, C. J. (1972). *AIChE. J.*, **18**, p. 513.
34. Del Valle, F. R. (1965). Ph.D. Thesis, Massachusetts Institute of Technology, Cambridge, Mass., USA.
35. Guerts, T. J., Walstra, P. and Mulder, H. (1974). *Neth. Milk Dairy J.*, **28**, p. 102.
36. Paulus, K. (1972). *Potato Research*, **15**, p. 209.
37. Urie, I. D. and Shahbenderian, A. P. (1968). *Process Biochem.*, June 1968, p. 39.
38. Karel, M. (1975). 'Stability of low and intermediate moisture foods', in: *Freeze Drying and Advanced Food Technology*, ed. S. A. Goldblith, L. Rey and W. W. Rothmayer, Academic Press, London, pp. 643–74.

DISCUSSION

Acraman: Do you know of any work that has been done on the use of amino acids to increase osmotic effect, and have you any comment to make on the potential use of these materials?

Karel: The best work I know on the use of amino acids to increase osmotic effect is the work of Dr Measures. The problem here in using a hydrolysate of some sort would be taste. At the concentrations of amino acids which would be necessary to achieve a substantial depression of water activity I think you might have a bitter taste. I don't know of anybody who has actually ventured to add amino acids to depress water.

Acraman: I was going to say that a relatively pure amino-acid solution can be almost tasteless.

Karel: The most economical approach would be to carry out a hydrolysis of a natural substance such as soy. In fact a fellow countryman of Dr Mossel's has done some work on controlled hydrolysis of soy proteins and it turns out that in order to get any kind of organoleptic acceptability you have to avoid a very low molecular weight cut. This is well known in texturising, especially in milk substitutes, which are being developed in the United States. As you say, if you could get very pure compounds, you could perhaps avoid the peptides. But it would be a very costly proposition.

Acraman: The other possibility, of course, would be screening to see if there were any synergistic effects.

Karel: Glycerol has been studied from that point of view and I think one or two amino acids. You have three factors here, first, solubility, second, molecular weight and third, deviation. Some of the less soluble amino acids just wouldn't work, because they are not soluble enough.

There are some very peculiar effects here, incidentally, that nobody knows very much about in terms of ionisable compounds—for instance, lactic acid is very effective in depressing water activity. It turns out that in some combinations it disappears completely, for instance citric acid completely negates the depressing activity of lactic acid. So I don't think enough is known. But I'd be worried about the taste.

Rolfe: Could they possibly increase non-enzymic browning in some cases, such as fruits—apples for example—where there was plenty of sugar?

Karel: Undoubtedly.

Acraman: You could say the same about the use of sugars.

Karel: Yes, exactly the same is true there, but not with sucrose, glycerol or sorbitol.

Jeffery: Do you know of any comparable work on the effectiveness of pectins and alginates and those sort of materials on water activity?

Karel: Yes. What I was talking about was simply the polyethylene glycol data of Bone. I was referring simply to the isotherm (that is water activity versus moisture content) for that substance. At a specific water activity, if one takes, say, the isotherms for compounds of different molecular weights, and counts the amount of water held at that fixed activity per hydrophilic group, it turns out that the polymers hold quite a bit. Isotherms are available for pectins, alginates, starch, dextrins, etc., and all of them hold quite a bit of water, but all of them also have a very high viscosity, which is the limiting factor. Cornstarch has a water content of about 16·5 grammes of water per 100 grammes of starch, and most polymers of glucose which are not crystalline (that is, not cellulose) would be similar. They would be too dry, but they would certainly suppress the water activity very nicely.

Jeffery: I was thinking in fact of a gelled form.

Karel: I don't quite follow you. Let's say you prepared a gel of pectin or cornstarch. No matter how you prepared it, by the time you achieved an activity of 0·7, the water content would be of the order of 15–20 %, which would be too dry to eat. However, there is some evidence on the formation of a certain kind of alginate gel-based food. You can stabilise the internal structure in some way and by a judicious operation, avoid the collapse of the gel in drying. But if you're going to stay at this activity, then these spaces are not going to be soft and moist. Now, the possibility does exist that if we could get other substances (for instance, conceivably, vegetable oil) to fill these spaces, we could have a plasticising action. This is one approach that in fact works. We have for years been eating low-moisture substances which appear soft because they are plasticised with lipids. But it's not due to the pectin or alginate polymers. These polymers, per unit hydrophilic group, are usually effective in depressing water activity, but they are also much more effective per unit hydrophilic group in increasing the viscosity. So that the race between these two is lost.

Sinskey: Can you clarify why lactic acid behaves as it does?

Karel: I don't know. I think it must have an effect in co-ordinating water in some manner which is more effective than other solutes of that size.

Leistner: You mentioned one or two recent papers that indicated that toxin production could occur at a lower water activity level than growth. Was this really toxin production, or was this just a persistence of the toxin that was produced before? Such a finding was reported by Lee, Staples and Olson, 1975.

Karel: I really mentioned this just as an aside. I am not a microbiologist. Theoretically, when you think about it, some metabolic activity at a very low level could conceivably occur resulting in the production of some compounds which are toxic even before cell replication occurs.

3

Some Introductory Thoughts on Intermediate Moisture Foods

J. N. ROBSON

Marks & Spencer Ltd, London, England

ABSTRACT

Intermediate moisture foods (IMF) for humans are introduced to the Symposium with some definitions and general observations on the historical development of the concept. The two types of IMF which emerge logically from this treatment are therefore the traditional and the new. The reasons for the evolution of the former are contrasted with the background to the present-day interest in the principle of IMF. Similarly contrasted are the methods of avoiding spoilage employed in IMF with the alternative safeguards available to fresh foods. There is speculation on the possible attitudes of consumers in general and 'consumerism' in particular to some of the technological objectives and devices used in the production of IMF. The conclusion is reached that for modern IMF for humans to be completely successful they should not merely offer alternative or more convenient forms of conventional and familar foods, but provide products which are completely new and different from, or are demonstrably better than, the traditional food. Savings in cost to the consumer are not, in themselves, sufficient to ensure commercial success.

INTRODUCTION

Every major scientific advance achieved by Man inevitably reverberates to the furthermost corners of technology. This is probably more true of space exploration than any other human achievement, and one of its 'spin-offs' is a renewal of interest in Intermediate Moisture Foods (IMF)—the subject of this Conference. Clearly the dry biscuits and iron rations of the polar explorers of the last century would have been inappropriate for the sophisticated lunar explorers of the last decade. Furthermore, food scientists would have been dragging their feet if they had not matched their technical skills with those of their contemporaries in other areas of science and engineering, by providing the astronauts with a varied and interesting diet displaying an inventiveness consistent with the rigid demands of the occasion.

The purpose of this contribution is to introduce the subject by way of general definitions and descriptions, and to offer some comments and speculation as to the possible development of IMF and their likely acceptance into the human diet. No attempt will be made to deal with the detailed science of the subject. The aspects are many and diverse, and they will be dealt with separately by workers with practical experience and precise information. It must also be stressed that this introduction will deal only with human foods; the next paper will report on pet foods.

Some of the views presented may be controversial: they are offered both in the spirit of healthy scientific discussion, and as a reminder that scientific achievement in food technology is not an end in itself. To achieve success, the final product must be acceptable to a critical and demanding consumer public which does not always share the scientist's optimistic evaluation of his own achievements!

DEFINITIONS

Many foods normally contain moisture levels of about 20–50 % by weight, and possess a water activity (a_w) of about 0·95–1·00 (*see* Tables 1 and 2). In such a state, the concentration of solutes in the water is not sufficient to discourage microbiological and biochemical activity and consequently deterioration and spoilage can occur under most ambient conditions.

If the concentration of the aqueous solution present in a food can be increased to a point where microbiological activity can be brought under control, several desirable features start to manifest themselves in the food.

TABLE 1

Fresh foods normally possessing water activities (a_w) *between* 0·95 *and* 1·00

Fresh meats
Fish
Shell fish
Poultry
Eggs
Vegetables
Fruits, juices
Milk
Butter, margarine

TABLE 2

Processed foods possessing a_w *levels at or about* 0·95

Bread
Sponge-type cakes
Some cooked sausages
Large canned hams

TABLE 3

Foods with a_w *levels below* 0·90

Salami
Matured cheese
'Dry' ham
Fruit cake
Marzipan, jams, etc.
Dried fruit

(a) *Spoilage* is reduced; food is conserved.
(b) *Safety* is improved; health hazards are diminished.
(c) *Shelf life* is increased; the product has greater convenience in use.
(d) *'Soft-moist' texture* is retained.

The description 'Intermediate Moisture Foods' has been applied to such products, and in general terms their a_w would probably lie in the range 0·65–0·85[1] (*i.e.* they would be in equilibrium with a relative humidity of 65–85%), and they contain some 15–30% moisture (*see* Table 3).

TRADITIONAL TYPES OF IMF

Attempts to achieve the desirable features listed above are, of course, not new. Certainly drying and the use of salt date back to Biblical times, and many of the foods which have evolved over the centuries as a result of these practices remain today as important constituents of the diet. In tracing the development of modern IMF it is useful, therefore, to be reminded of how our forebears tackled their problems, and to evaluate their achievements.

The earliest attempts to concentrate the solutes were by the simple drying process: this was originally applied to fruits and vegetables in many parts of the world, and remains of course the basis of an enormous and profitable food industry, in which the drying agent is still often the sun.

The concept of increasing the level of solutes in addition to removing some of the water then encouraged our forefathers to use sugar to produce jams, candied fruits, soft confectionery and jellies. They also learned more about using salt to treat meats, fish and sausages. Finally both salt and sugar were used together to make country or sweet cured hams and pemmican. Another development was the use of chopping and mincing to enable basic foods to be mixed together and handled and treated more easily. Thus for instance the large range of long-life sausages of the salami-type were produced; they provided a new type of food, were shelf-stable and nutritious. From them sprung a whole new delicatessen concept.

Baked products constitute a further branch of IMF in which cereal derivatives with a low and unappetising a_w are treated with water and other desirable additives and procedures and then heat treated in an oven to produce attractive foods, many of which fall in the IMF category.

These early developments in food technology achieved two goals. First, food could be safely stored; waste was avoided; there was something to eat at unseasonable times of the year. Secondly, completely new taste and texture sensations were achieved which in many cases enhanced the attractiveness of the food. Even today we thrill to the odour and flavour of newly-baked bread spread with fresh-fruit jam, or to the texture and taste of grilled bacon or kippers. The significance of the achievement of this novelty factor will be more apparent later.

MODERN TYPES OF IMF

The stimulus to apply modern technology to probe more deeply into the mysteries of water activity presumably derives from modern versions of the constraints which caused our forefathers to develop the conventional IMF reviewed above. Modern living, international economics, and world-wide food and health objectives have all conveyed new meanings to such words as Conservation, Safety and Durability. More specifically the continued concentration of large urban populations, the properly more demanding needs of the Armed Forces, and in the ultimate the tight specifications laid down by the US Space Programme are all good and sufficient reasons for bringing IMF technology up to date. Consequently new methods have been developed to achieve the necessary increase in the concentration of solutes in the water present and the resultant reduction of the water activity. The basic processes are of two types.

(a) *Adsorption* in which the food is dried (often freeze-dried) and then subjected to controlled re-humidification until the desired composition is achieved.

(b) *Desorption* by the infusion of the food in a solution of higher osmotic pressure so that at equilibrium the desired a_w is reached. This process can be accelerated by raising the temperature.[2]

Naturally, one can achieve any desired a_w by mixing together appropriate ingredients prepared by any of these methods and allowing them to equilibriate.

Drying alone often produces unacceptable textures,[3] and so the materials employed to achieve acceptability in IMF are many and various and will be dealt with elsewhere, but doubtless polyhydric alcohols including glycerol, sorbitol, mannitol and propylene glycol will be mentioned. Other functional components are also employed,[4] such as sorbate, antioxidants, plasticisers, emulsifiers, stabilisers, chelators and nutritive supplements, to say nothing of colours and flavours.

SPOILAGE HAZARDS

It seems appropriate to summarise briefly the principal food deterioration processes which must be brought under control in devising an IMF as follows.

(a) *Microbial.* Lower a_w will control most bacteria, many moulds and yeasts.

(b) *Oxidation.* The a_w range of IMF is probably the optimum for lipid oxidation.

(c) *Browning* (non-enzymatic). This is at a maximum at the lower end of the range of IMF. (Maillard reactions in solids proceed at maximum speed at a_w between 0·6 and 0·7.)[5]

Thus it can be seen that reducing a_w alone may well produce a food in which conditions for other forms of deterioration are approaching optimum levels.

Quality and cleanliness of raw materials and operations, a detailed study of the composition and interaction of constituents, the use of antioxidants, control of pH, careful selection and precise achievement of the actual a_w best suited to the product and the problem and precise specification of the packaging to be used, are among the agencies by which the IMF technologist can cope with these hazards.

IS IMF THE ONLY WAY?

While one can appreciate and enjoy the traditional, does one have to accept some of the technological gymnastics that combine to make modern IMF such complicated affairs? Table 4 shows an

IMF recipe for traditional roast beef.[6] Whilst it is appreciated that the US Air Force may have special problems, will this be the sort of formulation we will all be eating soon?

Fortunately there is another way. Fresh food can still be grown using scientific controls, delivered rapidly to the processor in a clean condition, hygienically processed, packed correctly, stored and

TABLE 4

Formula of ready-to-eat intermediate moisture roast beef cubes[a]

Ingredients	% by weight
Beef, cooked, ground, freeze-dried	51·00
Water, distilled	12·00
Water as steam	4·941 5
Glycerol	6·00
Pregelatinised starch	5·00
Gelatin (100 Bloom)	5·00
Non-dairy coffee whitener	3·50
Sorbitol, dry	3·00
Soup and gravy base, beef flavour	2·50
Sucrose	2·00
Salt	2·00
Hydrolysed vegetable protein, beef	2·00
Onions, dehydrated	0·50
Monosodium glutamate	0·25
Sorbic acid	0·20
Ascorbic acid	0·045
Black pepper	0·040
Ribotide	0·020
Citric acid	0·003 5
	100·000 0

[a] Developed by Swift & Company for US Air Force.

distributed at low temperatures, with controlled shelf life, and delivered fresh and sound to the eventual consumer. Prepared dishes, using conventional chef's recipes can be properly processed, similarly safeguarded, and retailed in the High Street as high quality convenience foods.

Just as with IMF, these alternatives demand care and control in technology, understanding and a sense of urgency and responsibility by all engaged in their production and distribution, and, it is submitted, will result in greater consumer satisfaction and acceptance.

QUALITY AND THE CONSUMER

To an increasing extent consumers—certainly in Western Europe and North America—are demanding quality in their foods. Certainly they have become more sophisticated and more critical. Indeed, as in other areas of science and technology, it might be argued that some traditional IMF might never have been developed in today's questioning and suspicious atmosphere.

By contrast, modern IMF will have to contend with the outspoken demands of the consumers of today which are as follows.

(a) The intrinsic qualities of fresh food, particularly freshness, flavour, succulence, texture.
(b) A reduction, not an increase in the numbers and quantities of additives employed.
(c) Convenience certainly, but not at the expense of quality.
(d) Improved nutritional standards. (Is this best achieved by producing fresh food, or by sophisticated processed foods with vitamins, minerals and other nutrients added?)
(e) The desire to understand, recognise and deal with hazards and perishability. Many consumers have equipped themselves with the ability to cope with such hazards (*i.e.* with refrigerator and freezer) and would rather feed the 'fresh' way than the 'chemical' way.

Although sometimes the consumers' jargon and accuracy can be open to question, the sentiment cannot pass unheeded. The technologists' reply must be professional, respectful and offer the advantages of novelty, convenience and satisfaction.

CONCLUSION

IMF intended for the human diet may find it difficult to penetrate the conventional food market unless they can offer a food sensation which is new and different from the old. We must seek foods which are as novel as bacon, smoked salmon, dried figs and fruit cake were when they first appeared. Cost will be an important, but not necessarily vital, factor. Cheapness with IMF (which is unlikely) will not ensure commercial success. Higher prices than the conventional food would be disastrous. As Heidelbaugh and Goldblith have said:[7] 'Highest profit margins go to those who effectively adapt new technology to meet consumer needs'. Do consumers need IMF?

REFERENCES

1. Heidelbaugh, N. D. and Karel, M. (1975). In: *Freeze Drying and Advanced Food Technology*, ed. S. A. Goldblith, L. Rey and W. W. Rothmayer, Academic Press, London, p. 620.
2. Hollis, F., Kaplow, M., Klose, R. and Halik, J. (1968, 1969). Tech. Repts. 69-26-FL and 70-12-FL, US Army Natick Labs., Mass.
3. Chordash, R. A. and Potter, N. N. (1972). *J. Milk Fd. Technol.*, **7**, p. 395.
4. Goldblith, S. A., Rey, L. and Rothmayer, W. W. (Eds.) (1975). *Freeze Drying and Advanced Food Technology*, Academic Press, London, p. 625.
5. Lea, C. H. and Hannan, R. S. (1945). *Biochim. biophys. Acta*, **3**, p. 313.
6. Goldblith, S. A., Rey, L. and Rothmayer, W. W. (Eds.) (1975). *Freeze Drying and Advanced Food Technology*, Academic Press, London, p. 626.
7. Heidelbaugh, N. D. and Goldblith, S. A. (1975). In: *Freeze Drying and Advanced Food Technology*, ed. S. A. Goldblith, L. Rey and W. W. Rothmayer, Academic Press, London, p. 683.

DISCUSSION

Karel: One of my colleagues, Paul Newberne, a veterinary pathologist, published a couple of years ago a paper which aroused a certain amount of controversy with pure meat cat-food producers, which showed that intermediate moisture dog food of the soft/moist type (this was for beagles) gave a superior performance to some other types. So I don't think there is much doubt that you can get a nutritionally adequate soft/moist food for animals.

My second comment is, while I agree with you that consumers are reluctant to accept less than top-grade equivalents of fresh foods, I would suggest that there are instances of people changing their allegiance from the traditional type of organoleptic acceptability to new types for the sake of convenience. Perhaps the hamburger is not quite the same thing as a gammon steak, but it is acceptable and convenient. I think we can achieve a convenient and acceptable food that doesn't have to be quite up to the standard of T-bone or porterhouse steak.

Robson: Yes, of course I agree the hamburger is a very desirable article. It is a very convenient way of making a food which is acceptable out of meat which is not of the highest quality, and therefore it is a sensible food to develop, and it is being accepted all over the world. What I'm trying to say is, if you say the hamburger is a new food, where is the equivalent of the hamburger? I'm not looking for an intermediate moisture eggs and bacon, because I've got eggs and bacon, and that's the way I want to go on eating them.

Chairman: One of the points you made about the use of additives in IMF was that it seemed almost essential, in view of the various reactions that take place (not only microbiological but chemical), that the emphasis of future thinking should be directed towards arresting these processes. Do you feel that it would be a retrograde step to develop even more additives?

Robson: I think as a food scientist I wouldn't necessarily consider it a retrograde step, providing we can develop the kind of food additives that do their job, do not have to be used in large quantities and are free from side-effects. Of course they would be entirely acceptable.

But I'm not here this morning to speak as a food scientist; I'm here to speak on behalf of the millions of people who buy these products, many of whom are very concerned about the enormous number of additives in their everyday food. You may not agree, you may think they are ill-advised, but people look down the list of ingredients on our products, and they write us letters about all the things they think shouldn't be there. I'm concerned about putting on to the market a range of foods in which that list of ingredients could get even longer.

Hardman: As a housewife, could I qualify one or two things? Marks and Spencer are dealing only with a small proportion of the population of women; now that more and more women are working, during the week at least they are looking for a convenience package. After all, if you are buying a package food, and you buy, say, protein in meat chunks, you know what you are buying, but if you buy stewed steak, it could be very variable.

Robson: In general it is not our experience that we fail to cater for the working housewife. I would say that something of the order of 70% of our lady customers are working people. I am merely trying to report on the facts as I see them, the facts that distil from a throughput of traffic of the order of 14 million people a week passing through our stores and registering their likes and dislikes. Of course there will be plenty of people who don't want to shop with us because they want to buy something we haven't got.

Blenford: Assuming that developments coming along do fulfil the requirements that you have defined for human IMF products, where would an IMF meeting all those requirements fit in? Is there a role for it in human food terms?

Robson: The answer must be yes. But I'm not sure if it will be a very successful marketing exercise in a country like this. It depends on what is produced, obviously. If you produce a cheaper version of smoked salmon which you can keep on the shelf for 12 months, then obviously you're going to have a lot of success. I think it would probably be more successful in countries where people are remote from the sources of food. A lot of it depends on the environment, the geographical location and the type of product.

4

Intermediate Moisture Petfoods

I. E. BURROWS and D. BARKER

*Pedigree Petfoods Ltd, Melton Mowbray,
Leicestershire, England*

ABSTRACT

Although intermediate moisture petfoods have been on the market for nearly thirteen years, some aspects of the technology of preserving meat products are much older. However, an understanding of the factors influencing microbial growth in intermediate moisture foods began with the introduction of the term 'water activity' by Scott in the 1950s. It was in the early 1960s that the first commercial intermediate moisture petfoods were introduced onto the market in the USA by General Foods. The product they marketed had an a_w of about 0·80. This a_w stops most food spoilage bacteria from growing but not moulds and yeasts. These were inhibited by including fungistats such as potassium sorbate in the formulation. Only by using fungistats are commercial long shelf life products possible, for without them only an a_w of less than 0·60 would give a shelf-stable product. Such low a_w's are not generally applicable to intermediate moisture foods, for this would correspond to a moisture content of below 20%.

There are two basic methods of preparing intermediate moisture petfoods: (a) making a slurry and extruding to form the final shape, or (b) taking whole chunks of meat or meat analogue and diffusing humectants into them. Only the first has been widely used in practice. A brief description is given of a commercial line using an extruder/ cooker for intermediate moisture petfood production.

INTRODUCTION

The preservation of meats and meat products by reducing their water activities can hardly be regarded as a new technology. The semi-drying or smoking of meats, additions of spices, etc., as carried out throughout recorded history (and probably before that) resulted in various recognisably intermediate moisture preserved products. With the widespread introduction of sugar into Europe in the seventeenth and eighteenth centuries a new 'curing' agent for meat was found, and resulted in the early forerunners of modern technology used for preparing intermediate moisture petfoods.

As in so many other aspects of technology the intrepid Victorians realised the potential of intermediate moisture technology about one hundred years before we Elizabethans have exploited it. Admiral Sir Edward Belcher, an Arctic explorer of the mid-nineteenth century, had the true English explorer's concern for the adequacy of his men's diet. He experimented with various concoctions involving sugar, treacle, nitrite, glycerol and molasses, for the preservation of meat for his expeditions during 1850–1860. Even this was not new since meat for the Admiralty had been preserved by rubbing with sugar and molasses in Jamaica 70 years before his expeditions. The meat was coated and rubbed with sugar until it acquired a 'coating like varnish'. Of the supplies that he took with him in 1852, Sir Edward sent a round of beef to the Admiralty 5 years and 8 months later, which apparently met their Lordships' approval in its good, fresh condition.[1] Modern intermediate moisture meat technology had arrived.

Food technologists often have a happy knack of forgetting the sister technology that goes hand in hand with the preservation of food, *i.e.* packaging. This is especially true of intermediate moisture petfoods, since unlike most human foods, petfoods are required to have an indefinite shelf life. However, this paper will only be concerned with the technological aspects of preserving foods from microbiological spoilage, but the importance of packaging should not be forgotten.

MICROBIOLOGICAL STABILITY

Before considering intermediate moisture petfoods in some detail it is worth while pausing to briefly consider the problems encountered in preserving meat products by intermediate moisture technology. The term 'water activity' was introduced by Scott in the 1950s.[2] Table 1 shows the water activity and moisture content of some common foods. The relationship between microbial growth and its control by reduction of water activity is well known. Thus a low

TABLE 1
Water activity and moisture content of common foods

	Moisture content	Water activity
% 100—	Fruits	0·97
90—		
80—	Eggs	0·97
70—		
	Meat	0·97
60—		
50—		
40—	Cheese	0·96
	Jams	0·82–0·94
30—		
	Intermediate moisture petfood	0·83
20—		
	Honey	0·75
10—		
	Sugar	0·1
0—		

Source: Reference 3.

water activity restricts the growth of micro-organisms, and for any given microbe there is a minimum water activity below which it will not grow (Table 2).

Water activity is controlled by the addition to the food of various solutes or humectants such as salt, sugars, polyhydric alcohols, etc. However, not all the inhibitory attributes of the solutes can be

ascribed to the simple 'binding' of water since some have microbiological activity of their own, *e.g.* propylene glycol. Further the
inhibitory effect of any solute can be profoundly modified by the
medium in which it is used, *i.e.* the control of water activity by any
given solute is not independent of the formulation of the food.[6]

TABLE 2

Limiting a_w *values for growth of micro-organisms associated with foods*

Minimum a_w value	Bacteria	Yeasts	Moulds
0·95	Pseudomonas		
0·94			Rhizopus Mucor
0·93	Clostridium		
0·92	Salmonella	Rhodotorula	
0·90		Saccharomyces	
0·88			Cladosporium
0·85			Penicillium
0·83	Staphylococcus		
0·75	Halophiles		
0·65			Aspergillus
0·62		Zygosaccharomyces	
0·60			Xeromyces

Source: References 3, 4 and 5.

It should also be remembered that water activity and water
(moisture) content are intimately linked in the control of microbiological activity. This is clearly illustrated by the sorption isotherms, where the actual water content and corresponding water
activity depend on whether the sample is on the adsorption or
desorption cycle (Fig. 1). Thus the higher water content at a given
water activity in general supports microbiological activity better
than at the lower water content level. This is clearly shown by the
work of Plitman[7] and is given in Fig. 2.

Another determinant factor to consider in the production of an
intermediate moisture food is of course its pH. In general micro-
organisms are preferentially encouraged at a pH range of 6·5–7·5,
i.e. around neutrality. The effect of water activity control on microbiological growth is greatly enhanced at low or acid pH values.[8]

However, translating this theory into a practical intermediate moisture product highlights another important factor. Moulds and yeasts are more resistant to low water activity than most bacteria, and some will grow at an a_w as low as 0·60. To inhibit fungal growth an a_w maximum of 0·60 would be necessary. Such low a_w's are not generally applicable to intermediate moisture foods, for this would

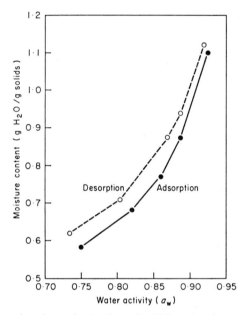

FIG. 1. Adsorption–desorption isotherm for I.M. pork cubes at 25°C prepared with glycerol.

correspond to total moisture contents of well below 20%, or an unacceptably high concentration of solutes. In general an a_w of around 0·80 is aimed at. This a_w will inhibit the important food spoilage bacteria but not the moulds and yeasts. In intermediate moisture petfoods this is overcome by using antimycotics which inhibit the growth that would occur below an a_w of 0·80.

To sum up, then, three main factors are important for the preparation of intermediate moisture food in order to control bacterial spoilage, *viz.* water activity, water content and pH. However, in order to use these factors to produce a succulent soft moist meat product at an a_w of 0·8–0·9 there remains a further problem. Moulds

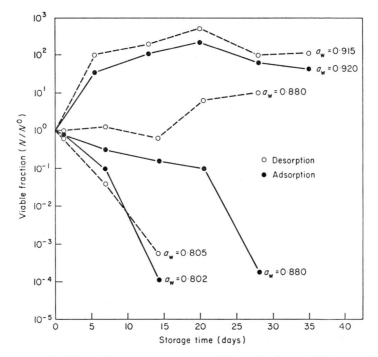

FIG. 2.   Viability of *Staphylococcus aureus* in I.M. pork cubes at 25°C prepared
with glycerol.

and yeasts being more robust than bacteria with regard to the water
activity at which they can live, are not inhibited at these water
activity levels. Thus the breakthrough which enabled the marketing
of a successful intermediate moisture meat petfood was the use of
acceptable antimycotics, in particular potassium sorbate. Consequently all products with water activity in the range 0·8–0·9, water
content 15–35% and pH 5·5–7·0 also contain antimycotics.

THE PRESERVATION AND PREPARATION OF
INTERMEDIATE MOISTURE PETFOODS

The prepared petfood market sector has been built up on products
that fulfil certain conditions. They have to be acceptable to the pet,
they have to have good nutritional value, they must offer the buyer a

perceived value for money, and the trade must be prepared to handle them. The question the petfood manufacturers must ask themselves is how far do intermediate moisture petfoods achieve these objectives. Clearly their continuing commercial success means that these objectives have been achieved in varying degrees. The significant point to bring out here is that the trade has been built up on products that have a very long shelf life. Although the average time for a commercial petfood to go from manufacturer to consumer may be less than 6 months in order to be acceptable to the trade a shelf life of significantly more than 12 months is required. Intermediate moisture petfoods need to have this almost indefinite shelf life to be successful on the market.

The technology outlined above has been used in various ways and this is conveniently reviewed by some of the patent literature available in this field (*see* Table 3).

TABLE 3

Some details of patents describing intermediate moisture food products[9]

Patent No.	Moisture (%)	pH	Humectant content (%)	Mycostats
1,043,585	15–30	6·0–7·0	15–35 sugar	Propylene glycol and potassium sorbate
1,217,662	35–45	<6·0	>10 sugar	Potassium sorbate
1,290,811	20–40	—	5–15 propylene glycol	Propylene glycol and potassium sorbate
1,251,357	15–45	—	>5 polyhydric alcohol	Propylene glycol and potassium sorbate

(1) *British Patent* 1,043,585—*Basic Gainesburger*

Here the preservation relies on high quantities of sugar (15–35%) to act as the humectant to control water activity where the moisture content can be in the range 15–30% at a pH of 6–7. Here General Foods have used potassium sorbate and propylene glycol as antimycotics. This has been the basis of a very successful product that has been on the market for some 12–13 years.

(2) *British Patent* 1,217,662

In this product General Foods used sugars as the humectant to control a_w in the moisture content range of 35–45%, *i.e.* slightly higher than in the basic Gainesburger but the preservation is controlled by lowering the pH to less than 6.

(3) *British Patent* 1,290,811

Ralston Purina uses propylene glycol as a humectant, which has special microbiological activity in its own right. The moisture content is controlled to 28–32% using between 5 and 15% of propylene glycol.

(4) *British Patent* 1,251,357

Here General Foods infuse whole pieces of food with sugar and polyhydric alcohols to control the water activity and an antimycotic to prevent mould growth. The final moisture content of the product can be in the range 15–45%.

Two basic methods can be used for the preparation of an intermediate moisture petfood.

- (a) Making a slurry of ingredients and extruding and/or expanding to form a patty or chunks.
- (b) Taking whole chunks of meat, or meat analogue and diffusing the humectants into them.

The first route used in the first three patents is the one that has been widely used in practice. The second route used in the fourth patent has been less successful.

A typical intermediate moisture petfood is made up of seven basic ingredients, protein, carbohydrates, fat, humectants, antimycotics, micronutrients (vitamins and minerals) and colouring agents. A typical product line using a cooker-extruder is shown in Fig. 3.

The protein is usually in the form of fresh meat or meat by-products and soya meal. The fresh meat is pasteurised in combination with an emulsifier and all the liquid and water soluble ingredients, such as the fat and humectants, at a temperature of about 100°C for 10 min. When the pasteurisation is complete the remaining ingredients such as any additional carbohydrate, the soya meal, micronutrients, colouring agents, etc., can be added. Much of the carbohydrate will have already been added in the form of humectants which are usually sugars or polyols.

When all the ingredients have been added and the mix is homogeneous, the dough-like mix is passed to a cooker-extruder (*see*

Fig. 3). If an unexpanded type of product is required only enough heat will be used to give the product a final cook. The product will be extruded at a low pressure and temperature through the appropriate shaped dies and cut with a rotating knife as it leaves the extruder. The hot, cut pieces can be formed into 'burger' shapes as

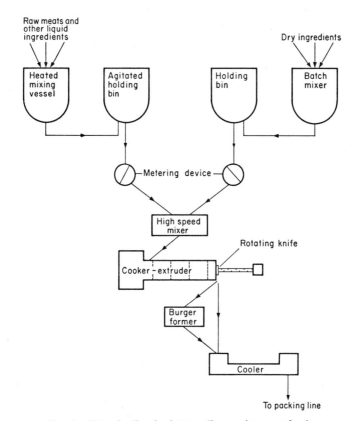

FIG. 3. Extruder line for intermediate moisture petfoods.

the original General Foods 'Gainesburger' or left as individual pieces. Both the 'burger' and the individual pieces need to be cooled before packing.

Many variations on this basic theme are used, but the most important one is expanding the cooked dough rather than straight cooking-extrusion. These formulations usually have more cereal content than their unexpanded counterparts. The cereal starch is gelatinised in the barrel of the cooker-extruder at temperatures of above 100°C and when the product leaves the extruder from the die it expands as the water vaporises. These products, like the previous ones, need to be cooled before packing.

CONCLUSIONS

We have come a long way since Admiral Sir Edward Belcher, but the road has taken us through to the long shelf life, very stable, inter-mediate moisture petfood that we see in the supermarket to-day. I wonder what the next step will be? Perhaps we shall find out in these two days.

REFERENCES

1. Morgan, J. (1864). *J. Royal Soc. Arts,* **XII.**
2. Scott, W. J. (1957). *Adv. Fd. Res.,* **7,** p. 83.
3. Haas, G. J. *et al.* (1975). *Food Prod. Dev.,* **9,** p. 86.
4. Corry, Janet E. J. (1973). In: *Progress in Industrial Microbiology,* Vol. 12, ed. D. J. D. Hockenhull, Churchill-Livingstone, p. 73.
5. Tatini, S. R. (1973). *J. Milk Food Tech.,* **36,** p. 559.
6. Mossel, D. A. A. (1974). In: *Water Relations of Foods,* ed. R. B. Duckworth, Academic Press, p. 347.
7. Plitman, M. *et al.* (1973). *J. Food Science,* **38,** p. 1004.
8. Rieman, H. *et al.* (1972). *J. Milk Food Tech.,* **35,** p. 514.
9. LaVon Wenger Company (1966). Petfood Industry, p. 8.

DISCUSSION

Smith: I've tasted a good number of these petfoods, and I've lived to tell the tale! But although the petfood industry have created an IM product that looks like meat, by no stretch of the imagination can they claim to have produced a *texture* which is like meat. Dogs and cats don't seem to be fussy about texture. I wonder whether in the course of your work you have evolved any textures which could be developed as an interesting new food for the human consumer, thus answering Mr Robson's rallying call to the food technologists to use IMF technologies to develop new products for the human food industry? I wonder whether, for example, the development of textured vegetable protein for human foods shouldn't be following the same lines as you have done in petfoods.

Barker: I can't say I really have. One of the problems with texture, or with giving foods textures, is that as soon as you start including higher levels of humectants, you start withdrawing the water, and the texturing agents that one would normally think of using (some of the gelling agents) rapidly start breaking down. We have played around with things like gluten to some degree; the ways that we've pushed these have of course been in the petfood applications. I have never seen any particular example for human foods.

Jeffery: Some humectants, such as glycerol and propylene glycol, have had effects on bowel movements in animals. Has this been a problem?

Barker: No, although at very high concentrations you could get difficulties—for example, if you push glycerol into animals at 20–30 % they don't like it, and they won't come back a second time. But at the levels we use them we haven't come across any problems. In fact we don't use glycerol in any of our products.

Jeffery: Or propylene glycol?

Barker: We do use that—at perhaps 5 %—but again, at low levels we find that there are no problems. Sugar is the humectant we rely upon most heavily. In the region of 20 % of sugar there are no problems.

5

Water Activity Concepts in Intermediate Moisture Foods

D. S. REID

Basic Studies Unit, Biosciences Division, Unilever Research Colworth/Welwyn Laboratory, Colworth House, Sharnbrook, Bedfordshire, England

ABSTRACT

The concept of water activity, a_w, occupies a key role in the formulation of Intermediate Moisture Foods. Since Scott's work pointing out a correlation between a_w and microbial growth, microbiologists have spent much time and effort in measuring and controlling it. This paper discusses the thermodynamic definition of water activity, pointing out some of its consequences, and in particular it compares the thermodynamic water activity with the quantity often measured, and labelled a_w, and asks the question—are these the same quantity?

INTRODUCTION

That the propensity of a foodstuff for bacteriological spoilage is related to the state of the constituent water, and not just simply the water content, has long been known by microbiologists, and there have been many studies which have emphasised this point. A landmark in such studies was provided by the work of Scott,[1] who showed clearly that there was a correlation between the thermodynamic water activity and microbial growth under certain circumstances. Scott's work was widely acclaimed, and led to a rapid expansion in the use of 'water activity' as one of the control variables in preservation technology. Unfortunately, though Scott was perfectly clear as to the nature of a_w, many workers who have followed in his footsteps

54

have had only a vague idea of the concept which they have been applying with such vigour. Since the reduced availability of water for bacterial spoilage is central to the concept of Intermediate Moisture Foods, 'water activity' is going to play an important role in this meeting. It is relevant, therefore, to look closely at the thermo-dynamic concept of water activity, and consider its relationship to water availability, and to the quantities frequently monitored by microbiologists.

THERMODYNAMIC ACTIVITY

There are many concepts of 'activity' which the practising scientist comes across in his work. Examples include radio *activity*, enzyme *activity*, etc. The term activity, therefore, has to be carefully defined in any application. When one uses the phrase 'water activity' by implication the word activity has its thermodynamic meaning. This carries with it certain consequences. It is convenient to consider the definition of activity, as stated by Lewis and Randall,[2] 'Activity is, at a given temperature, the ratio of the fugacity, f, of a substance in some given state, and its fugacity, f^0, in some state which, *for convenience*, has been chosen as a standard state'.

Several consequences of the definition are immediately apparent.

(1) As this is a thermodynamic concept, it refers only to equilib-rium.
(2) Activity is defined at a fixed temperature.
(3) Since the standard state is a matter of choice, one must specify which choice has been made.

Considering the definition in more detail, it refers to a quantity called fugacity. What is fugacity, and how can it be measured? Fugacity can be considered as being a measure of escaping tendency —a precise definition being out of place here. It is sufficient to consider it as having the form of a vapour pressure which has been corrected for any non-ideality of the vapour. Hence, provided this non-ideality is not too large, the fugacity can be substituted by the measured vapour pressure. This, fortunately, is true for aqueous systems, since at normal temperatures water vapour approximates to an ideal gas. Hence, for water

$$f = p \tag{1}$$
$$\text{fugacity} \quad \text{vapour pressure}$$

Since the activity is defined as a ratio of fugacities, the next task is to choose a standard state. There are two common choices:

(a) One chooses the ideal gas at unit fugacity as standard state. Then

$$a = f/f^0 = f/1 \approx p \tag{2}$$

This standard state is the usual choice for gaseous systems.

(b) One chooses the pure liquid solvent as standard state. Then

$$a = f/f^0 \approx p/p^0 \tag{3}$$

where p^0 is the vapour pressure of the pure solvent. This standard state is the usual choice for the solvent in a solution.

Clearly, if the water activity of a solution is to be measured, it is convenient to choose the pure solvent standard state. This particular choice of standard state has some consequences. For example, if in an ideal mixture of a fraction x_A of the molecules are of type A, the escaping tendency of A from the mixture will be a fraction x_A of the escaping tendency of pure A. This can be written

$$f_A = f_A{}^0 x_A \tag{4}$$

where $f_A{}^0$ is the fugacity of pure A. If we assume the vapour of A to behave as an ideal gas, we can also write

$$P_A = P_A{}^0 x_A \tag{5}$$

where $P_A{}^0$ is the vapour pressure of pure A. This is a statement of Raoult's law, which makes clear some of the conditions which must be fulfilled for Raoult's law to hold. From the definition of activity, and employing the pure solvent standard state, providing Raoult's law holds

$$a = P_A/P_A{}^0 = x_A \tag{6}$$

Thus, in an *ideal* mixture, the pure solvent standard state activity is given by the mole fraction, x, of the solvent in the mixture. In a non-ideal mixture, however,

$$a = P_A/P_A{}^0 \neq x_A \tag{7}$$

The activity, a, can be considered as being a measure of the 'effective concentration', provided the pure solvent standard state is being employed. In effect, it corrects the mole fraction for non-ideality in the mixture in the same way that fugacity corrects the vapour pressure for non-ideality in the vapour. Raoult's law, then, only applies when the mixture is ideal, and the activity on the pure solvent standard state is only equal to the mole fraction when the mixture is ideal. In Table 1, the range of applicability of Raoult's

TABLE 1

The variation in water activity (a_w) *of glucose and glycerol solutions with concentrations at* 25°C

		Glucose			Glycerol	
M	C (wt %)	a_w	x_w	C (wt %)	a_w	x_w
0·2	3·47	0·996 3	0·996 4	1·8	0·996 3	0·996 4
1·0	15·25	0·991 1	0·991 1	8·42	0·991 1	0·991 1
2·0	26·47	0·963 8	0·965 2	15·54	0·963 8	0·965 2
4·0	41·86	0·926 2	0·932 7	26·90	0·927 9	0·932 7
8·0	59·0	0·845 6	0·874 0	42·40	0·858 0	0·874 0
10·0	64·3	0·804 2	0·847 4	47·91	0·824 3	0·847 4

law is illustrated for aqueous glucose and glycerol solutions (often erroneously considered to be ideal mixtures). It is important to remember that Raoult's law no longer applies at concentrations of these solutes which produce water activities within the range of Intermediate Moisture Foods.

Consider now the consequences of the definition of activity, and its application to real systems. The pure solvent state will be used exclusively, unless otherwise noted. The activity on this scale can be equated with the equilibrium relative humidity, ERH, in aqueous systems. Bear in mind, though, that had the standard state been selected as the ideal gas at unit fugacity, the activity would be given by the equilibrium vapour pressure. It is for this reason that one must carefully specify the chosen standard state.

Figure 1 is a schematic diagram showing the variation of the vapour pressure of pure water with temperature. Also shown is the vapour pressure of water above some solution. The water activity at temperature T_1, is given by $(P/P^0)T_1$. Note that this activity refers only to T_1. If we wish to calculate the activity, a_w, at some other temperature T_2, this can be done, using relationships given in standard thermodynamic textbooks. However, this gives $(P/P^0)T_2$, *i.e.* the standard state is also at T_2. Water activity gives the escaping tendency of water from the solution *relative to* the escaping tendency of pure water *at the same temperature*.

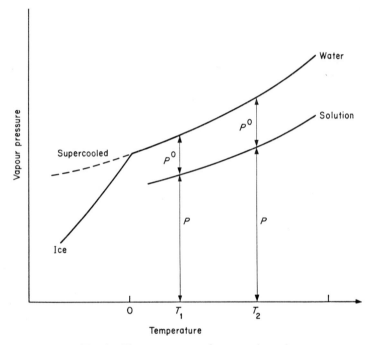

FIG. 1. Vapour pressure of water: schematic.

When using water activity as a criterion of bacteriological stability, this temperature restriction must be borne in mind. One must also ask whether the significant quantity is really the relative escaping tendency of water, or whether some measure of the absolute escaping tendency might not be more relevant in some cases. Another aspect of the definition is that it deals with equilibrium, and applies to systems at equilibrium, *i.e.* it applies only to systems where the escaping tendency (or fugacity) is equal in all phases. If equilibrium has not been attained, the definition does not apply. One might measure a relative humidity, but, if it is not *equilibrium* relative humidity it is not a measure of water activity, though it may still be an important quantity. One can conceive of many situations in which this restriction of the definition can be important. The following examples should illustrate some of the pitfalls which could be encountered in applying the concept of water activity.

(i) If a system is not at internal equilibrium, one might measure a steady vapour pressure (over the period of measurement) which is not the true vapour pressure of the system. An example of this might be pastry. Using the same ingredients, in the same proportions, the order of mixing can result in doughs which exhibit very different water vapour pressures, even though their compositions are identical. The relevant fact is whether the water is added to the flour before or after intimate mixing of the flour and fat. The water resides in different places before baking. The differing vapour pressures, however, do not represent equilibrium vapour pressures, since one, or both systems must be non-equilibrium, due to the presence of kinetic

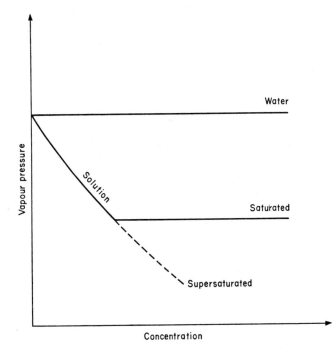

FIG. 2. The effect of supersaturation: schematic.

barriers to the diffusion of water. Indeed, since the situation is non-equilibrium a low measured vapour pressure does not necessarily indicate a low equilibrium vapour pressure. Conclusions drawn as to ease of preservation could be very wrong.

(ii) Another situation which could readily occur in a food system is a pseudo-equilibrium, *e.g.* a solution capable of supersaturation. This is illustrated in Fig. 2. The vapour pressure of the super-saturated solution is lower than that of the saturated solution. Thus the 'water activity' is also lower. Whether this observation is meaningful or not depends on the stability of the supersaturated solution. If crystallisation of the solute occurs, then the water activity will be that of the saturated solution. Whether one uses the 'water activity' of the supersaturated solution, or the true equilibrium water activity depends on the timescale. This means that in a food system the relative humidity must be measured as a function of storage time. It cannot just be assumed to be constant. If it is found to vary, then one cannot assume that it is a true measure of water activity at any time.

(iii) Figure 3 illustrates another aspect of the equilibrium condition. It shows the equilibrium vapour pressure of pure water, and three

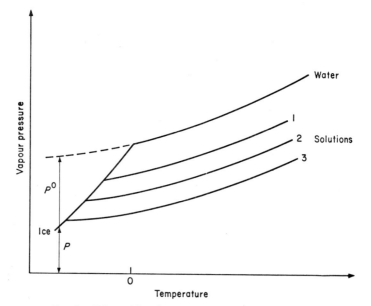

FIG. 3.   Effect of freezing on vapour pressure: schematic.

different solutions. After freezing, it can be seen that all these systems have the same equilibrium vapour pressure. They must therefore all have the same water activity. P^0 here is the vapour pressure of supercooled liquid water (dotted line). Hence, all frozen foods, etc., if at equilibrium, must have the same water vapour pressure, and hence the same water activity, provided that they are stored at the same temperature. At $-20°C$, a_w in a frozen aqueous system is 0·81. Hence frozen foods are a fine example of intermediate moisture foods (providing one does not class ice as moisture).

It is important to remember the restriction of the definition of activity to equilibrium. One is measuring relative escaping tendency, not escaping kinetics. Hence one must be concerned not only with the equilibration time of the measuring system (*i.e.* the response time) one must also bear in mind the equilibration time of the system being measured, and the perturbing effect of the measuring system. It is no good employing a sensor which reaches its maximum response in minutes if it takes the system being studied days (or even weeks) to establish thermodynamic equilibrium. One must always check that equilibrium has been attained, before quoting water activities. Otherwise it might be better to quote relative humidities, and give precise details of the conditions under which the relative humidity has been measured. Even if a system is at equilibrium before measurement, it is possible, if a small amount of water is lost or added whilst introducing it to the measuring system, and preparing for the vapour pressure determination, that re-equilibration could be very slow. Therefore a study of the changes which occur during storage could be distorted if the measuring system inadvertently perturbs the steady state. Such distortions could occur, for example, if the measuring chamber were large, and required a significant quantity of water vapour (in terms of the sample size) to fill it. Also, if evacuation of the space above the sample is required, significant dis-equilibrium could occur. All the vapour in the measuring chamber may have to come from the sample, and if the vaporisation kinetics are slow, and internal diffusion of water through the sample is slow, significant departures from equilibrium could exist for a considerable time. That such conditions could be encountered is evidenced by frequent observations of sorption hysteresis by workers studying the water sorption isotherms of foods.

Temperature also plays a significant role in a_w measurement. As indicated previously, a_w is defined as an isothermal concept. Close temperature control is required during measurement to minimise errors. It is of particular importance that the sample being measured is isothermal. If temperature gradients exist, significant errors can occur. A salutary illustration is provided by the following example. In a lighted display cabinet, it is not uncommon for a temperature differential of as much as 2°C to exist across a sample (*e.g.* a bottle or pack of some product). Table 2 lists the vapour pressure of

TABLE 2

Effect of a temperature differential on 'a_w' (see text for details)

Temp. (°C)	P^0 (mm Hg)	$P(a_w = 0.8)$ (mm Hg)	P(steady state) (mm Hg)	'a_w'
15	12·788	10·23	11·62	0·91
17	14·530	11·62	11·62	0·80
23	21·068	16·85	19·00	0·90
25	23·756	19·00	19·00	0·80
35	42·175	33·74	37·65	0·89
37	47·067	37·65	37·65	0·80

aqueous solutions at three sets of temperatures. In a sealed system, the vapour pressure at the higher temperature will be established as the steady state vapour pressure, and water will transfer to dilute the lower temperature solution until it has the same vapour pressure. Assuming we start with solutions of $a_w = 0.8$ in all cases, the table shows the steady state a_w's which will be achieved. The consequences of such a temperature gradient within the sample could, therefore, be grave, if 'a_w' is a controlling factor in microbiological stability.

Kinetic factors may also be of importance to the microbiology of systems. Since activity is an equilibrium concept, it has nothing to say about rates. Just because a system has a high water activity (and hence high escaping tendency of water) it does not follow that the kinetics are rapid. The rate of establishment of a steady vapour pressure, which is the quantity usually measured, is a much better indicator, but this is not necessarily related to the water activity. Tables of activities are not necessarily relevant.

It is possible to amplify the consequences of the definition of water activity in more detail, but the major points have been covered.

CONCLUSIONS

Activity is a thermodynamic concept, so if one is going to employ the term one must be aware of the requirements of the definition. The ERH, P^0 is indeed a measure of a_w, which can be looked on as an 'effective concentration'. However, this is not necessarily a measure of available water. If a_w is low, then available water will be low, but if a_w is high, the available water may still be low due to (a) the amount of water in the system, or (b) kinetic factors. A measure of the rate of establishment of a steady relative humidity is a meaningful quantity, but the steady value is not necessarily a_w, and should be renamed to avoid possible confusion, since thermodynamic tables list a_w. If order of mixing produces different steady vapour pressures, it is certain that at least one of the 'a_w' values is not a true water activity. One must distinguish between ERH and RH, and perhaps in so doing, new ideas for processing methods will come to light.

REFERENCES

1. Scott, W. J. (1957). In: *Advances in Food Research*, Vol. VII, ed. E. M. Mrak and G. F. Stewart, Academic Press, New York, p. 84.
2. Lewis, G. N. and Randall, M. revised by Pitzer, K. S. and Brewer, L. (1961). *Thermodynamics*, McGraw-Hill, London, p. 242.

DISCUSSION

Chairman: By considering water activity as such rather than the equilibrium relative humidity to which it is equivalent, are we not in danger of overlooking the equilibrium between food itself and its environment? In other words, I believe that if the equilibrium relative humidity of a particular food is less than the relative humidity in the atmosphere with which it is in contact, you will get migration of moisture from the atmosphere to the surface of the food until equilibrium is reached. You could well get conditions which would favour microbiological deterioration on the surface, whereas the bulk of the food is quite stable. I was wondering whether the attention given to water activity rather than to equilibrium relative humidity tended to obscure this relationship.

Reid: Just because you've got an equilibrium value that will be established in time doesn't mean that the surface can't reach a higher value—and if it does, you're liable to get surface spoilage. I'm just trying to point out that it's all very well using a concept such as water activity, but what you're interested in, in the end, is will this product keep, not what is the water activity.

Blanchfield: Could I refer to two very well-known instances, one of which illustrates the point that the Chairman has just mentioned, and the other the point Dr Reid made? The first is the classic case of glacé cherries, which from time to time people unwisely try to put in hermetically sealed packs like polythene bags—and cyclic changes in temperature, or temperature differentials in storage, give rise to local high water activity and fermentation. The second is the situation in a jam-filled biscuit. This is not primarily a microbiological problem, but a problem of deterioration in quality where the soluble solids of the jam filling have to be much higher than in a normal jam (and therefore the water activity lower), otherwise you get migration of moisture from the jam into the biscuit and deterioration follows.

Reid: I fully agree you have to be very careful, and watch exactly where the water goes. Shopkeepers have never learned to store products isothermally. It's all very well having a thermostat in the laboratory, but shops aren't laboratories.

Chairman: No. One has also got to consider tropical climates; all sorts of problems can arise due to humidity.

Karel: I should like to commend Dr Reid for considering the non-equilibrium aspects, which are very important, but I should like to express a very slight disagreement in an area in which I disclaim any expertise—microbiology. Your comment that frozen foods are lowered activity foods is correct, but I think you retreated too soon by saying that at the low temperature micro-organisms will not grow anyway. It has been shown that, if crystallisation of water is prevented, micro-organisms can in fact grow well below the freezing-point of water.

Reid: I meant that at $-20°C$ they won't grow.

Gould: Many meat products which rely for their stability and safety on lowered water activity are packed in hermetically-sealed packs, such as plastic vacuum packs, and stored in chill cabinets where the sort of temperature differential you mentioned does occur. Can you comment at all on the kinetics of water migration in that sort of pack, as opposed to the sort of pack in which there is air space?

Reid: Depending on how tight the pack is, the kinetics might be slowed down by the actual space available, but you've got to look at each individual case. Normally, most of the vapour transfer would be through the solids—but if the pack is slightly loose, even if it's a vacuum pack, then it gives a beautiful vapour transfer path on to the surface. If you look at some of the meats actually stored in supermarkets, you can get some green mouldy vacuum-packed hams. Usually the supermarket gets them off the shelf in the mornings, but I'm sure that there is a problem there which is not being fully tackled.

Roberts: Could you extend Dr Gould's question to consider a stack of packs of meat, all of which are tightly vacuum-packed, and the top one may be 2° or 10°C higher than the bottom one? So the top pack will have a higher a_w?

Reid: No, the top pack will have the same a_w as the bottom pack. As long as it's close to isothermal, it will just be a different temperature, but the same a_w. It's when you get a temperature gradient in the one pack that you get a vapour pressure established all down the pack, and so a_w increases all the way down.

Roberts: Ideally, of course, these cabinets should be at a constant temperature, but as you know very well there is often a difference between the top pack and packs right at the bottom. The greening you saw may or may not be spoilage; some very funny things can happen regarding colours produced through plastic laminates. There's one on the market where you can take a piece of perfectly good red meat, put a vacuum on it, and if you look at it in a certain lighting it's bright green. Take it out of the pack and it's red. It's just an optical effect.

6

The Significance of Water, Hydration and Aqueous Systems in Intermediate Moisture Foods

ALAN SUGGETT

*Unilever Research Colworth/Welwyn,
Sharnbrook, Bedfordshire, England*

ABSTRACT

The growth of micro-organisms in food systems can be minimised by reducing the availability of free water. In an equilibrium system the availability of water may be inferred from measurements of the water activity. However, in non-equilibrium systems (for example, many types of Intermediate Moisture Foods) the thermodynamic concept of water activity has no meaning. Water can, however, be effectively immobilised by virtue of the high activation barriers that can occur in non-equilibrium systems, so that this water does not in reasonable periods of time become available to micro-organisms.

'Water-binding' and 'hydration' are terms which are used by different people to refer to quite different phenomena. Some of the concepts and methods used in the food industry to assess 'water-binding' are re-examined with respect to both simple and multi-component systems. A method is described which utilises both nuclear magnetic and dielectric relaxation measurements to determine extents of hydration of some potential food humectants with rather less uncertainty and ambiguity than is currently customary. In three cases (glucose, sucrose, ribose) the hydration behaviour of the additive in concentrated aqueous solution (i.e. in an equilibrium situation) is compared to the corresponding behaviour in non-equilibrium situations.

INTRODUCTION

The reduction of microbial growth in food systems by lowering the 'water activity' is of course well known. However, as has been pointed out already, the use of the term 'water activity' should be restricted to systems in true thermodynamic equilibrium, and therefore one must be more than a little careful in the use of this term. There appear to be, after all, non-equilibrium ways of binding water—the water remaining effectively inaccessible to the micro-organism because of kinetic rather than thermodynamic factors. For example, the observation of a hysteresis loop in a hydration/dehydration experiment indicates immediately that, at least in one arm of the cycle, the system cannot be in equilibrium as the 'observation' of two alternative water activities at a single water content is clearly thermodynamically impossible.

So part of the art of Intermediate Moisture Food Technology seems to be the art of creating metastable systems and thus satisfying microbiological criteria by means of chemical ingenuity. Margarine and chocolate are two well known examples of food systems in which a great deal of work over many years has been channelled into ways of *avoiding* the true equilibrium state in which various undesirable crystallisation processes would have occurred. In Intermediate Moisture Foods we are more concerned with the non-equilibrium binding of water-hydration which according to the laws of thermodynamics should, at least in part, be available to micro-organisms, but because of high activation barriers is not readily released. This contribution to the Symposium will thus be directed towards the hydration of some potential ingredients of Intermediate Moisture Foods.

CONCEPTS OF HYDRATION

In their recent review of protein and polypeptide hydration, Kuntz and Kauzmann[1] used as an operational definition of bound water 'that water in the vicinity of the macromolecule whose properties differ detectably from those of bulk water in the same system'. Although such a definition has severe limitations in the sense that the estimation of the hydration depends very much on the 'property' which is being examined, it is nevertheless a useful starting point for our considerations—particularly as in the food industry the terms 'hydration' or 'hydratability' seem to mean almost all things to all men. For example:

(1) The term 'hydratability' is often used to imply something about the relative ease of solubilising the material. This in practice has probably more to do with the nature of the lattice forces in the solid than with the interactions with solvent. It is easy, after all, to think of very hydrophilic materials such as celluloses, amyloses which are essentially insoluble in water but on which solubility can be conferred by making the polymer less, rather than more, hydrophilic (*e.g.* by partial methylation). Some really quite hydrophobic polymers, *e.g.* poly(ethylene oxide) —(CH$_2$—CH$_2$—O—)$_n$ can be readily solubilised in water. In reality therefore, the hydration of the materials is only a tiny part of the solubilisation process. This is exemplified very well by the solubility behaviour of the inositols; while myo-inositol (Fig. 1) is quite soluble in water, changing the configuration of the single axial hydroxyl group (to scyllo-inositol) renders it virtually insoluble.

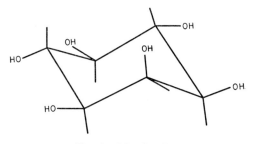

FIG. 1.   Myo-inositol.

(2) In rehydratable systems 'hydration' or 'water binding' are often used to describe the amount of water that is taken up when the material swells in excess water. Cross-linked dextrans have been used as model systems for such swelling phenomena. Again, however, this water does not come within our working definition of hydration as the vast bulk of the water is not significantly affected in any of its properties. As a general rule, the bulk of the water held in gels of all types (polysaccharide, protein, etc.) cannot be considered as hydration.[2,3]

(3) Some methods estimate water that is carried along by a solute in a dynamic experiment. This may include water molecules in intimate contact with the solute, but also in some cases water that is essentially trapped rather than bound. Thus hydrodynamic estimates

of the hydration of, for example, very flexible polymers may be grossly exaggerated.

(4) Even if one considers only the water intimately associated with the solute—by hydrogen-bonding for example—different techniques 'see' different things depending upon the timescale over which the system is examined. For example, the only kind of water that diffraction methods will 'see' is that so firmly attached that it is essentially part of the structure. With NMR, separate contributions from the 'bound' and 'free' water molecules can be observed so long as the water molecule resides on a binding site longer than say $\sim 10^{-3}$ s at a time. If the water exchange process is faster than this, then NMR will only detect an average property of all the water, and a shorter timescale technique, *e.g.* dielectric relaxation, would be needed to differentiate between the different states of the water. It is, however, important to recognise the fact that different methods with their different inherent timescales may see different degrees and extents of binding.

(5) The estimation (by NMR, calorimetry, etc.) of the so-called non-freezable water—the fraction which does not show normal freezing/melting behaviour—is widely used for 'hydration' estimation. It is undoubtedly worth remembering, however, that taking the amount of non-freezable water as an indication of ambient temperature hydration (rather like relative humidity measurements as an indication of a_w) can be very useful and convenient, but also contains implicit assumptions and hidden dangers.

Most of our specialist knowledge about water binding to biological molecules has been obtained in simple mixtures, and in general the results to be presented here fall into the same category. Much less is known about the competitive behaviour of different sorts of molecules for a limited supply of water—although later speakers may shed some light on this area.

HYDRATION OF SMALL SUGARS IN SOLUTION

There have been a number of attempts in recent years to determine the extents of hydration of carbohydrates from a range of bulk solution measurements (for a review *see* Reference 2, page 532) such as intrinsic viscosities, adiabatic compressibilities, etc. Water activity determinations from isopiestic studies have also been used. For example, Stokes and Robinson[4] suggested that aqueous solutions of sucrose and glucose behave semi-ideally (*i.e.* the solution is an ideal one provided due allowance is made for some of the solvent being 'removed' as hydration). From their data, hydration numbers of near 2 and 5 mol H_2O/mol sugar for glucose and sucrose at 25°C were extracted.[5] From available osmotic coefficient data, similar calculations can be performed for solutions of a number of simple sugars and related poly-ols, as shown in Table 1.

TABLE 1

Hydration numbers (at 25°C) calculated from activity data via the semi-ideal treatment

Sugar	Concentration (molal)	Hydration (mol H_2O/mol sugar)
Glycerol	3	1·1
	5	1·0
Mannitol	1	1·1
Xylose	2·8	1·3
Ribose	≤3	0
Glucose	3	1·9
	5	1·8
Sucrose	1	4·8
	2	4·8
Maltose	1·6	3·5
Raffinose	1	7·0

This sort of treatment is, however, an oversimplified one, as indicated by other thermodynamic studies.[6,7] Particularly curious is the indication[8] that D-ribose solutions behave completely ideally up to 3 molal in concentration (indicating on the basis of this treatment, zero hydration) whereas closely related molecules such as xylose show measurable deviations from unit activity. Such indications (Table 1) of the extent of hydration from water activity determinations must at best be treated as semi-quantitative.

In recent years relaxation spectroscopy has proven to be of great value in examining the state of water in carbohydrate systems,[5,9-11] and recently[12] a strategy for combining the best features of nuclear magnetic and dielectric relaxation techniques has been described. This parallel use of the two methods has eliminated many of the uncertainties and ambiguities which had previously been apparent in hydration studies performed via the individual techniques. The details of the combined relaxation approach need not be repeated here; suffice it to state that from it one can determine the 'primary hydration' of the sugars. Table 2 indicates some results for mono- and disaccharides at 5°C.

TABLE 2

Primary hydration of some simple sugars[12]
(sugar concentration 2M, $T = 5°C$)

Sugar	Hydration (mol H_2O/mol sugar)
Glucose	$3·7 \pm 0·2$
Mannose	$3·9 \pm 0·4$
Ribose	$2·5 \pm 0·4$
Maltose	$5·0 \pm 0·5$
Sucrose	$6·6 \pm 0·7$

It should be noted that variations (in both mono- and di-saccharides) from sugar to sugar indicate that the overall hydration of sugars cannot simply be the sum of the effects of the individual hydroxyl groups. These and other results tend to suggest that the stereochemical arrangement of the OH groups is important, and that equatorial hydroxyls in a pyranose sugar ring are very much preferred for strong hydration. As well as the primary hydration layer, the relaxation results suggest that the effects of the sugar–water interactions extend into a 'secondary hydration layer' in which the water molecules exchange between the 'bound' and 'bulk' states much more rapidly.

In relation to this Symposium, the question we need to ask now is whether there is any evidence for sugars holding on to their primary hydration in circumstances when, on the basis of the known equilibrium behaviour, it would not be expected. Some light can be thrown on this question by considering the behaviour of simple sugars in frozen aqueous solution. The thermal properties of frozen solutions of three simple sugars—glucose, ribose and sucrose—indicate[13] that the attainment of equilibrium at sub-zero temperatures is difficult, requiring days, weeks or even years depending upon the nature of the sugar. What is observed on freezing a solution of, say, glucose is the crystallisation of part of the water as ice and the formation of a second phase which may be a glass or a syrup depending upon the temperature. The compositions of the glassy phases for the three sugars are [glucose 3·7 ($\pm$0·6) H_2O], [ribose 2·9 ($\pm$0·6) H_2O] and [sucrose 6·6 ($\pm$1·0) H_2O]. The agreement between the amount of water held by the sugars in this non-equilibrium state and those indicated for the solution primary hydration in Table 2 is excellent, and probably not coincidental. Something of the strength of this water binding is indicated by the fact that the hydration water can withstand incorporation into the ice phase for very long periods despite its inherent only metastable state.

CONCLUSIONS

From current work in the area of the hydration properties of biological materials, three points are worthy of repetition:

(1) First, to reiterate the view expressed earlier that great care needs to be taken with the concept of water activity.

(2) It is possible to define reasonably clearly what one implies in a given situation by the use of the term 'hydration', but one must accept that different methods with their different inherent timescales are quite likely to 'disagree' quantitatively. The 'disagreement', however, only reflects the relative sensitivities of the methods to different degrees of binding.

(3) Estimates of hydration in equilibrium situations can be relevant to the understanding of the distribution of water between phases in non-equilibrium situations. However, probably more useful than a precise knowledge of the maximum hydration of food humectants would be a more extensive knowledge of their relative efficiencies in competing for a limited supply of water.

REFERENCES

1. Kuntz, I. D. and Kauzmann, W. (1974). *Adv. Prot. Chem.*, **28**, p. 239.
2. Suggett, A. In: *Water, A Comprehensive Treatise*, Vol. 4, ed. F. Franks, Plenum Press, New York, p. 519.
3. Suggett, A. (1975). In: *Water Relations of Foods*, ed. R. B. Duckworth, Academic Press, London, p. 23.

4. Stokes, R. H. and Robinson, R. A. (1966). *J. Phys. Chem.*, **70**, p. 2126.
5. Tait, M. J., Suggett, A., Franks, F. Ablett, S. and Quickenden, P. A. (1972). *J. Solution Chem.*, **1**, p. 131.
6. Franks, F., Ravenhill, J. R. and Reid, D. S. (1972). *J. Solution Chem.*, **1**.
7. Schonert, H. (1968). *Z. Phys. Chem.*, **61**, p. 262.
8. Uedaira, H. Personal communication in Ref. 2.
9. Franks, F., Reid, D. S. and Suggett, A. (1973). *J. Solution Chem.*, **2**, p. 99.
10. Suggett, A. and Clark, A. H. (1976). *J. Solution Chem.*, **5**, p. 1.
11. Suggett, A., Ablett, S. and Lillford, P. J. (1976). *J. Solution Chem.*, **5**, p. 17.
12. Suggett, A. (1976). *J. Solution Chem.*, **5**, p. 33.
13. Reid, D. S. unpublished.

DISCUSSION

Karel: I would like to point out that hydration per arbitrary unit (either per molecule of sugar, or per hydrophilic group) in IMF or in dehydrated foods is quite different from hydration in ideal solution. The controlling factor is often the internal 'surface' available for hydration. In amorphous systems produced by freezing and freeze drying only a fraction of —OH groups are available for hydration, and in crystalline sugars that fraction is exceedingly small, until the crystals are in fact disrupted (by H_2O sorption at high water activities).

Suggett: I appreciate that point very much. I don't want to over-emphasise the significance of simple trigger-point systems for complex intermediate moisture food combinations, except to say that it was indicative to me that if one could get non-equilibrium water-binding in such simple systems as this, then one must have this sort of problem arising in more complex systems.

Smith: You mentioned sugars in your paper, but have you done any work on the mesophase of protein dispersions which has been described by your colleague Dr Tooms?

Suggett: No.

Smith: Have you any comment, then, on whether this contributes, or might contribute, to the stability of intermediate moisture foods?

Suggett: I have my doubts, though I am not an expert in mesophases or soy proteins at all. I feel that probably for complex molecules like this, the state of preparation of the material is of paramount importance.

Chairman: You mentioned NMR and dielectric relaxation as methods for determining these non-equilibrium water-binding effects. Would you like to comment briefly on those methods and their relative advantages and disadvantages?

Suggett: The great advantage of NMR is the ability to adjust your system so that you are only looking at one component in that system. So that if in a simple sugar-based solution you want to look at the water, then you can put your sugar in ^{17}O for example, and then you can look at the properties of that by itself. Alternatively you can put your sugar into D_2O, and look at either the proton or the ^{13}C properties of the sugar. This can be a great advantage. Where it loses its advantages in the sort of systems I've been telling you about is, the time-scale of NMR is probably measured in milliseconds, and if this water pops off and on faster than milliseconds, then all NMR sees is some broad property of all this water, an average property; and although that gives us some indication of how it has changed, it doesn't tell us how much, or how strongly. It gives us, you might say, half the information.

The advantage of the dielectric technique is that it's a faster time-scale technique. One can look at exchange rates down to the order of $10^{-11}/s$ before the thing becomes blurred. The disadvantage is that it sees everything at once, so that the motion of the sugars in the water in whatever state are all superimposed on each other, and one can get a very complicated sort of spectral envelope. The combination that we've been able to use takes the advantages of NMR in an attempt to characterise the individual parts of that spectrum, the motion of the sugar, the average motional properties of the water, and uses that information to resolve, unambiguously, the dielectric spectrum. So it's a combination of the selectivity of NMR and the time-scale resolution of the dielectric method.

7

Measurement of Water Activity. Critical Appraisal of Methods

THELMA M. HARDMAN

*University of Reading, Chemistry Department,
Reading, Berks, England*

ABSTRACT

*Most foodstuffs continuously adjust their moisture contents by sorbing
or desorbing water to the atmosphere. In Food Technology both the
prevention of moisture exchanges, in the packaging and storage of
foods, and the controlled removal of water to reduce weight and extend
storage life, in dehydration and freeze drying, are important. The
concentration of water in the atmosphere varies over a wide range and
it is necessary to have an index of whether the food will sorb or desorb
moisture under given storage conditions.*

*The desorbable water present in a foodstuff may be expressed in
terms of the equilibrium relative humidity or ERH.*

$$ERH = (p_{equ}/p_{sat})_{T,P=1\,atm}$$

*where p_{equ} is the partial pressure of water vapour in equilibrium with
the sample in air at one atmosphere total pressure and temperature T;
p_{sat} is the saturation partial vapour pressure of water in air at a total
pressure of one atmosphere and temperature T. The ERH is temperature dependent.*

*A foodstuff in moist air will exchange water until the equilibrium
partial pressure at that temperature is equal to the partial pressure of
water in the moist air, so that the ERH value is a direct measure of
whether moisture will be sorbed or desorbed. The problem is to determine ERH values readily. The vapour pressure of water in equilibrium
with a foodstuff initially placed in an evacuated vessel can be measured*

75

manometrically. However, a reliable method is required which combines mobility with speed of measurement so that instant checks can be made anywhere in the laboratory or factory.

INTRODUCTION

A foodstuff containing moisture in contact with the ambient atmosphere will sorb or desorb moisture. The amount of desorbable water at a given temperature does not just depend on the actual concentration of water present in the sample, but is a sensitive function of the nature and concentration of water-soluble substances present. The amount and rate of loss or gain also depends on the concentration of water vapour present in the atmosphere.

The amount of water vapour in the atmosphere may be measured by its concentration or partial pressure. The partial pressure, p, of water vapour in a sample of air is *defined* as

$$p = yP \tag{1}$$

where y is the mole fraction of water in the gaseous phase and P is the total pressure of air plus water vapour. The partial pressure of water vapour in saturated air at pressure P is not the same as the vapour pressure of pure liquid water at that temperature. The difference is given by

$$\ln p_{sat}(P) - \ln p^0(p^0) = (P - p^0)V^0/RT \tag{2}$$

where $p_{sat}(P)$ is the partial pressure of water vapour in saturated air at total pressure P; $p^0(p^0)$ is the vapour pressure of water at the same temperature T; V^0 is the molar volume of liquid water at temperature T; R is the gas constant. (It has been assumed in writing eqn. (2) that the vapour phases are perfect gases; for real gases p_{sat} and p^0 should be replaced by their respective fugacities $p*_{sat}$ and $p^{0}*$.) At ordinary pressures, the quantity on either side of eqn. (2) is negligible. Thus for all practical purposes p_{sat} can be replaced by p^0, the vapour pressure of water at the same temperature, and the pressure dependence of the partial pressure of water vapour neglected.

As the amount of water lost from, or taken up by, a water-containing food depends on the nature and concentration of the water-soluble substances present, it is no use attempting to measure the quantity of water actually present in the foodstuff. Instead we need to know the weight of water desorbed into the vapour phase at equilibrium. This is an extensive quantity depending on the volume of the vapour phase. An intensive measure of the quantity of water in the vapour phase is the equilibrium partial pressure, p_{equ}. Thus the partial pressure, p_{equ}, of the water vapour in equilibrium with the food is taken as a measure of the concentration of desorbable water present. The rate of loss or gain depends on the value of p_{equ} in relation to the partial pressure of water vapour in the atmosphere. However, p_{equ} is a highly temperature dependent quantity, so that in practice, it is more convenient to find a quantity less dependent on temperature.

Consider the activity, a_w, of the water present in a solution, which is defined as

$$a_w = p_{equ}/p^0 \qquad (3)$$

where p_{equ} is the vapour pressure of water in equilibrium with the solution and p^0 is the vapour pressure of pure water at the same temperature and pressure as the solution. (Strictly the activity is the fugacity ratio.) Now the temperature dependence of the activity is given by

$$\left(\frac{\partial \ln a_w}{\partial^1/T}\right)_p = (H_{H_2O} - H_{H_2O}{}^0)/R \qquad (4)$$

where H_{H_2O} is the partial molar enthalpy of water in the solution and $H_{H_2O}{}^0$ is the molar enthalpy of water at the same temperature T. $H_{H_2O} - H_{H_2O}{}^0$ is called the relative partial molar enthalpy L_{H_2O}.

Dunning *et al.*[1] give for a saturated solution of sucrose at room temperature L_{H_2O}/J mol^{-1} is 0(150), which gives $da_w/dT \simeq 10^{-4}$ K^{-1}.

For a saturated sodium chloride solution[2] (6·1 mol kg^{-1}), L_{H_2O}/J mol^{-1} is 0(50); L_{H_2O} has a maximum value of 90 J mol^{-1} for a 4·6 mol kg^{-1} solution. Thus again the temperature dependence of the water activity is small. Now, as has been pointed out, the activity, a_w, as defined by eqn. (3), is strictly a fugacity ratio determined at a constant overall pressure, that of the solution. For practical purposes a quantity, called the equilibrium relative humidity, or ERH, is defined by

$$ERH = (p_{equ}/p_{sat})_{T, P = 1 atm} \qquad (5)$$

where p_{equ} is the partial pressure of water vapour in equilibrium
with the sample in air at one atmosphere total pressure and temperature T; p_{sat} is the solution partial pressure of water in air at a total
pressure of one atmosphere and temperature T.

From eqn. (2), the pressure dependence of both p_{sat} and p_{equ} is
negligible and p_{sat} may be replaced by p^0. The ERH is temperature
dependent, but, as shown by eqn. (4), this can often be ignored; p_{equ}
and p_{sat} must both refer to the same temperature T.

In certain circumstances the ERH is highly temperature dependent.
If a saturated solution in the presence of excess solute is heated, the
concentration of solute usually increases and hence the ERH will

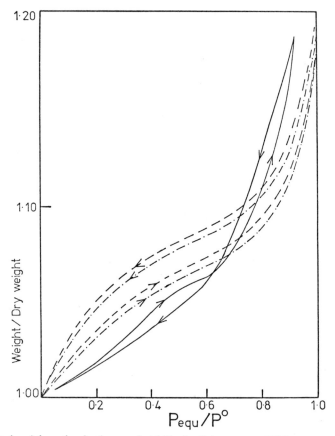

FIG. 1. Adsorption isotherms of stabilised cellulose; – – –, 25°C; – · – ·, 35°C;
——— 10^{-3} mol sucrose adsorbed on 1 g cellulose at 25°C.

change with increasing temperature. With many biological materials a different value of the equilibrium partial vapour pressure is reached depending on whether the material is sorbing or desorbing moisture, *i.e.* hysteresis occurs, and also the ERH is temperature dependent. In Fig. 1 are shown some of our own data[3] for cellulose at 25°C and 35°C; the ERH increases with increasing temperature. Isotherms for cellulose with adsorbed sucrose (10^{-3} mol of sucrose adsorbed on 1 g of cellulose) are also shown at 25°C, and illustrate the sensitivity of the ERH to the nature of the adsorbate. Instead of specifying the relative humidity of a sample of air, it is often useful to give the dew-point. The dew-point is the temperature at which saturation occurs when air is cooled without change in water content. The dew-point is an absolute measure of the water present in the air and from

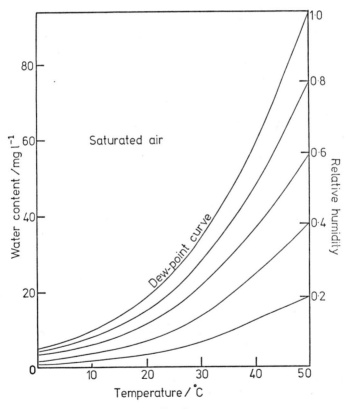

FIG. 2.

it the relative humidity at any temperature can be found from tables or a chart, shown in Fig. 2.

CLASSICAL METHODS OF DETERMINING ERH

A complete analysis of the equilibrium moisture content of a sample at a given temperature is given by its sorption isotherm. The isotherm shows the variation of equilibrium relative humidity with change in moisture content of the sample. Most foodstuffs show at least some hysteresis and it must be appreciated that a sample may have an ERH intermediate between that for sorption and desorption, depending on the fluctuations in atmospheric humidity which it has experienced. For many macromolecular materials, the sorption isotherms are not reproducible, *i.e.* repeated determinations of the sorption isotherm of the same sample give a changing series of sigmoid curves. Thus for some materials, particularly those which exhibit marked hysteresis effects, a knowledge of the moisture content does not necessarily give the ERH even if the sorption isotherm has been determined. Nevertheless, the sorption isotherm of a foodstuff containing water-soluble crystalline compounds, *e.g.* confectionery products, milk powders, can be useful; the isotherm may show sharp inflexions and discontinuities at certain humidities.

Bushuk and Winkler[4] used a McBain-Bakr sorption balance for determining the sorption isotherms of wheat flour, starch and gluten; the weight of a sample is determined by measuring the extension of a previously calibrated quartz spiral spring; the water vapour pressure at equilibrium is determined manometrically. A method demanding less sophisticated experimental techniques was used by Hellman *et al.*[5] on powdered starches. A weighed sample is stored in an enclosed container maintained at a known relative humidity, by a saturated salt solution, until a constant weight is obtained; the moisture content of the sample is then determined. This method has been extensively used, but the disadvantage is the slowness of equilibration as several days may be required. Makower and Dehority,[6] in studies on the sorption of dehydrated vegetables, evacuated the conditioning chamber and found that this halved the time required for equilibration.

In direct measurements of the equilibrium water vapour pressure an oil manometer should be used for measurements near room temperature. In order to avoid condensation of water vapour in the manometer, the manometric fluid adjacent to the sample should not be at a lower temperature than the sample. Makower and Meyers[7] used a vapour pressure apparatus for dehydrated vegetables and dried eggs; the water evaporated from the sample on evacuating the apparatus was collected in a cold trap; the ice was then evaporated and allowed to regain equilibrium with the sample, which took from 1 to 2 h. The disadvantages of this method are first that it is time consuming and secondly that as excessive water may be evaporated off on evacuation, a representative ERH may not be obtained for a sample with large hysteresis.

The equilibrium methods considered so far are slow as they are static methods and depend upon the time taken for the system to equilibrate. In a dynamic method of determining the equilibrium vapour pressure, air is repeatedly circulated over the sample in an enclosed system, which hastens the attainment of equilibrium. The water content of the air is determined by absorption in concentrated sulphuric acid and measuring the change in volume of the air. This method has been used by Jones[8] for confectionery products. It is an accurate method and although requiring considerable experimental skill, is less demanding than the static vapour pressure methods.

The above methods depend upon the establishment of equilibrium between the sample and vapour phase. A non-equilibrium method is the so-called 'sorption rate' method of Landrock and Proctor.[9] The rate of loss or gain of moisture by a set of identical samples of the same weight and surface area, each stored at a different relative humidity, depends on the vapour pressure difference between the sample and its environment. Smith[10] has applied this method very successfully to materials which readily form surface layers of syrup or crystals impeding moisture transfer so that equilibrium methods cannot be used. An ERH value can be obtained in 1 to 2 h with good precision.

Dew-point hygrometers provide a very accurate method of determining the moisture content of a sample of air. A dew-point method has been used by Pixton and Warburton[11] in conjunction with a separate measurement of moisture content to determine the complete sorption isotherms of cereals. Gough[12] used a similar method for determining the sorption isotherms for cereals, tea, coffee and cocoa, but hastened the attainment of equilibrium by circulating air through the sample with a peristaltic pump. Dew-point hygrometers are often used as standards for the calibration of other hygrometric instruments. The dew-point is detected by the deposition of dew on a silver mirror of accurately known temperature. For measurements of high accuracy, a photocell is used to detect the deposition of dew. Martin[13] has developed a highly sophisticated dew-point hygrometer for use as a laboratory standard. The mirror is made of copper/silver alloy and its temperature is carefully adjusted using a frigistor and electrical heater and measured with a thermocouple. A photocell is used to detect the dew-point, which is reproducible to a few hundredths of a degree even at $-15°C$.

SOME INSTRUMENTS FOR DETERMINING ERH

The methods of determining water activity described so far require laboratory facilities and skilled experimental technique. For an instrument to be used for routine sample control, it should be robust, have a rapid response time and require small sample headspace: it should also preferably be small and give a direct reading of ERH so that it is mobile and can be used by semi-skilled operators.

Dunmore[14] and Spencer-Gregory and Rourke[15] described hygrometers using a salt solution as a sensor, often referred to as electrolytic hygrometers. The salt solution, usually lithium chloride, loses or gains moisture until it has the same partial vapour pressure of water as the sample; measurement of conductivity gives the salt concentration at equilibrium. Several commercial instruments are available based on this principle. The sensor element which is impregnated with the salt differs in each instrument. The Sina equi-HYGRO-SCOPE[16] has been described in detail by Gröninger[17]; examples are given of sorption isotherms for various sugars which have been rapidly determined using this instrument. Doe[18] points out that although a temperature compensator is built into the instrument, the sensors are still sensitive to temperature and change calibration with age, and also that equilibrium must be established in the air-space between the sample and sensor. Hughes et al.[19] used a sensor element of this type as a probe; the sensor of the Honeywell W611A Portable Relative Humidity Readout Instrument[20] was inserted directly into samples of flour and rapid readings of the ERH were obtained. The disadvantages are that the probe values are temperature dependent and care must be taken not to contaminate the sensor. This method is based on the isopiestic method for determining activities of solutions. At equilibrium, the chemical potential of the water in the salt solution is the same as that in the food sample. Rigorous experimental criteria must be satisfied; the temperature of solution and sample must be the same and the solution must not be contaminated with other solutes. Also some time is required for equilibrium to be established as not only has the food sample to equilibrate to its ERH, but the salt solution also has to come to equilibrium with the food sample; the temperature at equilibrium of both sample and sensor must be that at which the sensor is calibrated.

In the Foxboro Dewcel,[21] the temperature of a saturated salt solution is raised until the chemical potential of the water in the saturated solution is equal to that of the food sample. The salt chosen is usually lithium chloride. A considerable amount of work has been done on sensors on unattended buoys at sea, over long periods, by C. K. Folland[22] of the Meteorological Office, Bracknell, England. He found that the sensor was very susceptible to contamination and the solution needed to be renewed every 2 months. Mossel and van Kuijk[23] used a sensor of this design to determine the ERH of foods from chocolate to sausage meat in the range 30–90% and obtained results in good agreement with a sorption method; the time to equilibrate was less than 1 h. Hedlin and Trofimenkoff[24] and Nelson and Amdur[25] also discuss the performance of hygrometers of this type. A commercial instrument of this type is the YSI Dew-point hygrometer.[26]

Several commercial instruments are available, which use sensors of anodised aluminium. This type of sensor was first developed by Jason[27] at the Torry Research Station, Aberdeen, and he has written a detailed review of their properties. Anodised aluminium oxide has a porous crystalline structure, which gives it an extremely high surface area, and is hygroscopic. The aluminium oxide layer is used as the moisture sensitive dielectric is a condenser of variable impedance. The porous oxide film is electrolytically deposited in an acid solution on an aluminium rod. An outer conducting layer, permeable to aqueous vapour, is added; this may be colloidal graphite or an evaporated metal film. The probes must be calibrated, but the response to changes in relative humidity is rapid; they are not suitable for measurements above 90% ERH as here the response is slow and irreversible drift occurs. Underwood and Houslip[28] found that the capacitance of a probe was temperature dependent. Efforts have been made to improve the long term stability, temperature dependence and ERH range of the probes by impregnating the oxide layer with salts, such as sodium tungstate, or by altering the structure of the oxide film. Thus, although there are several instruments on the market based on the same principle, each has its own characteristics. The 'Jason' sensor is marketed as the Jason hygrometer by Tinsley.[29] Reade[30] has used a Shaw hygrometer[31] to measure the ERH of cocoa and chocolate products. The outer electrode is a thin film of gold enveloping the aluminium oxide. He obtained ERH readings in a few minutes with a sensor that had been previously stabilised and calibrated with a salt solution of ERH close to that of the sample, but found the sensors to be temperature dependent. The MCM hygrometer[32] has a sensor produced by winding a fine insulated wire helically over an anodic layer which has been formed onto an aluminium rod. It is claimed to give good discrimination and covers a wide moisture range to near saturation levels of relative humidity. In the Panametrics model 1000 hygrometer,[33] the sensor is made of anodised aluminium foil covered with gold film; it is claimed to have long term calibration stability and to be temperature independent in the range -110 to $60°C$.

Another type of sensor which detects changes in relative humidity through changes in electrical resistance depends on the moisture adsorption of polystyrene. The sensor is a rectangular plastic wafer with surfaces covered with a chemically treated polystyrene co-polymer. The electrical resistance of the polystyrene is measured using an a.c. voltage to avoid polarisation effects. 'PCRC-11' and 'PCRC-55' sensors[34] differ considerably in their response to changes in relative humidity; the PCRC-11 is more sensitive than the PCRC-55 to changes in the region 0–50%, and less sensitive in the range 50–100%.

Gough[35] has done extensive tests on some of these commercial meters. He tested the Jason, Shaw, MCM, PCRC-11 and PCRC-55 sensors by subjecting them to a daily relative humidity cycle; the sensors were subjected to an alternating relative humidity of 45% and 70% for 16 days. These measurements showed no appreciable change in the calibration of the sensors, but the scatter in readings was about $\pm 3\%$ in all cases.

CONCLUSION

With careful checks of the calibration and temperature control, there is probably little to choose between a well designed commercial instrument in any of these categories. It is important to understand the characteristics of the sensor used and to bear this in mind when using the instrument. For a given foodstuff several sorption isotherms should first be determined so that the hysteresis behaviour is known before ERH measurements are made for process control. No commercial instrument can be better than the fundamental scientific principles on which it is based. In methods based on the sample (and sensor) reaching equilibrium with the ambient atmosphere, instantaneous measurement is not feasible. By actually inserting the probe into the food sample, rapid readings can be obtained, but these will not be as accurate as those obtained following the establishment of a true equilibrium. It is obviously desirable for the ambient atmosphere in contact with the sample and sensor to be as small as possible; in attaining an ERH value, the sample loses or gains moisture to the air and sensor, but as long as the sample space is small this will have negligible effect on the readings. The vapour pressure of water at 20°C is 2·34 kN m^{-2}, so that 100 cm^3 of saturated air contain $0(10^{-3}$ g) water.

Instruments using anodised aluminium sensors offer fast response time, compact probe-type sensors and little temperature dependence. However, the characteristics of these sensors depend critically on the method of manufacture so that different commercial instruments offer different advantages.

In order to ascertain the best method of determining the ERH of a given product, it is necessary to take into account both the shape of the sorption isotherm, so that it is known in what ERH range accurate discrimination is required, and the working temperature. It is advisable to carry out frequent calibration checks on any commercial instrument using, for example, a dew-point hygrometer or a salt solution. For the accurate determination of a sorption isotherm, one of the classical methods may be preferable.

REFERENCES

1. Dunning, W. J., Evans, H. C. and Taylor, M. (1951). *J. Chem. Soc.*, p. 2363.
2. Randall, M. and Bisson, C. S. (1920). *J. Am. Chem. Soc.*, **42**, p. 347.
3. Dobney, P. W., Cox, C. and Herrington, T. M. Unpublished work.
4. Bushuk, W. and Winkler, C. A. (1957). *Cereal Chem.*, **34**, p. 73.

5. Hellman, N. N., Melvin, E. H. and Boesch, T. F. (1952). *J. Am. Chem. Soc.*, **74**, p. 348.
6. Makower, B. and Dehority, G. L. (1943). *Ind. Engng Chem.*, **35**, p. 193.
7. Makower, B. and Meyers, S. (1943). *Proc. Inst. Fd. Technologists*, p. 156.
8. Jones, F. R. (1951). *J. Appl. Chem.*, 1 Suppl. issue No. 2, S144.
9. Landrock, A. H. and Proctor, B. E. (1951). *Mod. Packaging*, **24**, p. 123.
10. Smith, P. R. (1965). In: *Humidity and Moisture*, Vol. III, ed. A. Wexler and W. A. Wilderhack, Reinhold, New York, p. 487.
11. Pixton, S. W. and Warburton, Sylvia (1975). *J. Stored Prod. Res.*, **11**, p. 1.
12. Gough, M. C. (1975). *J. Stored Prod. Res.*, **11**, p. 161.
13. Martin, S. (1965). In: *Humidity and Moisture*, Vol. I, ed. A. Wexler and R. E. Ruskin, Reinhold, New York, p. 149.
14. Dunmore, F. W. (1939). *J. Res. natl. Bur. Stds.*, **23**, p. 701.
15. Spencer-Gregory, H. and Rourke, E. (1957). *Hygrometry*, Crosby Lockwood, London.
16. Sina, A. G., Zurich, Switzerland. Agents: Print Control Ltd, Buckingham Palace Road, London.
17. Gröninger, K. G. (1969). *B.F.M.I.R.A. Symp. Proc.*, No. 4, p. 16.
18. Doe, C. A. F. (1970). *B.F.M.I.R.A. Analyt. Methods Panel Mtg.*, October. Append. to Minute 78.
19. Hughes, F. J., Vaala, J. L. and Koch, R. B. (1965). In: *Humidity and Moisture*, Vol. II, ed. A. Wexler and E. J. Amdur, Reinhold, New York, p. 133.
20. Honeywell Controls Ltd, Charles Square, Bracknell, Berkshire.
21. Hickes, W. F. (1947). *Refrig. Engng*, **54**, p. 351.
22. Folland, C. K. (1972). *Proc. Wld. Met. Org. Tech. Conf.*, Tokyo, **2**, p. 186.
23. Mossel, D. A. A. and van Kuijk, H. J. L. (1955). *Fd. Res.*, **20**, p. 415.
24. Hedlin, C. P. and Trofimenkoff, F. N. (1965). In: *Humidity and Moisture*, Vol. I, ed. A. Wexler and R. E. Ruskin, Reinhold, New York, p. 627.
25. Nelson, D. E. and Amdur, E. J. (1965). In: *Humidity and Moisture*, Vol. I, ed. A. Wexler and R. E. Ruskin, Reinhold, New York, p. 617.
26. Shandon Scientific Company, Frimley Road, Camberley, Surrey.
27. Jason, A. C. (1965). In: *Humidity and Moisture*, Vol. I, ed. A. Wexler and R. E. Ruskin, Reinhold, New York, p. 372.
28. Underwood, C. R. and Houslip, R. C. (1955). *J. Sci. Instrum.*, **32**, p. 432.
29. H. Tinsley and Co. Ltd, Werndee Hall, South Norwood, London SE25 5LA.
30. Reade, M. G. (1970). *Confect. Prod.*, **36**, p. 619.
31. J. L. Shaw, Rawson Road, Westgate, Bradford.
32. Moisture Control and Measurement Ltd, Thorpe Arch Trading Estate, Boston Spa, Yorkshire.
33. Endress and Hauser Ltd, Southmoor Road, Wythenshawe, Manchester.

34. Phys. Chemical Research Corp., 36 East 20th Street, N.Y. 10003, USA.
35. Gough, M. C. (1974). *Trop. Stored Prod. Info.*, **27**, p. 19.

DISCUSSION

Leistner: I should like to make a comment on the electrolytic hygrometers you mentioned. What we are really trying to do is to put these hygrometers (the SINA instrument for instance) into the cooler and to measure the surface water activity of meat; and if we can measure it, and improve it, then this would mean a lot to the shelf life of refrigerated meat. Now we found that the water activity at 25°C and 5°C differentiates very little, but we had to calibrate the instrument at 5°C, because the characteristics of the instrument itself change. This has nothing to do with water activity, only with the calibration of the instrument. I think you pointed out a similar thing.

Hardman: Yes. This is something that a lot of people have commented on. One lady who wrote to me was very pleased that the instrument agreed with their method, but someone else had to calibrate their probes every day. The manufacturers claim their probes are independent of temperature, don't they?

Leistner: Perhaps I could add that the calibration of the SINA instrument is much improved now. We have a set-up with an ISO instrument where we use the SINA sensors. We have twelve SINA sensors on this ISO instrument and a digital read-out, with recording attached to it, which automatically calls for the different sensors. So we reduced the time we needed for reading values for meat (3 h) by having multiple sensors, and also with this instrument we can get a much better calibration than with the original SINA instrument.

Roberts: We have used SINA for many years. We keep the recorder and everything else in an incubator at a constant temperature, with very little temperature fluctuation, as temperature is very important. The calibration also changes in time, so we re-calibrate roughly every month over a series of saturated salt solutions. If you want to measure at another temperature, you have to re-calibrate at that temperature, and then if you put it back to the original temperature, you have to re-calibrate again. But knowing all of this, it is still quite a useful instrument.

I'd like to ask Professor Leistner about this time of 3 h. At the moment our probes require about 2 h, but it is very difficult to decide when the plateau is reached. I wonder whether in his experience this equilibration time becomes longer with a particular sensor, or whether he's happy to leave it at 3 h?

Leistner: Most of the time we are satisfied with the reading after 3 h. We record the curve, and if it reaches a plateau, most of the time it is after 3 h. But of course some of the sensors get tired after months of use, and then you just have to replace them because they respond much more slowly.

Karel: (1) The relation between a_w, T and μ is in fact recognised by many of us and we realise that the a_w concept has no fundamental meaning, but is simply a quantity conveniently correlated with some properties.

(2) In the 'Graphical Interpolation Method' of Landrock and Proctor it is not necessary to have absolutely the same areas of different samples, if, as should be done, (a) several humidities near the zero weight loss (gain) point are used, and (b) the estimation of the ERH is based on the approximation of the zero weight change point by interpolation, and *not* extrapolation. Extrapolation would assume two conditions which do not have to be true: (i) equal areas; (ii) the rate of approach to equilibrium is proportional to the 'distance from equilibrium'.

8

The Aqueous Environment for Chemical Change in Intermediate Moisture Foods

R. B. Duckworth, Joy Y. Allison and H. A. Anne Clapperton

*Department of Food Science and Nutrition,
University of Strathclyde, Glasgow, Scotland*

ABSTRACT

Interactions between constituent water and the solid components of foods can lead to marked changes in the physico-chemical properties of the water present. These effects extend through the intermediate moisture region and one aspect which is particularly important in relation to keeping quality, concerns the solvent properties of the aqueous fraction within this range.

The pattern of mobilisation of hydrogen-containing solutes in relation to water content can be examined by means of a simple wideline NMR technique. Using this method it can be shown that the behaviour of a given soluble substance is peculiar to that substance, but that when several different solutes are present various types of interaction can occur.

It is further shown that, when the test solutes are involved in particular reactions such as non-enzymic browning, the water content/reaction rate relationship is determined in each case by the pattern of mobilisation of reactants described by the NMR results.

In the context of Intermediate Moisture Foods, the influence on solute mobilisation of ingredients which have been or may be used as humectants is clearly of special interest. Some of these are liquid at normal temperatures and might therefore be expected to contribute to the total pool of solvent at any given hydration level. Results are described from experiments in which both mobilisation patterns and reaction rates have been determined for systems containing humectant materials of this kind.

The range of water content appropriate to intermediate moisture foods is a very interesting one from the physico-chemical viewpoint because when water is present in such proportions its properties, as we have already seen, are very strongly influenced by the solid substances with which it is associated. Although even within this range water is still the predominant molecular species present in terms of numbers, its molecules are hindered to different degrees in their rotational and translational freedom and this affects its behaviour in many different ways.

Several of the succeeding papers are to be concerned with the influences which these modifications have on the ability of the water present to support the growth and activity of micro-organisms in intermediate moisture foods. A properly formulated product of this type should, however, be effectively resistant to microbiological spoilage and if this is the case then deterioration in quality must result from chemical or physical change which will never be completely eliminated. Indeed, the ability of water to support chemical change is obviously linked with its fundamental biological roles as the universal solvent and as a 'structural' component in living systems. The aspects of the physico-chemical environment which are to be considered here are therefore relevant to biological as well as to chemical activity in intermediate moisture systems.

Water is, of course, itself involved directly as a reactant in hydrolytic reactions which can produce undesirable changes of various kinds during food storage, especially if the associated enzyme systems have not been effectively inactivated. However, the principal roles that water plays in relation to chemical reactivity in intermediate moisture foods are as a mobiliser and solvent for other reacting species.

The extent to which moisture can support the freedom of movement of soluble food constituents is strongly influenced by the proportion of water present, and major changes in the condition of constituent water, which affect its ability to support the free movement of reactant solutes, take place over the intermediate moisture range. Considering the progressive hydration of an initially dry system, there appear to be two particular levels of hydration at which highly significant changes occur in the mobility of soluble solid constituents. The first is at a surprisingly low moisture content, little higher than the monomolecular layer level, at which it has been shown by tracer methods that a very slow movement of labelled test solutes such as sugars is rendered possible.[1-3] This phenomenon can be detected at water contents below the intermediate moisture range and clearly must contribute to the progress of chemical reactions in relatively dry systems. It should be emphasised, however, that the resulting rate of movement is very slow and the process may perhaps be likened to that which would occur in an extremely viscous solution.

The degree of molecular mobility associated with this slow diffusive process is much too small to permit any contribution by the hydrogen protons of the molecules concerned with the sharp 'liquid state' NMR signal produced by some of the absorbed water at these levels of hydration. However, it can be shown that for any added H-containing test solute there is reached on further hydration a particular point at which the solute itself begins to make an additive contribution to the liquid state signal (*see* Fig. 1). This represents the second significant hydration level in respect of the mobilisation of the respective solute. It would appear to correspond to the point at which true dissolution of the solute begins, permitting a much higher degree of free molecular movement.

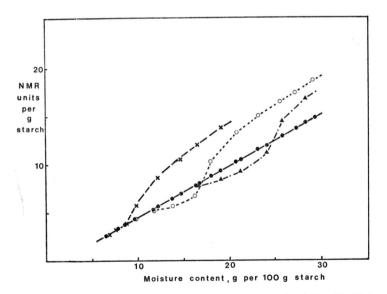

FIG. 1. Mobilisation patterns of acetamide, proline and lysine hydrochloride in hydrated gelatinised potato starch (25°C). Control starch ●, + acetamide ×, + proline ○, + lysine ▲.

Examination of the behaviour of a wide range of highly-soluble low-molecular-weight substances in hydrated model systems, as well as in some foods, has shown that different substances become mobilised, in this sense, at very different levels—though for the main part these fall within the intermediate moisture range.[4,5] For example, Fig. 1 illustrates some results for acetamide, proline and lysine hydrochloride in a hydrated (gelatinised) potato starch system. In the cases of the proline and the lysine there is a range of moisture content, immediately below the point at which the addition of the solute causes an incremental increase in NMR signal, over which a small reduction in signal size below that of the starch control is to be seen. This phenomenon is associated with the formation of crystalline hydrates in which a part of the water of hydration is preferentially bound within the test solute in the solid state (one molecule of water per amino acid molecule is so bound in the case of proline; three molecules of water per molecule in the case of lysine).

The precise behaviour of a given substance can be influenced by the form in which it is initially present in the system. In Fig. 2, for example, are shown results for glucose following its introduction in the predominantly amorphous form (prepared by freeze-drying), the

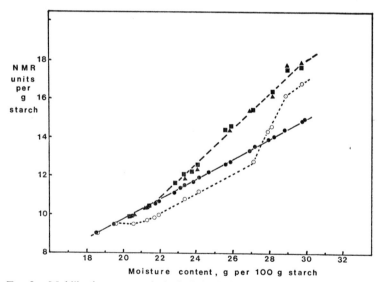

FIG. 2.   Mobilisation patterns in hydrated gelatinised potato starch of glucose, initially present in different physical forms (25°C). Control starch ●, + amorphous glucose ▲, + anhydrous glucose ○, + glucose monohydrate ■.

anhydrous crystalline form or as the crystalline monohydrate respectively. The formation of the crystalline hydrate, when starting from the crystalline anhydrous form, is evident as for proline and lysine in Fig. 1, but when amorphous glucose is used this becomes dissolved directly with no hydrate formation and mobilisation occurs, as for the glucose monohydrate itself, at a moisture level only slightly higher than that at which the anhydrous glucose begins to show the reduction in signal associated with hydrate formation.

The pattern of mobilisation for a particular solute may also be affected by the presence of other soluble substances. Various kinds of interaction can occur and the different types of behaviour found are illustrated diagrammatically in Fig. 3. In some cases no interaction occurs, the behaviour of one of a pair of solutes being

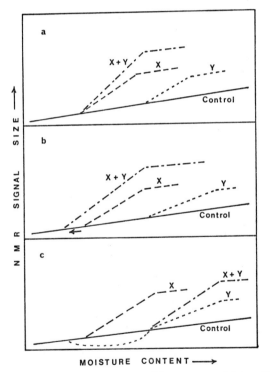

Fig. 3. Diagrammatic representation of different types of interaction between mobilising solute species. (a) Synergistic effect, *e.g.* sucrose and ascorbic acid; (b) synergistic effect with lowering of mobilisation point, *e.g.* proline and glucose; (c) antagonistic effect, *e.g.* sucrose and glucose.

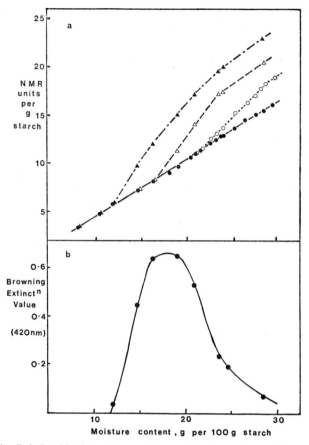

FIG. 4. Relationship between reactant mobilisation and reaction rate. (a) Mobilisation of γ-amino-butyric acid, glucose and a mixture of the two in hydrated gelatinised potato starch. Control starch ●, γ-amino-butyric acid △, glucose hydrate ○, γ-amino-butyric acid + glucose hydrate, ▲. (b) Browning extinction values of water extracts of the samples used for the readings in (a) after seven days at 25°C.

unaffected by the presence of the other. More commonly, however, there is a synergistic effect, the substance with the higher individual mobilisation point apparently becoming dissolved at a lower hydration level along with the other soluble species present. This may begin at the normal individual mobilisation point of the latter (Fig. 3a) or at an even lower moisture content (Fig. 3b), the detailed results for a particular case of this kind, involving glucose and γ-amino-butyric acid, being illustrated in Fig. 4a. Finally, an antagonistic interaction may occur in which, in the presence of both solutes of a pair, dissolution occurs only when the hydration level reaches or exceeds that normally necessary for the substance having the higher mobilisation point of the two (Fig. 3c).

Investigations of this kind have been made on several individual solutes and combinations of solutes which are involved in chemical changes associated with loss of quality in intermediate moisture foods, such as non-enzymic browning, loss of ascorbic acid, etc. Where parallel studies of mobilisation and of reaction rate have been carried out, especially large and sharp increases in rates of reaction have invariably been found to accompany an increase in moisture content beyond the determined mobilisation points of the respective reactants. Figure 4 illustrates such a relationship for the non-enzymic browning reaction in a simple glucose/amino acid/starch system. A similarly striking agreement between the pattern of mobilisation of ascorbic acid and its rate of loss in savoy cabbage and in potato starch in the presence and absence of added glycerol, from the work of Seow,[6] is shown in Fig. 5. It has also been found that

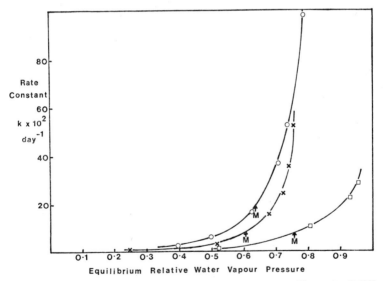

FIG. 5. Rates of ascorbic acid loss in dehydrated savoy cabbage ○, (25°C) potato starch gel, □ (45°C), and glycerated potato starch gel, × (45°C) in relation to ascorbic acid mobilisation and water activity. M: mobilisation point of ascorbic acid.

where, for any reason, the mobilisation behaviour of a reactant or combination of reactants is modified, this is always associated with a parallel change in respect of the rate of reaction for the species concerned.

Considerations of this kind obviously have an important bearing on the chemical stability of intermediate moisture foods and, since in practically all cases these products are prepared by mixing different ingredients, rather than by partial dehydration of the main food ingredients themselves, some measure of control over the physico-chemical conditions within the mixture is generally possible.

Earlier speakers have surveyed the range of substances which have been used as additives in IM foods for the purposes of appropriately adjusting the water activity and textural characteristics. Among these so-called humectants, are represented compounds of a number of different chemical types. Sugars, di-, tri- and poly-hydric alcohols and salts have been the main materials used. All are necessarily highly soluble in or miscible with water. Physically they are of two kinds: those such as the sugars, salts and the sugar alcohols—sorbitol, mannitol, etc., are crystalline solids at normal temperatures, while the glycols and glycerol are liquids readily miscible with water

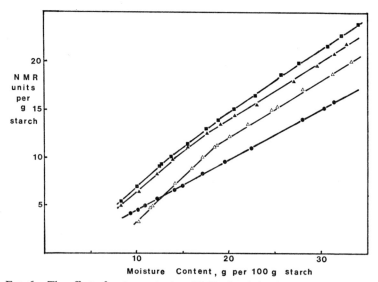

FIG. 6.   The effect of water content on NMR signal size for gelatinised potato starch ●, and for the similar starch containing 10% of glycerol ▲, sodium lactate Δ, and propylene glycol ■.

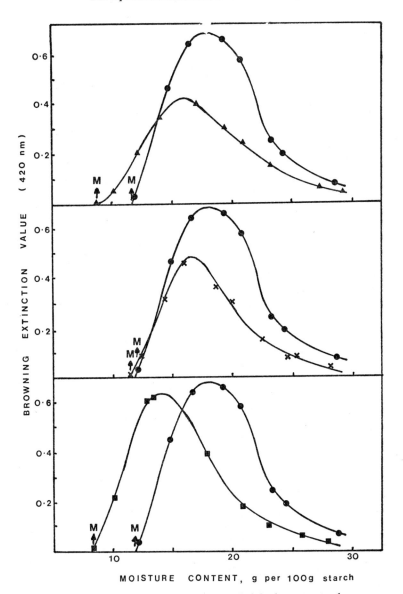

FIG. 7. Rates of non-enzymic browning in gelatinised potato starch, as compared with similar starch containing (a) 10% glycerol ▲, (b) 10% sodium lactate × and (c) 10% propylene glycol ◼, in relation to reactant mobilisation and water content. M: mobilisation point of reactants.

in all proportions. The former must be dissolved in water in order to exert their effects while the latter, being water-miscible liquids, can, of course, serve to actually increase the amount of liquid solvent phase at a given hydration level. This effect is borne out by the data illustrated in Fig. 6 where it can be seen that the size of the liquid state NMR signal is increased in the presence of such liquid humectants. At higher moisture contents, above about 20 g per 100 g dry starch, the increase in each case is around the theoretical, assuming a full contribution from the hydrogen protons of the humectant present. It is, however, interesting to note that at lower moisture levels there are indications that the molecules of the humectant are subject to restrictive influences by the solid absorbent in a similar way to the binding effect on water molecules at lower levels. This is particularly marked in the case of sodium lactate where the NMR signal actually falls below that of the starch control when the moisture content is reduced below about 11·5%.

The influence of the presence of liquid humectant (to the extent of 10% by weight of the solid absorbent) on the mobilisation of a combination of browning reactants (glucose and γ-amino butyric acid) and on the resulting pattern of non-enzymic browning is illustrated in Fig. 7. In each case, the humectant has caused a lowering of the mobilisation point of the reactants but because of the factors alluded to in the previous paragraph, together with the fact that this particular combination of solutes becomes mobilised at a relatively low level in the control material, the differences are not very great. In spite of this, the effects on the pattern of browning are quite clear and the differences in this regard are sufficiently large to be highly significant in relation to the keeping quality of products of this general kind within the intermediate moisture region.

Bearing in mind that by the use of appropriate combinations, adjustments of mobilisation behaviour can be induced both upwards and downwards within this hydration range, the scope for bringing about beneficial effects on keeping quality by manipulation of the aqueous environment is obviously considerable.

ACKNOWLEDGEMENT

The authors wish to acknowledge that much of the work described in this paper was carried out with support from the J. Sainsbury Centenary Grant and one of us (J.Y.A.) is in fact employed under this grant.

REFERENCES

1. Duckworth, R. B. (1962). In: *Recent Advances in Food Science*, Vol. 2, ed. J. Hawthorn and J. M. Leitch, Butterworths, London, p. 46.
2. Duckworth, R. B. (1963). *Proc. Nutr. Soc.*, **22**, p. 182.
3. Duckworth, R. B. and Smith, G. M. (1963). In: *Recent Advances in Food Science*, Vol. 3, ed. J. M. Leitch and D. N. Rhodes, Butterworths, London, p. 230.
4. Duckworth, R. B. (1972). *Proc. Inst. Fd Sci. Tech.*, **5**, p. 60.
5. Duckworth, R. B. and Kelly, Carole E. (1973). *J. Fd. Technol.*, **8**, p. 105.
6. Seow, C. C. (1975). Ph.D. Thesis, Strathclyde University.

9

Chemical and Non-Enzymic Changes in Intermediate Moisture Foods

J. C. WILLIAMS

Tate & Lyle Ltd, Philip Lyle Memorial Research Laboratory, Reading, Berks, England

ABSTRACT

The major components of intermediate moisture foods (carbohydrates, proteins and lipids) and also some of the minor components (e.g. ascorbic acid and carotenoids) can undergo chemical changes during processing and storage. The water content of the foods greatly affects the rates of these chemical reactions.

The lipid components can suffer oxidation, which occurs by a free radical mechanism and is retarded as the water content is reduced. The Maillard reaction (non-enzymic browning) covers the reactions between carbohydrates and amino acids or proteins, and is near to its maximum rate in the range of water activities found in intermediate moisture foods. It begins with the formation of glycosylamines which subsequently rearrange and degrade to unsaturated carbonyl compounds. The later stages of the reaction are not well-defined but lead to the formation of volatile materials, which can cause off-flavours; and pigments. The latter are not simple substances but mixtures of high molecular weight, highly unsaturated, polycarboxylic acids.

Inhibition of the Maillard reaction is desirable in view of the losses caused in nutritive value together with the possible generation of off-flavours and diminished visual appeal of the product. Sulphur dioxide, in addition to its anti-microbial action, is an efficient inhibitor through its addition to the carbonyl intermediates. Some products of the Maillard reaction can themselves inhibit the oxidation of lipid components.

INTRODUCTION

Intermediate moisture foods are specially formulated to achieve a low water content to reduce spoilage caused by microbial growth, but otherwise have generally the same components as conventional foodstuffs. Although they are products of modern technology the chemical reactions of their main components (lipids, carbohydrates, proteins) are well known. The oxidation of lipids has been investigated by the edible oils and fats industry; while Maillard[1] laid the foundations of studies of non-enzymic browning; the interaction of carbohydrates with amino acids or proteins. These reactions are associated with losses of nutritive value in foods and changes in their flavour and appearance affecting their 'consumer appeal'. The Maillard reaction has been studied in the food industry as a route to flavour development during processing, while sugar producers have investigated its role in the generation of colour during sugar refining.

Both lipid oxidation and non-enzymic browning are sensitive to water content and from this aspect their occurrence in intermediate moisture foods is particularly important. However, the comparatively recent development of these foods means that relatively little work has been done on the reactions of their components in systems with a low water content. Most of our knowledge comes from studies of model systems or from work on other foodstuffs.

This paper is a brief, general review of the chemical changes involving food components, indicating how the results may apply to intermediate moisture foods. More detailed accounts are available in the recent comprehensive reviews by Labuza[2] on oxidation; Hurst[3] on non-enzymic browning; and Adrian[4] on the nutritional consequences of the Maillard reaction.

OXIDATIVE REACTIONS

Lipids, especially those containing polyunsaturated fatty acids, are the components of foods most susceptible to oxidation. The reaction involves free radicals and is catalysed by traces of heavy metals. Once the free radicals have been formed (which can be by the action of radiation, mechanical action, or by freezing or dehydration) an autocatalytic reaction can set in, with the reaction products catalysing the reaction so that its rate increases with time. The main reaction chain involves the lipid and oxygen (Reactions 1 and 2 in Fig. 1). Initially the rate is slow as the hydroperoxides build up and decompose monomolecularly (Reaction 3). When the hydroperoxide concentration is high enough bimolecular decomposition sets in (Reaction 4), which adds more lipid radicals to the chain reaction. The reaction only ends when the recombination of radicals gives relatively unreactive products.[5]

1. $R^\bullet + O_2 \longrightarrow ROO^\bullet$

2. $RH + ROO^\bullet \longrightarrow ROOH + R^\bullet$

3. $ROOH \longrightarrow RO^\bullet + {}^\bullet OH$

4. $2ROOH \longrightarrow ROO^\bullet + RO^\bullet + H_2O$

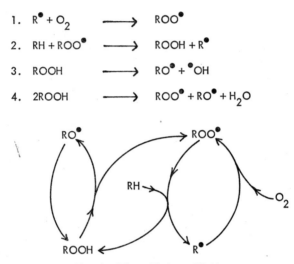

FIG. 1.   The oxidation of lipids.

The Effect of Water

The influence of water on the reaction is complex but studies by Karel and co-workers[5-8] have revealed the important aspects. Water can speed up the reaction by increasing the mobility of reactants and bringing catalysts into solution. It also swells the solid matrices in a system and exposes new surfaces for catalysis. On the other hand the presence of water may retard oxidation by hydrating or diluting heavy metal catalysts or even precipitating them as hydroxides. Water hydrogen bonds with hydroperoxides and slows down the peroxide decomposition steps. It can also promote radical recombination and thus terminate the reaction chain.

The combination of these accelerating and retarding effects results in a minimum oxidation rate at a certain water activity; the actual value being dependent on the system. Work on model systems and on actual foodstuffs shows a decrease in oxygen uptake as water activity increases from zero to 0·4–0·5 (Fig. 2), followed by a rise as the water activity increases further. One system showed a further decrease in rate at water activities 0·68–0·85; this was attributed to the relatively high content of trace metals, which were less active as catalysts at the highest water activities.[2] Intermediate moisture foods generally are in the range where oxidation is increasing in rate with increasing water activity.

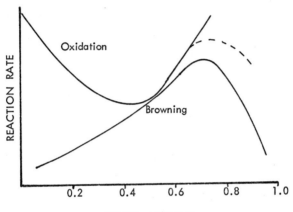

FIG. 2. The variation of oxidation and browning with water activity.

The actual water content is also important. In a given food system, because of sorption hysteresis, two different water contents can lead to the same water activity. Foods prepared by rehumidifying a dry mix (adsorption method) contain less water and thus oxidise much less rapidly than foods produced by directly mixing partially dried components (desorption systems).[9]

The Effects of Oxidation

The oxidation of fats leads to polymerisation and rancidity; polymerisation occurs by the recombination of lipid radicals and rancidity by the formation of volatile carbonyl compounds. The effects extend to other components of the food. Proteins are attacked by the free radical intermediates inducing cross-linking and toughening. The aldehydic and ketonic oxidation products which produce rancidity can enter into a Maillard reaction with amino acids and proteins, described below.

Ascorbic acid (vitamin C) also is destroyed by oxidation, the complex degradation reaction involving free radicals. The rate of destruction increases with increasing water content into the intermediate moisture range, and this change in rate has been related to the viscosity of the aqueous phase.[10] This viscosity decreases with increasing water content thus giving reactants greater mobility.

The Control of Oxidation

For a particular moisture range, oxidative deterioration of foods may be controlled by suitable packaging, by lower storage temperatures or by the use of antioxidants.The first involves vacuum packing coupled with oxygen impermeable packing materials. Antioxidants may be fat soluble free radical scavengers (*e.g.* butylated hydroxy anisole) or water soluble metal chelators (*e.g.* EDTA or citric acid). In model systems the chelators tend to become more effective at higher water activities[11] but in actual foods they are less effective than model studies would indicate.[9] Products of the Maillard reaction also have antioxidant activity.[12] The coating of vitamin C with an edible non-water permeable material has been suggested as a means of minimising its loss by oxidation.[2]

NON-ENZYMIC BROWNING

Non-enzymic browning is not a single reaction but a group of chemical changes involving aldehydic or ketonic materials and amino compounds which react to produce coloured polymeric products. The carbonyl compounds reacting in foodstuffs may be carbohydrates or the oxidation products of lipids; while the amino function can be provided by amino acids or proteins or by naturally occurring amines. However, according to conventional usage non-enzymic browning is the reaction between a reducing sugar and an amino acid; also called the Maillard reaction. The earlier stages of this reaction have been studied in depth and a general scheme of the initial reactions is given in Fig. 3.

The main stages in browning are:

(1) The reaction of an aldose with the amino group of an amino acid to form an aldosylamino acid.

(2) An Amadori rearrangement which gives a ketose amino acid.

(3) Addition of a second molecule of aldose and further rearrangement results in a diketoseamino acid.

(4) The ketoseamino acids decompose to give carbonyl intermediates. (These are underlined in Fig. 3.)

(5) These carbonyl compounds react further, often with amino acids, to give brown pigments.

Stages 1–4 have been well investigated in model systems and in foods, and the intermediates identified. They can be illustrated by the reaction between glucose and glycine.

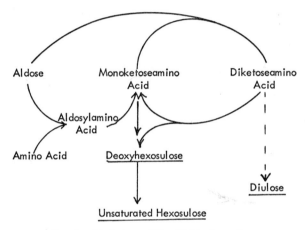

FIG. 3.   First stage of the Maillard reaction.

The Formation of Glucosylglycine and Fructoseglycines (Fig. 4)

The first step of the reaction is reversible and as water is one of the products its presence tends to inhibit the formation of glucosylglycine (I). Therefore the reaction will be faster at lower water concentrations. Glucosylglycine rapidly undergoes an Amadori rearrangement to give fructoseglycine (II a ketoseamino acid). This rearrangement needs an acid catalyst, a role played by the amino acid itself. Fructoseglycine (and any other ketoseamino formed from a primary amine) can react with another glucose molecule when a further Amadori rearrangement gives difructoseglycine (III). Monoketoseamino acids have been isolated by Anet and Reynolds[13] from browned fruit purees stored at 70% RH; and diketoseamino acids

J. C. Williams

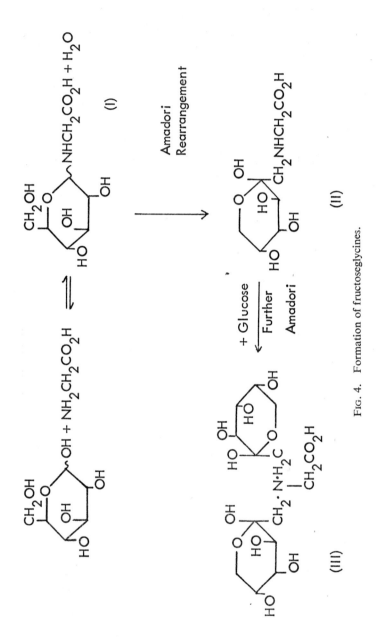

Fig. 4. Formation of fructoseglycines.

were detected in the same system.[14] Fructoseglycines have been synthesised and their browning properties studied.[14,15]

The Decomposition of Fructoseglycine

Fructoseglycine may decompose either by 1,2-enolisation or 2,3-enolisation.[16] The first pathway (Fig. 5) is judged to be the predominant reaction under the mild conditions prevailing in food

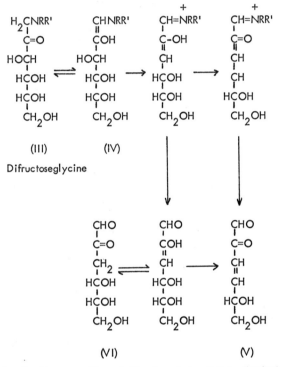

(III)   (IV)

Difructoseglycine

(VI)   (V)

FIG. 5.   Decomposition of difructoseglycine (1,2-enolisation).

systems. Difructoseglycine decomposes rapidly to monofructose-glycine; 3-deoxyglucosulose (VI);[17] and an unsaturated osulose (V).[18] Monofructoseglycine, on decomposition, gives compounds (VI) and (V) but does so more slowly than the diketoseamine.[15] The amino acid is liberated unchanged.

2,3-Enolisation (Fig. 6) leads to the formation of a 2,4-diulose (VII) *via* the relatively unstable 2,3-diulose (VIII). These are less important in the formation of pigments but are implicated in the production of flavour volatiles.[19]

The 3-deoxyosuloses, being relatively stable compounds, have been detected in experimental systems and in foods.[20] They have been synthesised and shown to decompose to give brown pigments. Unsaturated osuloses have been found only in experimental systems.

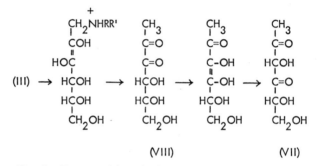

FIG. 6.   Decomposition of difructoseglycine (2,3-enolisation).

The carbonyl intermediates of the Maillard reaction are also produced by the degradation of aldoses in the absence of amino acids, but the reaction needs higher pHs[21] than are generally found in foods. Up to this stage the amino acid acts essentially as a catalyst of sugar decomposition, converting the aldose into more reactive compounds.

The Formation of Pigments

The next stage of the reaction is more complex and less well defined. Pigment formation is believed to involve aldol condensations of the carbonyl intermediates or their further reaction products. Amino acids enter the reaction again at this stage and give rise to nitrogen containing pigments; these are often termed melanoidins. Work in our laboratories indicates the involvement of the enolic form of a dideoxytriketohexose as a key intermediate in the pigment formation in alkaline degradation systems.[22] This could give pigments with the observed properties by successive aldol condensations, dehydrations and benzilic acid-type rearrangements. Although 5-hydroxymethylfurfural is a possible decomposition product of 3-deoxyhexosulose (VI)[23] it does not appear to be a precursor of pigment formation except possibly at low pH.[24]

The Reactions of other Carbohydrates and Amino Acids

The reaction scheme presented above is based on investigations of model glucose/glycine systems. Where other aldoses are concerned the major differences are in the rate of reaction; pentoses (xylose and ribose) brown more rapidly than hexoses.[25] There is evidence that the browning of ketoses (fructose) differs from that of aldoses. The initially formed fructosylamino acid undergoes a Heyns rearrangement to give aldoseamino acids. A new asymmetric centre is created and so fructose gives a mixture of glucoseglycine and mannoseglycine, together with a small amount of fructoseglycine. Aldoseamino acids are more stable than the corresponding ketoseamino acids. Fructose browns more slowly than glucose and measurements of amino acid losses during the reaction indicate that it proceeds by routes different from the browning of aldoses.[25] This difference deserves further investigation because fructose is a major food sugar, both in its own right and as a hydrolysis product of sucrose. The rate of browning of non-reducing disaccharides (*e.g.* sucrose) and polysaccharides can be limited by the rate of their hydrolysis to reducing sugars. Ascorbic acid browns by a mechanism which is different again from glucose, and there are indications that amino acids are not necessarily involved in the earlier stages.[26]

The nature of the amino acids involved also affects the rate of the reaction; the further the amino group is from the carboxyl, the greater the rate of browning.[27] γ-Aminobutyric acid browns more rapidly than α-aminobutyric, and lysine, with an additional ε amino group, browns more rapidly than nor-leucine. The reaction of the ε amino group of lysine in proteins taking part in the browning reaction in foods causes losses in lysine and reduces the nutritional value of proteins.

The Properties of Pigments

Although only small quantities of pigments are formed, their intense coloration greatly affects the appearance of foods. The brown colour is caused by a featureless absorption spectrum in the visible region which is made up from the overlapping absorptions of many chromophores. The investigation of pigments formed in foods is complicated by the inclusion of polysaccharides and proteins, but even those formed in model sugar/amino acid systems are by no means simple single substances. They are mixtures of compounds with basically similar chemical structures but differing in such properties as molecular weight (which ranges upwards from the low hundreds).[28] Chemically the pigments from model systems are unsaturated polycarboxylic acids; extensively conjugated, with the carboxyl groups included in the conjugation. Hydroxyl, enolic and amino functions are also present and in the case of pigments formed in the presence of basic amino acids (lysine) they have zwitterionic properties.[29] Strictly, it is incorrect to refer to the pigments as polymers because there is probably no single repeating unit in the molecule.

The Production and Nature of Flavours

As well as high molecular weight coloured products the Maillard reaction also leads to volatile materials with flavour imparting properties. During cooking and processing generation of these materials often leads to the development of desirable characteristic flavours, for example, during the baking of bread or the roasting of cocoa beans. Flavours arising during storage are less desirable as they will change the original character of the foodstuff.

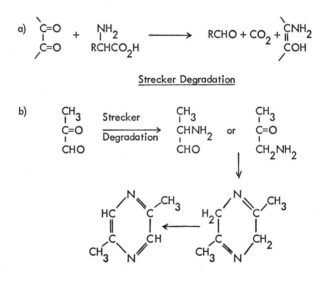

FIG. 7.   Flavour forming reactions.

Reynolds[19] has reviewed the subject of flavour development and identifies the major reaction pathways leading to flavour volatiles as the 1,2- and 2,3-enolisation steps in the decomposition of ketose-amino acids described earlier. Of these the 1,2-enolisation is the less important, giving hydroxymethylfurfural (from hexoses) and furfural (from pentoses). The 3-deoxyosuloses can react with amino compounds to give pyrrole aldehydes. 2,3-Enolisation gives a wider range of products including dihydropyranones and furanones.

Osuloses and other dicarbonyl compounds can take part in a Strecker degradation resulting in the decarboxylation of amino acids and formation of aldehydes (Fig. 7a). The aldehydes so formed are not necessarily directly responsible for flavours but the enolamines can condense to give substituted pyrazines which frequently occur as flavour volatiles. The Strecker product from the simple dicarbonyl compound pyruvaldehyde, itself a product of sugar decomposition, can condense to give dimethylpyrazine (Fig. 7b).[30]

Most of the work on the formation of flavours has been done on heated samples—either foods or model systems. The relevance of the results to the milder conditions found in the storage of foods is indicated by Tatum *et al.*[31] who identified furfurals, furanones and pyrrole aldehydes in a dried orange juice which had browned during storage at 37·5°C.

Physical Factors Influencing the Maillard Reaction

Temperature, pH and water activity are all important in determining the rate of non-enzymic browning. The rate of browning increases rapidly with increasing temperature. The activation energies of various stages of the reaction have been measured, as well as the apparent value for browning as a whole.[20] From these activation energies a rate change with temperature of 3–4 times for a 10°C change can be calculated. This change with temperature depends on water activity. The activation energy decreases with increasing water activity,[32] as does the effect of temperature on the rate of formation of Maillard intermediates.[12]

Increasing the pH also increases the rate of browning.[33] The reaction is slow below pH 5–6 and then increases rapidly with increasing pH. pH can also influence the course of the reaction; under alkaline conditions browning can also occur by routes that do not involve nitrogen containing intermediates. The degradation of the carbohydrates is brought about by hydroxyl ions to give the carbonyl intermediates formed in the Maillard reaction.[21]

The effect of water is more complicated and naturally of great importance to the stability of intermediate moisture foods. Reynolds[20] has noted work on foods showing changes in browning with water content. Labuza *et al.*[34] describe a maximum in the browning rate at water contents in the intermediate moisture range (Fig. 2). Model studies (Eichner,[12] McWeeny[35]) confirm this. They used amino acid/glucose/cellulose systems at various water activities and noted maxima in the rate of browning. (At a_w 0·75 for glucose/lysine—40 h at 40°C; and at a_w 0·55 for glucose/glycine—192 h at 38°C.) Both authors record that the position of the maximum changes as the reaction proceeds. Eichner established this by studying fructoselysine which browned fastest at a_w 0·4. He concluded that at higher water activities the course of browning does not involve the ketoseamino acid itself but the 1,2-eneaminol (IV) which is an intermediate in its formation by the Amadori rearrangement.

The observed browning maxima have been attributed to a balance of viscosity controlled diffusion; dilution; and mass action effects. At low water activities the slow diffusion of reactants limits the rate. As the water content increases freer diffusion enables faster reaction to take place, until at the upper end dilution of the reactants again slows it down. Also the higher concentrations of water retard those reversible reaction steps which produce water, *e.g.* the initial condensation stage. Up to 3·5 moles of water are formed per mole of sugar consumed in non-enzymic browning.

The Control of Non-enzymic Browning

The rate of browning may be controlled by adjusting the parameters described above. This approach has obvious limitations but a further degree of control may be achieved by chemical means; in particular by the addition of sulphur dioxide or sulphites. These can act as inhibitors of microbial growth as well as decreasing the browning rate.

The 'free sulphur dioxide' content of a system slowly decreases during the course of non-enzymic browning in the presence of sulphites. In some cases the browning is completely inhibited until the sulphite level drops nearly to zero (*e.g.* with glucose and amino acids). In others the browning is merely retarded (*e.g.* with ascorbic acid and amino acids). Sulphites are able also to bleach the final brown pigment. McWeeny *et al.*[36] attribute the different effects of sulphites to differences in the intermediates involved in colour formation.

The intermediates most likely to be influenced by the presence of sulphite are the 3-deoxyosuloses (VI) and the unsaturated osuloses (V). The former will combine reversibly with sulphite and retard the reaction. In the latter case an addition compound is irreversibly

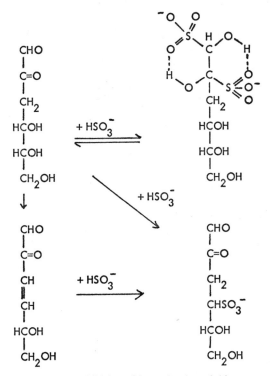

FIG. 8. Inhibition of browning by sulphite.

formed with the sulphite, thus stabilising this intermediate and inhibiting browning until the sulphite is consumed. The products of addition have in fact been isolated from model systems[26,37] and identified in a real food system[38] (Fig. 8).

Although sulphur dioxide and its derivatives are effective in reducing the browning of foodstuffs there is a growing body of food regulations tending to reduce or prevent its use. There is also some experimental evidence for the existence of slightly toxic components in stored sulphited foods.[39] The search for alternative inhibitors continues but at present such alternatives are unacceptable on the grounds of toxicity, *e.g.* cyanides, dimedone, hydroxylamine, hydrazines, mercaptans, bromine. It is interesting to note that stannous salts not only inhibit browning in model systems but also prevent amino acid loss from proteins.[40] Other agents only inhibit the browning process, while amino acid loss still occurs.

Antioxidant Activity

Maillard intermediates have been shown to have antioxidant activity. Eichner[12] describes model experiments where browning products from glucose and glycine reduce the oxygen uptake and peroxide formation of linoleic acid derivatives, and suggests that the 1,2-eneaminols (IV) combine with peroxides or free radicals to retard the oxidation process. Suitably controlled Maillard degradation in the food processing stages could bring great benefits in enhanced storage stability.

THE EFFECTS OF CHEMICAL CHANGES ON FOODSTUFFS

The effects of chemical changes can be summarised:

(1) Loss of consumer appeal leading to wastage.
(2) Loss of nutritive value and vitamin activity.
(3) Possible toxic effects.

Consumer Appeal

The production of off-flavours by the Maillard reaction and rancidity by lipid oxidation has already been mentioned. In addition undesirable colour changes are produced, not only by browning, but also by pigment oxidation; the oxidation of myoglobin to give a brown colour to meats is an example.[2] Toughening of proteins, also a factor in consumer rejection, arises both from oxidative and free radical reactions, and from the cross-linking of proteins by the Maillard reaction. This leads also to a reduction in protein digestibility.

Nutritive Losses

As has been noted earlier the Maillard reaction joins with oxidation in the destruction of ascorbic acid. This is particularly rapid by both mechanisms in the region of water activities which includes intermediate moisture foods. The browning reactions can be seen also as the chief causes of loss of nutritive value in foods through loss of sugars and especially of essential amino acids. The latter are lost by being made nutritionally unavailable. Basic amino acids are particularly susceptible to loss on account of their greater reactivity; lysine loss being especially serious in view of its nutritional significance. Sulphur containing amino acids are also easily lost.

Adrian[4] lists types of foods in order of their sensitivity to damage by the Maillard reaction, the important factor being the availability of carbohydrates able to enter into the reaction.

(a) Dairy products are especially susceptible on account of the lactose content and the relative instability of the proteins.

(b) Cereals are readily damaged as part of their starch is hydrolysable to reducing sugars.

(c) Fishmeals rich in nucleic acids are readily damaged because of their ribose content. (Pentoses are especially reactive in the Maillard reaction.)

(d) Legumes and yeast products are reasonably stable, having low levels of reducing sugars.

(e) Meats are resistant to damage, both through their lack of reducing sugars and their acidity.

In the earlier stages of the Maillard reaction amino acids are still recoverable by chemical hydrolysis but are resistant to enzymic hydrolysis *in vitro*. These amino acids are not nutritionally available. Lysine rich foods are especially susceptible to loss of lysine.[41]

In addition to reducing the availability of amino acids there is evidence that the Maillard reaction produces materials which can hinder the assimilation of proteins. Adding amino acids to a food to restore those destroyed during heating does not necessarily restore the whole protein value.[42] The influence of Maillard products on the utilisation of protein can be so great as to cause up to 40% drop in growth rate of rats fed 0·2% of a glucose/glycine reaction mixture in a casein containing diet. Retained dietary nitrogen fell from 49% to 31%.[43] The Maillard intermediates causing this effect have not been identified.

Toxicity

Retardation of nitrogen assimilation could be described as a form of toxicity. In addition to this, Maillard products fed to rats on a protein free diet caused actual weight loss. Organ enlargements and pregnancy disorders have also been reported with such diets.[4] Measurements of LD_{50} show a reduction from 20 g/kg to 4·1 g/kg (in the case of lysine) when glucose/amino acid mixtures are heated. Lysine reaction products were the most toxic.[43] Thermally oxidised fats also are known to cause cellular damage and organ enlargement in experimental animals.[44]

In conclusion it must be emphasised that much of the work on chemical changes in food systems has been done either on model systems to simplify interpretation, or under relatively harsh conditions such as high temperatures to produce readily measurable results. Thus the findings, especially on such matters as toxicity, can only be considered as indications of what may occur in intermediate moisture foods under relatively mild storage conditions. The nutritive values and possible toxicities of foods which have undergone the chemical changes found at intermediate moisture levels need to be examined further before definite conclusions can be drawn about the significance of these changes.

REFERENCES

1. Maillard, L. C. (1912). *Compt. rend.*, **154**, p. 66.
2. Labuza, T. P. (1975). In: *Water Relations of Foods*, ed. R. B. Duckworth, Academic Press, London, p. 455.
3. Hurst, D. T. (1972). *British Food Manufacturing Industries Research Association, Scientific and Technical Surveys No. 75*. (Recent Developments in the Study of Non-Enzymic Browning and its Inhibition by Sulphur Dioxide.)
4. Adrian, J. (1974). *World Review of Nutrition and Dietetics*, **19**, p. 71.
5. Maloney, J., Labuza, T. P., Wallace, D. H. and Karel, M. (1966). *J. Fd. Sci.*, **31**, p. 878.
6. Labuza, T. P., Maloney, J. and Karel, M. (1966). *J. Fd. Sci.*, **31**, p. 885.
7. Heidelbaugh, N. D. and Karel, M. (1970). *J. Am. Oil Chem. Soc.*, **47**, p. 539.
8. Chou, H. E., Acott, K. and Labuza, T. P. (1973). *J. Fd. Sci.*, **38**, p. 316.
9. Labuza, T. P., McNally, L., Gallagher, D., Hawkes, J. and Hurtado, F. (1972). *J. Fd. Sci.*, **37**, p. 154.
10. Lee, S. H. and Labuza, T. P. (1975). *J. Fd. Sci.*, **40**, p. 370.
11. Tjhio, K. H., Labuza, T. P. and Karel, M. (1969). *J. Am. Oil Chem. Soc.*, **46**, p. 597.

12. Eichner, K. (1975). In: *Water Relations of Foods*, ed. R. B. Duckworth, Academic Press, London, p. 417.
13. Anet, E. F. L. J. and Reynolds, T. M. (1957). *Aust. J. Chem.*, 10, p. 182.
14. Anet, E. F. L. J. (1959). *Aust. J. Chem.*, 12, p. 280.
15. Anet, E. F. L. J. (1959). *Aust. J. Chem.*, 12, p. 491.
16. Reynolds, T. M. (1965). *Adv. Fd. Res.*, 14, p. 167.
17. Anet, E. F. L. J. (1960). *Aust. J. Chem.*, 13, p. 396.
18. Anet, E. F. L. J. (1962). *Aust. J. Chem.*, 15, p. 503.
19. Reynolds, T. M. (1970). *Fd. Tech. Aust.*, 22, p. 610.
20. Reynolds, T. M. (1963). *Adv. Fd. Res.*, 12, p. 1.
21. Anet, E. F. L. J. (1964). *Adv. Carbohyd. Chem.*, 19, p. 181.
22. Fleming, M., Parker, K. J. and Williams, J. C. (1968). *I.S.S.C.T. Proceedings, 13th Congress Taiwan*, p. 1781.
23. Anet, E. F. L. J. (1961). *Aust. J. Chem.*, 14, p. 295.
24. McWeeny, D. J. and Burton, H. S. (1963). *J. Sci. Fd. Agric.*, 14, p. 291.
25. Spark, A. A. (1969). *J. Sci. Fd. Agric.*, 20, p. 308.
26. Wedzicha, B. L. and McWeeny, D. J. (1974). *J. Sci. Fd. Agric.*, 25, p. 577.
27. Lento, H. G., Underwood, J. C. and Willits, C. O. (1958). *Fd. Res.*, 23, p. 68.
28. Williams, J. C. (1974). *I.S.S.C.T. Proceedings, 15th Congress Durban*, p. 1402.
29. Cookson, D., Parker, K. J. and Williams, J. C. (1970). *Proceedings Tech. Sess. on Cane Sugar Ref. Res.*, p. 103.
30. Dawes, I. W. and Edwards, R. A. (1966). *Chem. and Ind.*, p. 2203.
31. Tatum, J. H., Shaw, P. E. and Berry, R. E. (1967). *J. Agric. Fd. Chem.*, 15, p. 773.
32. Hendel, C. E., Silveira, V. G. and Harrington, W. W. (1955). *Fd. Technol.*, 9, p. 433.
33. Wolfrom, M. L., Kolb, D. K. and Langer, A. W. (1953). *J. Am. Chem. Soc.*, 75, p. 3471.
34. Labuza, T. P., Tannenbaum, S. R. and Karel, M. (1970). *Fd. Technol.*, 24, p. 543.
35. McWeeny, D. T. (1973). In: *Molecular Structure and Function of Food Carbohydrate*, ed. G. G. Birch and L. F. Green, Applied Science Publishers Ltd, London, p. 21.
36. McWeeny, D. J., Knowles, M. E. and Hearne, J. F. (1974). *J. Sci. Fd. Agric.*, 25, p. 735.
37. Knowles, M. E. (1971). *Chem. and Ind.*, p. 910.
38. Wedzicha, B. L. and McWeeny, D. J. (1974). *J. Sci. Fd. Agric.*, 25, p. 589.
39. Hedin, P. A. (1962). *J. Nutr.*, 77, p. 471.
40. Adrian, J. and Favier, J. C. (1961). *Ann. Nutrit.*, 15, p. 181.
41. Frangne, R. and Adrian, J. (1962). *Ann. Nutrit.*, 26, p. 97.
42. Rau, M. N., Sreenivas, H., Swaminathan, M., Carpenter, K. J. and Morgan, C. B. (1963). *J. Sci. Fd. Agric.*, 14, p. 544.
43. Adrian, J., Petit, L. and Godon, B. (1962). *Compt. rend.*, 255, p. 391.
44. Andia, A. M. G. and Street, J. C. (1975). *J. Agric. Fd. Chem.*, 23, p. 173.

DISCUSSION

Johnson: I notice you mentioned sulphur dioxide as inhibiting browning reaction by combining with carbonyl groups. It has been suggested by Song and Chichester that sulphur dioxide inhibits the browning reaction by acting as a free radical acceptor. Would you care to comment?

Williams: This is becoming one of the vexed questions in this field. Song and Chichester's conclusions are based on the fact that benzyl peroxide can inhibit browning reaction, as it's a radical producer, and on the fact that some free radicals have been detected in amino-acid/sugar systems.

Johnson: The browning reaction is also catalysed by small quantities of oxygen.

Williams: Yes, in some cases this is so. But I gather that the consensus of opinion is in favour of the carbonyl compounds rather than the free radicals. However, the field is wide open.

Barker: You were talking about pH as a control of browning. What sort of reaction have you found with respect to pH?

Williams: American studies, quite a few years ago, showed that at round about pH 5 browning is very low. Our own studies have gone up into the outlying region, and we have found that at pH 9·5 browning is really at its maximum. This is in very high water activity systems. But I'm not sure if there are studies that have examined the effect of pH at different water activities.

Smith: I understood that in Dr Duckworth's paper he said that he had measured the mobilisation point by adding water to dry crystals. Could he tell us if there is any significant difference in the mobilisation point when you remove the water from the same system?

Duckworth: The mobilisation point was determined by adding a test solute to a system which was already hydrated, not water directly to a solute.

Smith: I'm trying to think as a practical food technologist. If you dry a food material and add water back to it, that's one way of arriving at intermediate moisture. If I'm drying foodstuffs down to the same moisture level, will the mobilisation point differ in the reverse direction?

Duckworth: This is one of those cases where you may have some hysteresis effect in relation to the hydration of the absorbent. It is possible that this could be so. The systems that we've studied have all been hydrated from an almost dry state, but they have been thereafter left for at least 6 days for the equilibration of the system to occur, that is for the water—given that you are hydrating from the dry state at least—to have become equilibrated with the system. Does that answer your question?

Smith: I don't think so.

Karel: I'd like to add to Professor Duckworth's account of this subject. Large hysteresis effects in dissolution of sugar crystals have been observed by us and others, and are in fact affected not only by time, temperature and initial state of sugar (amorphous, crystalline) but also by other components of the system. For instance, we observe that Avicel retards transformation of amorphous to crystalline sucrose.

Duckworth: I'm sure this is the case. The fact is that our own data relate to systems that have been hydrated up from the lower side. One could also examine the situation from the other side, but we have not in fact done this.

Obanu: It has been observed by Professor Labuza that in the presence of glycerol the rate of non-enzymic browning was maximal at a lower a_w than usual (I think it was 0·43). Do you think that, besides increasing mobility, glycerol could have any direct role in non-enzymic browning?

Williams: This is quite a new one to me; Professor Karel mentioned it last night, but I had not heard of it before. It would seem a profitable direction for future research, to investigate whether there's any actual chemical involvement here.

Obanu: The reason I ask is that in our own laboratories we have found that just mixing lysine with glycerol gave some browning, at of course a high temperature (we used 38° and 65°C). We then tried a greater concentration of glycerol with a protein (gelatin), and we got the same thing. We tried casein—it was visible, but we couldn't extract the brown pigment.

Duckworth: There was on one of my slides an example of the effect of glycerol on the browning in that model system. The rate of browning was in fact, in that case, lower in the presence of glycerol.

10

The Stability of Intermediate Moisture Foods with Respect to Micro-organisms

L. LEISTNER and W. RÖDEL

Bundesanstalt für Fleischforschung, Kulmbach,
Bundesrepublik Deutschland

ABSTRACT

The a_w of food influences the multiplication and metabolic activity (including toxin production) of micro-organisms, also their survival and resistance. In the a_w range of IMF (0·90–0·60) some bacteria (Pediococcus, Streptococcus, Micrococcus, Lactobacillus, Vibrio, Staphylococcus), yeasts (Hansenula, Candida, Hanseniaspora, Torulopsis, Debaryomyces, Saccharomyces) and moulds (Cladosporium, Paecilomyces, Penicillium, Aspergillus, Emericella, Eremascus, Wallemia, Eurotium, Chrysosporium, Monascus) may multiply. Most of these organisms cause spoilage, some produce toxins (Staphylococcus, Paecilomyces, Penicillium, Aspergillus, Emericella, Eurotium). On the other hand, well adapted strains of Lactobacillaceae or Streptococcaceae as well as selected moulds might also in IMF be desirable as competitive microflora and thus be used as starter cultures. An inhibition of micro-organisms in IMF cannot solely depend on the a_w, but the pH, Eh, temperature, preservatives and the competitive microflora might be of importance too. How many of these 'hurdles' and at what level they are needed for the stability of IMF depends not only on the types but also to a large extent on the number of organisms present. Where feasible, the raw material should be heat-processed. The preparation of IMF should be done under hygienic conditions and refrigeration to insure a low initial count of a_w-tolerant organisms. If the palatability of the products permits, the a_w of IMF should be below 0·85 or the pH below 5·0, since either of these 'hurdles' protects the product against staphylococcal enterotoxin *production. If possible, IMF should be packaged in evacuated containers or pouches which are impermeable to oxygen. A low Eh of the product inhibits mould growth and staphylococcal enterotoxin production. The addition of toxicologically acceptable fungistatic substances to IMF will improve the stability of the products with respect to moulds and yeasts. IMF shouldn't need refrigeration. However, the shelf-life of these foods is prolonged if they are stored below room temperature.*

INTRODUCTION

The a_w of a food influences the multiplication[1] and metabolic activity (including toxin production) of micro-organisms, also their survival and resistance. This is true not only for organisms that cause spoilage and food-poisoning, but also for those which are desirable for the fermentation of certain foods. Microbial spoilage, food-poisoning and fermentation take place if the a_w of the substrate is favourable for the multiplication and metabolic activity of the organisms involved. Most organisms occurring in foods proliferate at a high a_w; only a few require a low a_w for growth. Thus, if the a_w decreases, then fewer genera of micro-organisms are able to multiply on or in a food.

In traditional processes a decrease in a_w of a food and thereby an extension of its shelf-life are accomplished by drying, salting, addition of sugar or freezing. Some of these processes are applied in combination. The principle of newly developed processes, which are used in the production of intermediate moisture foods (IMF), is to decrease the a_w below a level where most pathogenic micro-organisms cannot grow but still have enough water present in the product for palatability. Furthermore, inhibition of undesirable micro-organisms in IMF is not solely caused by a decrease in a_w, but is influenced by pH, *Eh*, temperature, preservatives or a competitive microflora.

According to the a_w, foods may be divided into three categories:

(1) High moisture foods (HMF): $a_w = 1.0–0.90$
(2) Intermediate moisture foods (IMF): $a_w = 0.90–0.60$
(3) Low moisture foods (LMF): $a_w = 0.60–0.00$

Depending on the a_w of a food, its deterioration during storage is influenced by different chemical, physical or biological reactions. In low moisture foods (LMF) lipid-oxidation, non-enzymatic browning, losses in water soluble nutrients (*e.g.* vitamins) and deterioration by enzymatic activity may occur, but micro-organisms are inhibited by the a_w of these foods. The stability of intermediate moisture foods (IMF) is already much influenced by micro-organisms and for the shelf-life of many high moisture foods (HMF) micro-organisms are decisive.

TOLERANCE OF MICRO-ORGANISMS TO a_w

In general, of the micro-organisms associated with foods, moulds are more tolerant of a decreased a_w than yeasts, and yeasts are more tolerant than bacteria. In Table 1 the minimal a_w required for the growth of a number of genera of bacteria, yeasts and moulds which are recovered from foods, is listed. This table has been compiled from the data reported by many authors.[1-37]

The a_w requirements of some micro-organisms reported by different authors are not always in agreement; therefore, the data in Table 1 are based partially on a compromise and have to be regarded as incomplete. In many studies the a_w of the substrates for the organisms investigated was adjusted with sodium chloride. If the authors reported only the NaCl tolerance of the organisms studied, the corresponding a_w was estimated. It should be mentioned, that the minimum a_w requirements of organisms may vary somewhat depending upon the solute used to adjust the a_w or the moisture content of the substrate.[38,39] If fermentable carbohydrates are used to adjust the a_w of the substrate, then organisms producing acid from these carbohydrates will not tolerate such a low a_w as on substrates with a higher pH.[36] The minimum a_w requirement is also influenced by the method of preparation of the food system. Foods prepared to a given a_w by desorption or adsorption processes for example, exhibit different characteristics for growth of micro-organisms.[40,41] A food prepared by desorption has a higher moisture content at a given a_w than a food prepared by adsorption and organisms have a higher a_w requirement for growth if the food is prepared by adsorption.[42]

Most data in Table 1 were obtained by investigating the a_w tolerance of the studied organisms under otherwise optimal growth conditions using an artificial substrate with the a_w adjusted with

TABLE 1

Minimal a$_w$ for multiplication of micro-organisms associated with foods

a$_w$	Bacteria	Yeasts	Moulds
0·98	Clostridium (1), Pseudomonas[a]	—	—
0·97	Clostridium (2)	—	—
0·96	Flavobacterium, Klebsiella, Lactobacillus,[a] Proteus,[a] Pseudomonas,[a] Shigella	—	—
0·95	Alcaligenes, Bacillus, Citrobacter, Clostridium (3), Enterobacter, Escherichia, Proteus, Pseudomonas, Salmonella, Serratia, Vibrio	—	—
0·94	Lactobacillus, Microbacterium, Pediococcus, Streptococcus,[a] Vibrio[a]	—	—
0·93	Lactobacillus,[a] Streptococcus	—	Rhizopus, Mucor
0·92	—	Rhodotorula, Pichia	—
0·91	Corynebacterium, Staphylococcus (4), Streptococcus[a]	—	—
0·90	Lactobacillus,[a] Micrococcus, Pediococcus, Vibrio[a]	Hansenula, Saccharomyces	—
0·88	—	Candida, Debaryomyces, Hanseniaspora, Torulopsis	Cladosporium
0·87	—	Debaryomyces[a]	—
0·86	Staphylococcus (5)	—	Paecilomyces
0·80	—	Saccharomyces[a]	Aspergillus, Penicillium, Emericella, Eremascus
0·75	Halophilic bacteria	—	Aspergillus[a] Wallemia
0·70	—	—	Eurotium, Chrysosporium
0·62	—	Saccharomyces[a]	Eurotium,[a] Monascus

[a] Some strains; (1) = Clostridium botulinum type C; (2) = Cl. botulinum type E
and some strains of Cl. perfringens; (3) = Cl. botulinum type A and B and
Cl. perfringens; (4) = anaerobic; (5) = aerobic.

additives or by desorption. The a_w tolerance of the organisms will decrease if other factors, such as temperature, redox-potential and pH, are not optimal, as is often the case, if foods are the substrate. In addition, food products often contain preservatives (e.g. nitrite, sorbic or propionic acid) and sometimes competitive organisms and this will cause a further increase in the a_w sensitivity of the listed micro-organisms.

From Table 1 it is possible to conclude that substrates with a_w of <0.95 inhibit multiplication of most Gram-negative bacteria as well as spore-forming bacteria of the genera *Bacillus* and *Clostridium*, and also apparently inhibit germination of bacterial spores. Some Gram-positive bacteria which are desirable for the fermentation of meats, i.e. representatives of the genera *Lactobacillus*, *Pediococcus* or *Micrococcus*, tolerate a much lower a_w than 0.95. Certainly, well-adapted strains of bacteria, for instance in curing brines, are able to grow at an a_w at which most representatives of their genera would be inhibited. Yeasts and moulds of the genera *Debaryomyces* and *Penicillium*, which are important for the fermentation of certain sausages and could be used as starter cultures for IMF, multiply and are metabolically active at remarkably low a_w levels too.

Of the food-poisoning bacteria, representatives of the genus *Shigella* are inhibited by an $a_w < 0.96$ (Ref. 36) and other Gram-negative rods <0.95; the latter was demonstrated for *Salmonella*,[5,8,15,36,43] enteropathogenic *Escherichia coli*[36] and *Vibrio parahaemolyticus*.[44] However, some strains of *V. parahaemolyticus* require an $a_w < 0.94$ for inhibition.[35] The growth and toxin production of *Clostridium botulinum* type C is inhibited below an a_w of 0.98 (Ref. 24), of *Cl. botulinum* type E < 0.97 (Refs. 23, 21, 28), and of *Cl. botulinum* type A and B (Refs. 45, 46, 21) and *Cl. perfringens*[29] <0.95. Undoubtedly, of the food-poisoning bacteria the lowest a_w is tolerated by *Staphylococcus aureus*. Under anaerobic conditions this organism is reported to be inhibited at $a_w < 0.91$ (Ref. 1), but aerobically at only <0.86 (Refs. 1, 11, 12, 19).

Some strains of *Staph. aureus* produce enterotoxins; their classification (A, B, C_1, C_2, D, E, F) is based on reactions of these toxins with specific antibodies. Types A and D cause most outbreaks of food poisoning.[47-49] Several authors[50,26,51-54,33,34] related both staphylococcal growth and enterotoxin production to sodium chloride concentration or a_w. It was found that the production of enterotoxin B[50,26,51,33] and enterotoxin C[54] by *Staph. aureus* cease at an a_w of 0·94. However, enterotoxin A might also be produced at an $a_w < 0·90$ (Ref. 34). Preliminary data of Troller[34] indicate that the effect of a_w on enterotoxin C production is similar to that on enterotoxin A, and the author concluded that reliance cannot be placed on the reduction of a_w alone as a means of preventing the formation of enterotoxins A and C by *Staph. aureus*. Furthermore, no loss of enterotoxins A and C was observed as a result of suspension in substrates poised at low a_w levels.[34,55] Recently enterotoxin A and B production by *Staph. aureus* has been reported in potato doughs and shrimp slurries by Troller and Stinson.[56] These authors could detect no enterotoxin A in their glycerol-treated shrimp slurries at a_w 0·93, the same level where growth of *Staph. aureus* had decreased considerably. In contrast, in the glycerol-treated potato doughs, enterotoxin A production occurred at an a_w level of 0·93 but not at 0·88 even with 10^7 viable cells/ml recovered. In the case of enterotoxin B production, the limiting a_w level was 0·93 for glycerol-treated shrimp slurries but 0·97 for the potato doughs.

Information on the a_w requirements for mycotoxin production is scarce. Mycotoxins are frequently produced at sub-optimal growth temperatures,[57] and sometimes are also favoured by sub-optimal a_w (Ref. 58). On the other hand, in many instances mycotoxin formation will probably be limited at higher a_w levels, rather than the growth of the toxinogenic mould. In peanuts aflatoxins are produced within 14 days at 25°C at an a_w of 0·86 (Ref. 59); as limiting RH (a_w) for aflatoxin production in peanuts at 20°C Diener and Davis[60] reported 83% $(a_w$ 0·83). In the study by Bacon *et al.*[58] with poultry feed inoculated with *Aspergillus ochraceus* it was observed that penicillic acid began to accumulate at an a_w of 0·80 at 22° and 30°C, whereas ochratoxin A began to accumulate at an a_w of 0·85 at 30°C; maximum production of penicillic acid occurred at 22°C and an a_w of 0·90 and of ochratoxin A at 30°C and an a_w of 0·95. From the data available, it is possible to conclude that the production of some mycotoxins could occur in IMF which support mould growth.

In considering the data available and by taking into account that some species or strains of micro-organisms are tolerant of a lower a_w than other members of the genus, it may be concluded that in the a_w range of IMF (0·90–0·60) the bacteria, yeasts and moulds listed in Table 2 are of significance. These bacteria are able to multiply in the a_w range 0·90–0·80, yeasts and moulds in the range 0·90–0·60.

Most organisms listed in Table 2 cause spoilage, some produce toxins (*Staphylococcus, Paecilomyces, Penicillium, Aspergillus, Emericella, Eurotium*), and a few species of the genus *Candida* may be pathogenic. On the other hand, well adapted strains, *e.g.* of the

TABLE 2

Micro-organisms of potential significance for IMF

Bacteria	Yeasts	Moulds
Pediococcus	*Hansenula*	*Cladosporium*
Streptococcus	*Candida*	*Paecilomyces*
Micrococcus	*Hanseniaspora*	*Penicillium*
Lactobacillus	*Torulopsis*	*Aspergillus*
Vibrio	*Debaryomyces*	*Emericella*
Staphylococcus	*Saccharomyces*	*Eremascus*
Halophilic bacteria		*Wallemia*
		Eurotium
		Chrysosporium
		Monascus

genera *Lactobacillus* and *Penicillium*, might also be desirable in IMF as competitive microflora and thus serve as starter cultures. Certainly, all growth of undesirable micro-organisms in IMF should be inhibited, and the production of toxins (enterotoxins and mycotoxins) must be prevented.

HURDLE EFFECT ON IMF

The inhibition of micro-organisms in IMF does not solely depend on the a_w, but the pH, Eh, t-value, F-value, preservatives and the competitive microflora might be of importance too. How many of these 'hurdles' and at what level they are needed for a sufficient inhibition of micro-organisms during the desired storage period of IMF (*e.g.* six months), depends not only on the types but also much on the number of organisms present. It is possible to inhibit a low number of organisms present in an IMF at the beginning of storage with fewer and much lower 'hurdles' than are required for the inhibition of a large number of organisms of the same type. This emphasises the need for using raw materials with low counts of organisms and hygienic or even aseptic procedures in the preparation of IMF, especially if the products are not traditional products. As Labuza[42] points out, one problem with IMF is that to obtain stability with respect to moulds, the a_w should be reduced below 0·70. This, however, creates a dry, unpalatable food. Thus, it is desirable to keep IMF above this level; however, they must also be kept below a_w 0·85, in order to inhibit the growth of *Staphylococcus aureus*. Table 3 indicates the effectiveness of factors other than the a_w for the inhibition of a_w-tolerant organisms (*see* Table 2) in IMF.

TABLE 3

Effectiveness of several factors for the inhibition of a_w *tolerant microorganisms in IMF*

Organisms	pH-value	*Eh*-value	*t*-value	*F*-value	Sorbate	Pimaricin	Competitive microflora
Bacteria	±	±	±	+	±	−	±
Yeasts	−	±	−	+	±	±	±
Moulds	−	+	−	+	+	+	±

+ = inhibition; − = no inhibition; ± = some inhibition; *t*-value = effect of storage temperature; *F*-value = thermal process.

As Table 3 indicates some a_w-tolerant bacteria are inhibited by a low pH, this includes the genera *Vibrio*, *Micrococcus* and *Staphylococcus*. Therefore, the pH of an IMF should be as low as palatability permits; whenever possible, below pH 5·0. At this pH growth and, therefore, also enterotoxin production by *Staphylococcus aureus* cease. However, some representatives of the genus *Micrococcus* are inhibited only at a pH below 4·5.[61] For the inhibition of other a_w-tolerant bacteria (*Pediococcus*, *Streptococcus*, *Lactobacillus*) as well as for yeasts and moulds a much lower pH would be necessary, which impairs the taste of the products. It should be mentioned that the growth of lactic, acetic and butyric acid bacteria as well as the growth of yeasts and moulds is favoured in the pH range 6·0–3·0.[62]

Only representatives of the genus *Micrococcus* are inhibited by a low redox potential (*Eh*) of the a_w-tolerant bacteria, since the others are facultatively anaerobic. However, it should be remembered that *Staphylococcus aureus* is, under anaerobic conditions, already inhibited by an $a_w < 0.91$ (Ref. 1). Also yeasts apparently tolerate a much lower a_w level aerobically than anaerobically. Most mould growth is prevented by a low *Eh*. Therefore, IMF should be packaged in evacuated containers or pouches which are impermeable to oxygen.

By refrigeration, *i.e.* a low *t*-value, of the a_w-tolerant organism, *Staphylococcus aureus* is inhibited at 7°C (Refs. 63, 64), and enterotoxin B production is prevented below 10°C. For the inhibition of the genus *Lactobacillus* a temperature below 1°C (Ref. 65), for yeasts below -12°C (Ref. 66) and for moulds below -18°C (Ref. 66) is required. Since IMF should be shelf-stable, unfrozen, and even unrefrigerated, the *t*-value has not much importance for the storage of these foods. However, in order to ensure a low initial count of micro-organisms, IMF should be prepared under refrigeration. For the same reason, it would be advisable to precook the ingredients of IMF. The a_w-tolerant organisms are not heat-resistant, and, therefore, a low *F*-value, *i.e.* an internal temperature of 85°C, is sufficient for elimination of these organisms in the raw materials. However, this temperature is required, because the heat resistance of micro-organisms increases somewhat with decreasing a_w (Refs. 67, 68, 42). Since some micro-organisms, including *Salmonella* and *Staphylococcus*, may have the maximum heat resistance in the a_w range of IMF, it was suggested by Labuza[42] that components such as meat, eggs, etc., which are at high a_w should be heat-pasteurised prior to combination with the a_w-lowering agents and other dry components of IMF. This should ensure maximum heat inactivation of organisms by a relatively mild heat process.

With fungistatic substances, such as potassium sorbate[69,70] pimaricin,[71-73] parabens, glycols, glycerol and butanediol,[42] the growth of moulds and to some extent also of yeasts and bacteria is inhibited in IMF, and, therefore, these substances could be useful.

In some traditional products in the IMF a_w range the competitive microflora, especially representatives of the genus *Lactobacillus*, contribute to the stability. It seems advisable that by using selected strains of bacteria or moulds as starter cultures, which must be well-adapted to a low a_w, the stability of newly developed IMF could also be improved.

MICROBIOLOGY OF IMF

It is useful to differentiate between traditional and newly developed IMF. Both product groups are in the a_w range of 0·90–0·60. However, the traditional IMF, such as certain meat and bakery products, as well as dried fruits and jams, are processed by the withdrawal of water by desorption or adsorption and/or the addition of conventional legally approved additives (salts, sugar, fat, etc.). On the other hand, the newly developed IMF are processed by using additives, such as glycerol, glycols and sorbitol as humectants, and sorbate, pimaricin and parabens as preservatives; these substances are at the present time at least partially not approved by the food law of several countries.[74,42] Newly developed IMF are processed either by desorption or adsorption of water or a combination of both processes.[75,42] In Tables 4 and 5, the a_w range and the inherent 'hurdles' are listed for some traditional and newly developed IMF.

TABLE 4

a_w *range and inherent 'hurdles' of some traditional IMF*

Products	a_w range	Inherent hurdles
Jams	0·90–0·80	a_w, pH, *Eh*, *F*, pres.[a]
Meats	0·90–0·60	a_w, p*H*, (*Eh*), *t*, pres.,[a] c.m.[b]
Cake and pastry	0·90–0·60	a_w, (*t*), *F*, pres.[a]
Dried fruits	0·75–0·60	a_w, pH, (*F*), pres.[a]
Frozen foods	0·90–0·60	a_w, *t*

[a] Preservatives (such as sorbic acid, nitrite).
[b] Competitive microflora (Lactobacillaceae, Streptococcaceae, moulds).

The microbial stability of traditional IMF allows prolonged storage of these products without refrigeration for a considerable time. Thus, much could be learned from the empirical 'hurdles' built into traditional products for the protection of newly developed IMF against spoilage and food-poisoning. In traditional IMF bacteria are occasionally of significance for spoilage and food-poisoning; in some products (*e.g.* fermented sausages) a competitive microflora supports the stability of the food. In general yeasts and, especially, moulds are the major spoilage factors of traditional IMF. Yeasts cause spoilage in syrups, confectionery products, jams and dried fruits[79]; while moulds spoil meats, jams, cake and pastry as

TABLE 5

a_w *and inherent 'hurdles' of some newly developed IMF*

Products	a_w	Inherent hurdles
Sweet and sour pork (1)	0·85	a_w, pH, (*Eh*), *F*, pres.[a]
Chicken dish, ready-to-eat (2)	0·85	a_w, *F*, pres.[a]
Sliced and dried bologna (3)	0·85	a_w, *Eh*, *F*, pres.[a]
Hennican (4)	0·85	a_w, (pH), *Eh*, (*F*), pres.[a]
Diced carrots (5)	0·77	a_w, (*F*), pres.[a]

(1) = Brockmann;[76] (2) = Lück;[75] (3) = Pavey;[77] (4) = Labuza;[42] (5) = Kaplow;[78] [a] = preservatives (such as sorbic acid, propylene glycol, glycerol, nitrite).

well as dried fruits. Moulds are also the main microbial problem for newly developed IMF.[42] Fungistatic substances, such as sorbic or propionic acid, improve the stability of several traditional IMF and are used to prolong the shelf-life of bakery and meat products, as well as dried fruits.[80] The packaging of products like jams, meat or bakery products in evacuated containers or pouches which are impermeable to oxygen also improves the protection against mould spoilage. If mould growth occurs the shelf-life of traditional IMF is not only jeopardised, but also the possibility arises, as has been proven in country-cured hams and fermented sausages, that myco-toxins are penetrating into the products. Traditional and newly developed IMF alike should be protected against spoilage and food-poisoning by a combination of 'hurdles' which ensure the desired and necessary microbial stability of the products.

It should be mentioned that frozen foods, at a certain temperature, are also in the range of IMF, since freezing is equal to drying. The a_w of a food decreases with the freezing temperature. At a tempera-ture of $-11°C$ the a_w of many frozen foods is about 0·90, at $-23°C$ about 0·80, and at $-30°C$ about 0·75.[81,6,82,83] Probably, the growth of some micro-organisms in frozen foods is not limited by the temperature but by the a_w of the substrate.[6,84]

RECOMMENDATIONS FOR IMF

The raw material used for the production of traditional and newly developed IMF should contain low counts of micro-organisms, especially of those types of bacteria, yeasts and moulds which tolerate a low a_w. Where feasible, the raw material in the preparation of the IMF should be heat-processed to destroy undesirable microorganisms as well as microbial enzymes which deteriorate the products.

The preparation of newly developed IMF should be done by handling the heated raw materials under hygienic or even aseptic conditions and under refrigeration to ensure a low initial count of a_w tolerant organisms.

If the palatability of the products permits, the a_w of IMF should be <0·85 or the pH <5·0, since either of these 'hurdles' protects the product against food-poisoning by *Staphylococcus aureus*.

If possible, IMF should be packaged in evacuated containers or pouches which are impermeable to oxygen. A low *Eh* of the product inhibits mould growth, which is the major risk for the spoilage and poisoning of IMF. The addition of toxicologically acceptable fungistatic substances to IMF, such as sorbic acid, propylene glycol, glycerol, parabens, diols, will improve the stability of the products in respect to moulds and yeasts.

The usefulness of starter cultures, using selected strains of *Lactobacillaceae* or *Streptococcaceae* as well as moulds, which tolerate a low a_w, should be explored for newly developed IMF, since this competitive microflora supports the microbial stability of traditional IMF.

It should be possible to store IMF without refrigeration; however, it is obvious that not only the chemical and physical but also the microbial deterioration of these products is inhibited and thus the shelf-life prolonged if IMF are stored below room temperature.

REFERENCES

1. Scott, W. J. (1953). *Aust. J. Biol. Sci.*, **6**, p. 549.
2. Snow, D. (1949). *Ann. appl. Biol.*, **36**, p. 1.
3. Burcik, E. (1950). *Arch. Microbiol.*, **15**, p. 203.
4. Bullock, K. and Tallentire, A. (1952). *J. Pharm. Pharmacol.*, **4**, p. 917.
5. Christian, J. H. B. and Scott, W. J. (1953). *Aust. J. Biol. Sci.*, **6**, p. 565.
6. Scott, W. J. (1957). In: *Advances in Food Research*, Vol .7, ed. E. M. Mrak and G. F. Stewart, Academic Press, New York, p. 83.
7. Williams, O. B. and Purnell, H. G. (1953). *Food Res.*, **18**, p. 35.
8. Christian, J. H. B. (1955). *Aust. J. Biol. Sci.*, **8**, p. 75.

9. Beers, R. J. (1957). In: *Spores*, ed. H. O. Halvorson, American Institute of Biological Science, Washington, USA.
10. Wodzinski, R. J. and Frazier, W. C. (1960). *J. Bacteriol.*, **79**, p. 572.
11. Christian, J. H. B. and Waltho, J. A. (1962). *J. appl. Bacteriol.*, **25**, p. 369.
12. Christian, J. H. B. and Waltho, J. A. (1964). *J. Gen. Microbiol.*, **35**, p. 205.
13. Lanigan, G. W. (1963). *Aust. J. Biol. Sci.*, **16**, p. 606.
14. Riemann, H. (1963). *Food Technol.*, **17**, p. 39.
15. Blanche Koelensmid, W. A. A. and van Rhee, R. (1964). *Ann. Inst. Pasteur.*, **15**, p. 85.
16. Gough, B. J. and Alford, J. A. (1965). *J. Food Sci.*, **30**, p. 1025.
17. Hobbs, B. C. (1965). *J. appl. Microbiol.*, **28**, p. 74.
18. Kim, C. H. (1965). *Diss. Abstracts*, **26**, p. 1288.
19. Matz, S. A. (1965). In: *Water in Foods*, The AVI-Publishing Company, Inc., Westport, Connecticut, p. 249.
20. Brownlie, L. E. (1966). *J. appl. Bacteriol.*, **29**, p. 447.
21. Ohye, D. F. and Christian, J. H. B. (1966). *Proc. 5th Int. Sympos. Food Microbiol.*, *Moscow*, p. 217.
22. Ohye, D. F., Christian, J. H. B. and Scott, W. J. (1966). *Proc. 5th Int. Sympos. Food Microbiol.*, *Moscow*, p. 136.
23. Segner, W. P., Schmidt, C. F. and Boltz, J. K. (1966). *Appl. Microbiol.*, **14**, p. 49.
24. Segner, W. P., Schmidt, C. F. and Boltz, J. K. (1971). *Appl. Microbiol.*, **22**, p. 1025.
25. Baird-Parker, A. C. and Freame, B. (1967). *J. appl. Bacteriol.*, **30**, p. 420.
26. McLean, R. A., Lilly, H. D. and Alford, J. A. (1968). *J. Bacteriol.*, **95**, p. 1207.
27. Pitt, J. I. and Christian, J. H. B. (1968). *Appl. Microbiol.*, **16**, p. 1853.
28. Pivnick, H. and Thatcher, F. S. (1968). In: *The Safety of Foods*, ed. J. C. Ayres, F. R. Blood, C. O. Chichester, H. D. Graham, R. S. Miccutcheon, J. J. Powers, B. S. Schweigert, A. D. Stevens and G. Zweig, The AVI-Publishing Company, Inc., Westport, Connecticut, p. 121.
29. Kang, C. K., Woodburn, M., Pagenkopf, A. and Cheney, R. (1969). *Appl. Microbiol.*, **18**, p. 798.
30. Mossel, D. A. A. (1969). *Alimenta*, **8**, p. 8.
31. Bem, Z. and Leistner, L. (1970). *Fleischwirtschaft*, **50**, p. 492.
32. Strong, D. H., Foster, E. F. and Duncan, C. L. (1970). *Appl. Microbiol.*, **19**, p. 980.
33. Troller, J. A. (1971). *Appl. Microbiol.*, **21**, p. 435.
34. Troller, J. A. (1972). *Appl. Microbiol.*, **24**, p. 440.
35. Rödel, W., Herzog, H. and Leistner, L. (1973). *Fleischwirtschaft*, **53**, p. 1301.
36. Tomčov, D., Bem, Z. and Leistner, L. (1974). *RIM*, **6**, p. 3.
37. Pitt, J. I. (1975). In: *Water Relations of Foods*, ed. R. B. Duckworth, Academic Press, London.

38. Marshall, B. J., Ohye, D. F. and Christian, J. H. B. (1971). *Appl. Microbiol.*, **21**, p. 363.
39. Kushner, D. J. (1971). In: *Inhibition and Destruction of the Microbial Cell*, ed. W. B. Hugo, Academic Press, London.
40. Labuza, T. P., McNally, L., Gallagher, D., Hawkes, J. and Hurtado, F. (1972). *J. Food Sci.*, **37**, p. 154.
41. Plitman, M., Park, Y., Gomez, R. and Sinskey, A. J. (1973). *J. Food Sci.*, **38**, p. 1004.
42. Labuza, T. P. (1974). *Storage stability and improvement of intermediate moisture foods*, Phase II. NASA, Food and Nutrition Office. Contract NAS 9-12560. Houston, Texas.
43. Hansen, N. H. and Riemann, H. (1962). *Fleischwirtschaft*, **14**, p. 861.
44. Beuchat, L. R. (1974). *Appl. Microbiol.*, **27**, p. 1075.
45. Greenberg, R. A., Silliker, J. H. and Fatta, L. D. (1959). *Food Technol.*, **13**, p. 509.
46. Anderton, J. I. (1963). *Scientific and Technical Surveys* No. 40. The British Food Manufacturing Industries Research Association, Leatherhead, Surrey, England, p. 1.
47. Casman, E. P., Bennet, K. W., Dorsey, A. E. and Issa, J. A. (1967). *J. Bacteriol.*, **94**, p. 1875.
48. Toshach, S. and Thorsteinson, S. (1972). *Can. J. Public Health*, **63**, p. 58.
49. Wieneke, A. A. (1974). *J. Hyg. Camb.*, **73**, p. 255.
50. Genigeorgis, C. and Sadler, W. W. (1966). *J. Bacteriol.*, **92**, p. 1383.
51. Genigeorgis, C., Riemann, H. and Sadler, W. W. (1969). *J. Food Sci.*, **34**, p. 62.
52. Hojvat, S. A. and Jackson, H. (1969). *J. Inst. Can. Sci. Technol. Aliment.*, **2**, p. 56.
53. Markus, Z. H. and Silverman, G. J. (1970). *Appl. Microbiol.*, **20**, p. 492.
54. Genigeorgis, C., Foda, M. S., Mantis, A. and Sadler, W. W. (1971). *Appl. Microbiol.*, **21**, p. 862.
55. Lee, W. H., Staples, C. L. and Olson, J. C., Jr. (1975). *J. Food Sci.*, **40**, p. 119.
56. Troller, J. A. and Stinson, J. V. (1975). *J. Food Sci.*, **40**, p. 802.
57. Jarvis, B. (1971). *J. appl. Bacteriol.*, **34**, p. 199.
58. Bacon, C. W., Sweeney, J. G., Robbins, J. D. and Burdick, D. (1973). *Appl. Microbiol.*, **26**, p. 155.
59. Sanders, T. H., Davis, N. D. and Diener, U. L. (1968). *J. Amer. Oil Chem. Soc.*, **45**, p. 683.
60. Diener, U. L. and Davis, N. D. (1970). *J. Amer. Oil Chem. Soc.*, **47**, p. 347.
61. Lerche, M. (1957). *Berliner Münchener tierärztl. Wschr.*, **70**, p. 13.
62. Böhringer, P. (1962). In: *Die Hefen*, Band II, *Technologie der Hefen*, ed. F. Reiff, R. Kautzmann, H. Lüers and M. Lindemann, Verlag Hans Carl, Nürnberg.
63. Angelotti, R., Foter, M. J. and Lewis, K. H. (1961). *Amer. J. Public Health*, **51**, p. 76.

64. Riemann, H., Lee, W. H. and Genigeorgis, C. (1972). *J. Milk Food Technol.*, **35**, p. 514.
65. Allen, J. R. and Foster, E. M. (1960). *Food Res.*, **25**, p. 19.
66. Schmidt-Lorenz, W. (1970). *Alimenta*, **9**, p. 32.
67. Vrchlabský, J. and Leistner, L. (1970). *Fleischwirtschaft*, **50**, p. 1237.
68. Vrchlabský, J. and Leistner, L. (1971). *Fleischwirtschaft*, **51**, p. 1368.
69. Lück, E. (1972). In: *Sorbinsäure*, Band II, *Biochemie-Mikrobiologie*, B. Behr's Verlag, Hamburg.
70. Leistner, L., Maing, I. Y. and Bergmann, E. (1975). *Fleischwirtschaft*, **55**, p. 559.
71. Moerman, P. C. (1966). *Vlees*, **8**, p. 73.
72. Moerman, P. C. (1967). *Vleesdistr. Vleestechnol.*, **2**, p. 243.
73. Hechelmann, H. and Leistner, L. (1969). *Fleischwirtschaft*, **49**, p. 1639.
74. Lück, E. (1973). In: *Sorbinsäure*, Band IV, *Lebensmittelrechtliche Zulassungen*, B. Behr's Verlag, Hamburg.
75. Lück, E. (1973). *Ernährungswirtschaft/Lebensmitteltechnik*, **5**, p. 346.
76. Brockmann, M. C. (1970). *Food Technol.*, **24**, p. 61.
77. Pavey, R. K. (1972). Report for US Army Natick Laboratories, Technical Report 73-17-Fl. Natick, Massachusetts, USA.
78. Kaplow, M. (1970). *Food Technol.*, **24**, p. 53.
79. Walker, H. W. and Ayres, J. C. (1970). In: *The Yeasts*, Vol. 3, *Yeast Technology*, ed. A. H. Rose and J. S. Harrison, Academic Press, London and New York.
80. Lück, E. (1970). In: *Sorbinsäure*, Band III, *Technologie*, B. Behr's Verlag, Hamburg.
81. Moran, T. (1935). Report of the Food Investigation Board for the year 1935 (1936), H.M. Stationery Office, London, p. 20.
82. Storey, R. M. and Stainsby, G. (1970). *J. Food Technol.*, **5**, p. 157.
83. Fennema, O. and Berny, L. A. (1974). *Proc. 4th Int. Congr. Food Sci. and Technol.*, Madrid, Work Documents Topic 2, p. 12.
84. Leistner, L. and Rödel, W. (1975). *Deutsche Zschr. Lebensmitteltechnol.*, **26**, p. 169.

DISCUSSION

Blanchfield: I was very interested in this hurdle concept, and in the possibility that the existence of one hurdle may permit the height of the next to be lower than it would otherwise have to be. Could you please enlarge on the possibility that in a canned, cured meat product, other things being equal, and if one could reduce the water activity, one might be able to reduce the minimum safe heat process in the canning operation?

Leistner: It is possible, for instance, to reduce the water activity of canned liver sausage below 0·95, and this would be enough to inhibit the germination of bacillacae spores. This can be done by adding 4·5% of salt and 44% fat. In this instance it works very well with a heat treatment of only 100°C, giving storage stability at 37°C. There are only a very few products, however, to which you can add so much fat that you can achieve a water activity of below 0·95.

Gould: Could you explain your statement that fat has an indirect effect on the water activity of meat products? Do you mean that the fat will simply replace some of the water, or are you suggesting a more specific effect?

Leistner: No, it is just an indirect effect, because there is not much water in the fat. If you add to a certain amount of food, let us say, a certain amount of salt, this salt will concentrate in the lean part, and the brine phase will be more concentrated in the lean part, and so the fat indirectly influences the water activity. One of the main factors in the water activity adjustment of meat products is fat.

Seiler: I was wondering to what extent the difference in water activity between the outside surface of a meat product and the inside of the product has been taken into account? I noticed that in one of your slides you had a water activity of round about 0·88 to 0·9, and you said there wouldn't be any trouble from yeast or bacteria. I wondered whether perhaps the surface of these products was at a lower water activity, and you didn't get mould because of that.

Leistner: Of course the surface water activity is of great importance for most spoilage problems in meats, and so we try first of all to measure surface water activity. The surface is in a dynamic state, therefore you need to have an open a_w measurement device, where this dynamic flow is not disturbed; otherwise, if you have a closed system, after a short while you are just measuring the water activity at the interior. We now have an open system whereby we can measure the water activity of the surface, and we think shelf-life capability of fresh meat can be considerably improved by adjusting this surface water activity. For instance, in Canada shrouds are dipped in a brine solution, and placed on the carcase, thus lowering the surface water activity. On the other hand there are now new casings which are not permeable to water vapour, and these casings are used for Bologna-type sausages. They keep from about 14 days to 3 weeks because the water activity on the surface is much lower than it would be with natural casings. This makes a lot of difference to the keeping quality, especially of products such as Bologna, liver or some types of blood sausages. So I think the best approach towards improving the shelf-life of meat is to measure and control the surface water activity.

Jeffery: You mentioned the effect of pH. Have you also studied the type of acid used to achieve that pH? You mentioned lactic acid particularly as being very effective, but have you also studied other acids and their effects?

Leistner: There are two different things here. First, you have the effect the acid has in itself on depression of a_w. Secondly, you have the effect the acid has on pH. In our opinion, if you have a food which has a water activity below 0·95, and a pH below 5·2, this food doesn't need any refrigeration; it is a shelf-stable product.

Chairman: I think the question was, was there any effect of the molecular structure of the acid used at a given pH? For instance, citric acid as contrasted with tartaric acid?

Leistner: No. We have not in fact studied this as far as molecular structure is concerned.

Tilbury: I can give a reference for this—a paper published by Pitt last year (Pitt, J. I., 1974, *Food Technol. (Australia)*, **26**, p. 238) on the effects of both mineral and organic acids on the inhibition of yeasts. He was working at low values, about pH 2–4. As I recall, acetic was considerably more inhibitory than some of the mineral acids.

Jarvis: There is quite a lot of published information about the effects of acids in culture media for moulds and yeasts, showing that specific types of organic acids have a greater or lesser effect at equivalent pH values.

Blanchfield: I can add that in the area of pickles and sauces the nature of the acid is far more important than any pH effect in inhibiting, particularly, yeasts. In fact in the case of acetic acid and its effectiveness, it is the undissociated acid molecule that exercises the inhibitory effect and not the pH.

Karel: Lubieniecka Von Schellhorn did some work in Munich many years ago on the effects of specific fatty acids independent of pH on water activity.

Leistner: So far as meats are concerned, we studied the effects of tartaric, lactic, citric and acetic acids (these are permitted acids in Germany), with regard to mould inhibition and acetic acid was by far the best.

de Groote: The tolerance of micro-organisms towards water activity depends on the nature of the humectants. Do you know to which biological factors this is correlated?

Leistner: What I can say to this is just speculation. It seems that some humectants are more toxic than others. For example, certain organisms will tolerate a very high salt concentration, and others will not, but will tolerate a very high sugar concentration. I don't know whether this is a membrane, or an osmotic effect—but it seems that some organisms are more tolerant of one humectant than they are of others.

11

The Microbial Stability of Intermediate Moisture Foods with Respect to Yeasts

R. H. TILBURY

Tate and Lyle Limited, Group Research and Development,
PO Box, 68, Reading, Berks, England

ABSTRACT

Intermediate moisture foods generally possess a_w *values between* 0·60 *and* 0·85, *which inhibits growth of bacteria but permits growth of xerophilic fungi. Within this group are the so-called osmotolerant yeasts, which may be defined empirically as those yeasts capable of growth at* a_w *values below* 0·85. *A brief review is given of the occurrence of osmotolerant yeast spoilage in a wide range of traditional intermediate moisture foods, with special reference to recent outbreaks. Ecological factors which influence the growth of osmotolerant yeasts are discussed in order to elucidate those factors which predispose intermediate moisture foods to yeast spoilage. Sources of osmotolerant yeast contamination and vectors of infection are mentioned. Special aspects of the physiology of osmotolerant yeasts are described, including the effect of* a_w *and different solutes on growth limits, growth optima, growth rates and heat resistance. This information is used to predict the effect of the composition of 'novel' intermediate moisture foods on their susceptibility to yeast spoilage. Current views on the mechanisms of osmotolerance are briefly reviewed. Methods for prevention of yeast spoilage of intermediate moisture foods are discussed, especially the use of heat-processing and chemical preservatives. Finally, certain practical problems are mentioned, concerning media and methods for the isolation and recovery of osmotolerant yeasts, and the methodology of stability tests for intermediate moisture foods.*

INTRODUCTION

For the purposes of this review intermediate moisture foods (IMF's) are taken to be those possessing a water activity (a_w) within the range 0·60–0·85. The scope will include finished foods, raw materials and model systems.

One of the advantages of IMF's is that bacterial growth does not occur below an a_w of 0·85. Most yeasts and moulds are similarly inhibited, but certain species can tolerate high solute concentrations. Fortunately, pathogenic yeasts do not grow at low a_w values so the effect of yeast growth in IMF's is essentially one of spoilage. Yeasts capable of growth at low a_w values or high solute concentrations have been variously classified as: osmophilic,[1] osmotophilic,[2] osmotolerant,[3] osmoduric,[2] osmotrophic[4] and xerophilic.[5] A discussion of the origins and merits of these alternatives is outside the scope of this review. However, it should be mentioned that although the term 'osmophilic' yeast is most commonly used and will be adopted in this paper, it is misleading for two reasons. First, it is now generally agreed that a_w, not osmotic pressure, is the principal factor governing the water relations of micro-organisms.[1,6,7] Secondly, 'osmophilic' yeasts do not have a general requirement for decreased a_w but merely tolerate drier conditions better than do non-osmophilic yeasts.[3] Hence the terms 'osmotolerant' or 'sugar-tolerant' are more accurate than 'osmophilic'.

Various definitions of osmophilic yeast have been proposed, usually based on an organism's ability to grow at a particular a_w value or sugar concentration. Christian[1] defined osmophilic yeasts as those capable of multiplication in concentrated syrups of a_w below 0·85, whilst Scarr and Rose[8] chose a limit of 65°Brix sucrose, equivalent to an a_w of 0·865 at 25°. An a_w of 0·87 was regarded by Mossel[9] as the lowest limit for growth of non-osmophilic yeasts. van der Walt[2] recommended the use of agar media containing 50% w/w and 60% w/w glucose to distinguish between 'osmotolerant' and 'osmotophilic' yeasts, equivalent to a_w values of approximately 0·90 and 0·85 respectively. In the sugar industry, osmophilic yeasts are conveniently defined in practical terms, as those capable of growth in a saturated sucrose solution. This is approximately 67°Brix at 25°, equivalent to an a_w of 0·85. Most recently, Pitt[5] defined xerophilic fungi, including osmophilic yeasts, as those 'capable of growth, under at least one set of environmental conditions, at an a_w below

0·85'. Choice of this limit was empirical, but in view of its practical value, it will be used here.

Since the classical paper by Scott[6] in 1957, there have been published several excellent reviews dealing with osmophilic yeasts and/or their role in food spoilage, notably those of Ingram;[10,11] Christian;[1] Onishi;[12] Walker and Ayres[13] and Kushner.[14] The Ph.D. theses of Anand,[15] Koh[16] and Corry[17] contain useful critical

TABLE 1

Traditional IMF's susceptible to spoilage by osmophilic yeasts

Product type	Examples	Water content (% w/w)	Solute content (% w/w)	Water activity a_w
1. Syrups, sugars,	Raw cane sugar	0·4–0·7	99·3–99·6	0·60–0·75
sweet spreads	Refined sucrose syrup	33·3	66·7	0·85
and preserves	Glucose or invert syrup	20·0	80·0	0·72
	Barley syrup; malt			
	extract	20–25	75–80	0·70–0·80
	Maple syrup	26–36	64–74	0·70–0·80
	Honey, jam,			
	marmalade	20–35	65–80	0·75–0·80
2. Fruit juice	Orange juice	35	65	0·80–0·84
concentrates	Raspberry	35	65	0·79–0·80
3. Confectionery	Marzipan	15–17	83–85	0·75–0·80
products	Glacé cherries	30	70	0·75
	Toffees and caramels	8	92	0·60–0·65
4. Bakery products	Fruit cakes	20–28	72–80	0·73–0·83
	Christmas pudding	20–25	75–80	0·70–0·77
5. Dairy	Sweetened condensed			
products	milk	30	70	0·83
6. Dried fruits	Prunes and figs	20	80	0·68
	Dates	12–25	75–88	0·60–0·65
7. Cereals	Flour, rice, pulses	16–19	81–84	0·80–0·87
	Rolled oats	10	90	0·65–0·75
8. Brined and	Lactic acid			
pickled	fermentations—			
vegetables;	cucumbers, olives;			
sauces	acetic acid pickles	76–90	10–24	0·79–0·94
9. Meats	Fermented sausages,	74	26	0·83
	e.g. Hungarian			
	salami, county-			
	cured hams			0·87

Data extracted from References 5, 7, 14, 43, 44.

reviews, mainly concerned with physiological aspects of osmophilic yeasts. Spoilage of foods of plant origin by xerophilic fungi has recently been reviewed by Pitt,[5] and Mossel[7] discussed the inter-relationships between water and micro-organisms in foods. This review will concentrate on special aspects relevant to the development of new IMF's mainly covering literature published in the last decade.

Many foods preserved by the traditional methods of sugaring, salting, drying and curing fall within our definition of IMF's. Although these methods of food preservation were developed empirically it is now known that the underlying principle is that of a lowering of the a_w to a level which inhibits or retards microbial growth. Table 1 lists some of these traditional IMF's in terms of their moisture content and a_w. Spoilage of many of these foods by osmophilic yeasts is well known.[13] Here we will describe those species which occur most frequently in spoilt IMF's, and describe the ecology of these organisms. Then some recent examples of spoilage outbreaks will be quoted, followed by a discussion of physiology, control methods and methodology.

PRINCIPAL SPECIES OF OSMOPHILIC YEAST

Table 2 lists those species of osmophilic yeast which are most commonly associated with spoilage of traditional IMF's. The data are partly extracted from the 1970 review by Walker and Ayres[13] and partly from additional or more recent publications. The yeasts are named and classified according to Lodder,[20] but common synonyms and names of perfect/imperfect forms are included for ease of reference to earlier literature.

Some attempt has been made to indicate the sugar and salt tolerance of the organisms, using maximum concentrations cited for the species in Lodder.[20] This information is incomplete as in some genera only salt tolerance is quoted, in others only sugar tolerance, and in several genera combined salt and sugar tolerance is tested. In Lodder, sugar tolerance is given in terms of ability to grow in media containing 50% and 60% w/w glucose,[2] equivalent to a_w values of about 0·90 and 0·845 respectively; these values are not necessarily the maximum sugar concentration tolerated. For comparison, a_w values of salt concentrations are as follows: 10% w/v = a_w 0·94;

TABLE 2

Common osmotolerant and osmophilic yeasts, according to the classification methods and descriptions of Lodder[20]

Organism	Synonyms; perfect/imperfect forms	a_w Tolerance maxm concn for growth		Type of commodities commonly spoilt		Recent references
		Glucose (% w/w)	NaCl (% w/w)	High sugar	High salt	
Candida catenulata					+	13
C. guilliermondii	P.Pi. guilliermondii	57^a	12	++		8, 22, 24, 68
C. krusei			13	++	+	13, 68
C. lipolytica			10	+	+	13
C. parapsilosis			14			22, 24
C. tropicalis		60	17	+++		13, 68, 69
C. valida	P.Pi. membranefaciens		13	++	++	13, 25
C. zeylanoides			9			13
Citeromyces matritensis	I.T. globosa	57^a; 5+	13	+++		8, 68
Debaryomyces hansenii	I.T. candida	50	10	+++	+	5, 13, 21, 28
Endomycopsis burtonii	E. chodatii	50		+++		13, 68
Hansenula anomala var. anomala	I.C. pelliculosa	0·75^b; 5+		+++	+	13, 21, 22, 25, 28, 37
H. polymorpha		5+	10	+++		24
H. subpelliculosa		5+	10	+++		13, 21, 24, 28
Kloeckera apiculata		50	10	+	+	25
Pichia farinosa		50		+++		13, 21, 22
Pi. guilliermondii	I.C. guilliermondii	50		+		8, 22, 24, 68

Perfect form	Imperfect form					References
Pi. membranefaciens		50		+	+	13, 25
Pi. ohmeri		50		+	+	13, 68
Saccharomyces bailii var. bailii	I.C. valida	50		+	+	4, 5, 13, 24, 25
S. bailii var. osmophilus	I.E. ohmeri	60		+	+	37, 45
S. bisporus var. bisporus	S. acidifaciens; S. elegans	50		+	+	4, 5, 21, 24, 25
S. bisporus var. mellis	S. mellis	0·70[b]; 60		+		28, 37
S. microellipsoides var. osmophilus		60		+		4
S. rosei		60		+	+	4, 13, 22, 68
S. rouxii	many Tygosacch. spp.	0·65; 60		+	+	4, 5, 12 13, 21, 28, 36 22, 24, 25, 37, 44, 68
Schizosaccharomyces octosporus		50		+		13, 68
Sc. pombe		50		+		68
Torulopsis apicola	T. bacillaris	57[a]	11	+		8
T. candida	P.D. hansenii	0·65[b]	21	+	+	5, 13
	T. famata	75		+		21, 28, 68
T. colliculosa			13	+		42
T. dattila			15	+		13, 22, 24, 68, 69
T. etchellsii		0·70[b]	21	+	+	13, 21, 28, 68, 69
T. glabrata			13	+		22, 68
T. kestoni		57[a]	11	+		8
T. lactis-condensi		57[a]	11	+		8, 13
T. magnoliae				+		24
T. versatilis	Brett. versatilis	0·70[c]	13	+	+	13, 21, 24, 28, 69

I = Imperfect form.
P = Perfect form.
[a] = 57% w/w glucose = a_w 0·865. Data taken from Scarr and Rose.[8]
[b] = Minimum a_w for growth in sucrose/glycerol syrups, determined by Tilbury.[21]
[c] = Minimum a_w for fermentation in fructose syrups, determined by Windisch and Neumann.[22]

$15\% = 0.895$ and $20\% = 0.845$. Additional information on sugar tolerance is taken from three sources: Scarr and Rose[8] identified yeasts capable of growth in 65% w/w sucrose syrups; Tilbury[21] determined the minimum a_w for growth in sucrose/glycerol syrups and Windisch and Neumann[22] tested isolates for ability to ferment fructose solutions containing 45, 60 and 75% sugar. According to the terminology of van der Walt,[2] yeasts that can grow at concentrations of 50% but not 60% w/w glucose are called osmoduric or osmotolerant, whereas those capable of growth at 60% w/w glucose are osmotophilic. This principle was adopted by Davenport[23-25] but the names were shortened to 'osmotolerant' and 'osmophilic'. On this basis, only some of the species listed in Table 2 may be classified as truly osmophilic. According to Davenport,[25] the principal osmophilic yeasts are as follows: S. rouxii, S. bailii var. osmophilus; S. bisporus var. mellis; T. lactis-condensi; Schizosacch. pombe; D. hansenii/T. candida; Pi. ohmeri and H. anomala var.

TABLE 3

Some physiological properties of osmophilic yeasts[20]

Physiological characteristic		S.bailii var. osmo- philus	S.bisporus var. mellis	S.rouxii	D. hansenii and T. candida	H. anomala var. anomala
Sugar fermentation and assimilation	glucose	F	F	F	FVW; A	F
	galactose	AV	AV	A	FVW; A	F
	sucrose	FV; AV	FV; AV,W	FV; AV	FVW; A	F
	maltose	NA	NA	F	FVW; A	FV; A
	lactose	NA	NA	NA	AV	NA
	raffinose	FV; AV	NA	NA	A	F
Carbon assimilation	soluble starch	NA	NA	NA	AV	A
	ethanol	A	A	AV	A	A
	glycerol	A	A	AV	A	A
	sorbitol	A	A	A	A	A
Assimilation of KNO_3		NA	NA	NA	NA	A
Growth in vitamin-free med.		—	—	—	V	+
Growth at 37°C		—	—	—	V	V

F = fermented and assimilated; NA = not assimilated; A = assimilated but not fermented; W = weak; V = variable: some strains positive, others negative.

anomala. Many species can tolerate high concentrations of both sugar and salt.

Some important physiological properties of the main osmophilic yeasts are summarised in Table 3.[20] This information is useful in assessing the spoilage potential of particular IMF's by osmophilic yeasts.

ECOLOGY OF OSMOPHILIC YEAST SPOILAGE

A detailed account of the factors predisposing foods towards spoilage by yeasts was given by Ingram.[11] Special features relevant to osmophilic yeasts and IMF's will be discussed here, using the terminology suggested by Mossel.[9]

Before microbial spoilage can occur, the IMF must be contaminated by organisms capable of growth in the food. Such organisms, called the 'spoilage association',[9] may form only a small part of the initial microflora. Their subsequent growth depends upon four groups of factors, *viz.* intrinsic, processing, extrinsic and implicit.

Initial Contamination

Contamination of foods by osmophilic yeasts can arise by various means. Intrinsic infection of the food itself may occur, *e.g.* mummified fruits,[23] but it is thought to be rare for this to be the sole important source of infection.[11] Although yeasts are widely distributed in the air, osmophilic yeast infection is not normally airborne. Tilbury[21] isolated small numbers of osmophilic yeasts in the air in raw cane sugar factories, but concluded that they did not significantly contaminate raw sugar. Scarr and Rose[8] isolated a new species of osmophilic yeast, *Torulopsis kestoni*, together with *Saccharomyces florentinus* from the air. Little is known about the occurrence of osmophilic yeasts in soil or water; Lochead and Farrell[26] frequently isolated them from soil in an apiary, but Davenport[23] found them to be relatively rare in vineyard soil. It is well known[11,13,27] that insects such as bees, wasps and fruit-flies carry an indigenous population of osmophilic yeasts and that they have a significant role in transmission of infection to nectaries, fruits, honey, etc. In our laboratories *T. apicola*, *T. candida* and *S. rouxii* have been isolated from the abdominal contents of bees and wasps.[8,28] It is thought that such insects may help spread osmophilic yeast infection in piles of raw sugar at refineries. Doubtless human carriers may also be important in certain instances, *e.g.* dried fruits.[11] The major sources of contamination of IMF by osmophilic yeasts are probably physical contact with already spoiled food or unclean equipment,[11] *e.g.* residues of infected raw sugar on dirty processing plant (chutes, conveyors, scales, etc.) were shown to be the principal source of contamination for raw cane sugar.[21]

Intrinsic Factors

These are the expression of the physical properties and the chemical composition of the food itself. Perhaps the most important factor is water activity, although the effect of a given a_w value on microbes can vary greatly with several other parameters of the food environment,[7] *e.g.* the nature of the solute or 'total solids' in the food; storage temperature; composition of the gaseous phase and time of exposure. Osmophilic yeasts can, by definition, grow at a_w values below 0·85, but their rate of growth is directly proportional to the a_w, and minimum a_w values vary with the strain of organism, nature of the 'total solids' and other ecological factors. In general, the lower the a_w of the food the longer its microbiological shelf-life and the fewer the strains of yeast able to grow in it.

At high levels of a_w, the effects of pH, acidity and buffering capacity of food on osmophilic yeasts are the same as for non-osmophilic yeasts, *i.e.* growth usually occurs over the range pH 2·0–7·0 with an optimum pH of 4·0–4·5. Hence the spoilage of medium and high acid foods, such as fruit juice concentrates and pickles, is usually caused by yeasts rather than by less acid-tolerant bacteria. It is thought that a reduction in pH below the optimum reduces the maximum concentration of sugar tolerated;[29] similarly, it is likely that a reduction in a_w of the food lessens the tolerance of osmophilic yeasts to high acidity. Nevertheless, a few strains are able to tolerate both low a_w and high acidity, *e.g.* fermentation of 65°Brix concentrated lemon juice at pH 2·0 by certain *Saccharomyces* strains.[29]

The redox potential (*Eh*) of a food influences the type of spoilage organism which develops, but since *Eh* is related to the oxygen tension of the atmosphere in which the food is stored, this will be discussed under 'extrinsic' parameters.

The chemical composition of an IMF affects its spoilage potential by osmophilic yeasts primarily with regard to the influence of 'total solids' on its a_w. A secondary factor is nutrient availability. In general, osmophilic yeasts are not fastidious in their nutritional requirements and they are able to grow on a wide range of foods. All osmophilic yeasts can utilise some simple sugars as a carbon source, *e.g.* glucose, fructose, maltose or sucrose, whilst some can also assimilate organic acids such as lactic and acetic; a few can hydrolyse starch. In contrast to many bacteria, yeasts are not proteolytic but can feebly attack a wide range of organic nitrogen compounds. Yeasts generally need only small amounts of nitrogenous compounds for growth, and are definitely fermentative rather than putrefactive. Consequently, foods with a high C/N ratio tend to be spoilt by yeasts, whereas foods with a high N/C ratio tend to be spoilt by bacteria. Similarly, yeasts need only small amounts of minerals for growth. As a group, yeasts possess good vitamin-synthesising ability and hence are largely independent of an external supply;[11] many osmophilic yeasts can grow in vitamin-free media.

TABLE 4

Growth of osmophilic yeasts in 'nitrogen-free' sucrose medium[a] at 27°C[28]

		Count/ml	
	Initial	6 weeks	
		Air	Helium
Sacch. rouxii	60	5 000	5 000
Torulopsis kestoni	50	5 000	5 000

[a] Medium composition: Pure sucrose saturated solution: 1·0 litre; $MgSO_4 . 7H_2O$: 1·0 g; KH_2PO_4: 2·0 g.

A good illustration of the ability of osmophilic yeasts to grow in foods high in carbohydrate but low in nitrogen, minerals and vitamins is provided by the occurrence of yeast spoilage in refined sugar syrups. Table 4 shows the slow growth of two osmophilic yeasts in a 'nitrogen-free' sucrose medium, whereas Table 5 shows the beneficial effect on growth of trace amounts of phosphate.[28] On one occasion spoilage was observed in damp crystalline refined, white sugar; *T. apicola* was the causative organism. Natural antimicrobial substances may occur in IMF's and help to inhibit growth of spoilage yeasts, *e.g.* furfural and its derivatives produced in concentrated sugar syrups which have browned during storage.[30]

Finally, there is evidence that the structure and physical form of an IMF can influence the spoilage flora. Christian[1] noted that osmophilic yeasts, in contrast to xerophilic moulds, may grow in liquid media at a_w values below 0·65, but not below a_w 0·75 on solid media. Possibly yeasts are less able than moulds to colonise solid substrates due to their lack of motility and non-mycelial mode of growth. An alternative explanation may be that the total water content is greater in liquids than in solids at the same a_w. It has been

TABLE 5

Effect of phosphate on growth[a] of osmophilic yeasts at 27°C[28]

| | Initial | Count/ml | | | |
		0	10	20	30
Sacch. rouxii	2	$1·0 \times 10^3$	$1·0 \times 10^6$	$2·0 \times 10^7$	$3·0 \times 10^7$
Torulopsis kestoni	5	0	$4·0 \times 10^6$	$6·0 \times 10^7$	$2·0 \times 10^7$

Count/ml — 3 weeks — Phosphate (ppm)

[a] Medium composition: Pure sucrose saturated solution: 1·0 litre; $(NH_4)_2SO_4$: 3·75 g; $Mg SO_4 . 7H_2O$: 0·6 g.

shown that total water content as well as a_w influences microbial growth response,[31] and that the minimal a_w for growth is higher in IMF's whose water content is adjusted by adsorption than by desorption. Additionally, oxygen tension varies with the substrate of a food and plays an important part in selection of the spoilage flora of IMF's (*vide infra*). In nature, the combination of these factors results in the fact that spoilage of 'solid' IMF's like cereals, nuts and dried fruits tends to be caused by xerophilic moulds, whereas 'liquid' IMF's like fruit juice concentrates, syrups, jams and brines tend to be caused by osmophilic yeasts.

Processing Factors

Changes in microflora may result from the mode of processing of a food. In traditional IMF's the main effect of processing is to reduce a_w, as in drying, salting and candying; also, a reduction in pH may be achieved by addition of organic acids or lactic fermentation as in fermented sausages, sauerkraut, yoghurt and pickles; both these effects are discussed elsewhere.

Production of many traditional IMF's involves a heat-processing step, *e.g.* vacuum evaporation of syrups and fruit juice concentrates; heating of liquids to dissolve solid sugars as in jams and confectionery products. Pasteurisation is not the primary objective of these heating processes, but since vegetative cells of osmophilic yeasts have D values at 65°C of less than 2 min, they are readily killed.[32,33] Yeast ascospores are only slightly more heat-resistant than the vegetative cells.[34] Bacterial spores may readily survive such heat treatments, but they are unable to germinate and grow at a_w's below 0·89.[35] Hence the main spoilage risk of heat-processed IMF's is post-process contamination by osmophilic yeasts and xerophilic moulds. Other relevant factors are first, the heat resistance of osmophilic yeasts is greatly increased in the presence of high solute concentrations;[11,32,33] secondly, thermally-damaged cells are generally more susceptible to other unfavourable external conditions, such as reduced a_w.[9]

Little is known about survival and growth of osmophilic yeasts in IMF's processed by ionising radiations, beyond the general statement that a reduction in a_w may sometimes enhance and sometimes reduce lethality to micro-organisms.[7]

Extrinsic Factors

These comprise the temperature, humidity and gaseous composition of the atmosphere in which an IMF is stored, together with the duration of storage.

IMF's are generally intended to be stable at ambient temperatures and are not normally refrigerated or frozen. Osmophilic yeasts are similar to mesophilic yeasts in that they grow over the range 0–40°C with an optimum temperature of about 27°. In general, an increase in temperature increases the sugar concentration (and reduces the optimum a_w) and reduces the range of concentration tolerated.[29] In the same way, both the optimum and maximum temperature increase with sugar concentration (and reduction in a_w); this may explain why osmophilic spoilage, of dried fruits, etc., is usually associated with hot climatic conditions.[11] Recent examples cited[8] are *S. rouxii* and *T. kestoni* which grow at 37°C on osmophilic agar (45% w/w sugar) but not on media containing 2% sugar. The phenomenon may explain the existence of apparently obligately osmophilic yeasts.[10,12] Osmophilic yeasts probably behave like moulds in that they are most tolerant of low a_w near their optimum growth temperature.[5]

An important phenomenon occurs when a packaged IMF is stored at fluctuating temperatures. This results in moisture migration so that certain parts of the food increase in a_w at the expense of others,[7] leading to considerable local shifts in both growth rate and selection of microbial types.

The gaseous environment during storage of IMF's influences microbial stability by virtue of its relative humidity, oxygen content and CO_2 content. In a closed system, moisture vapour in the atmosphere rapidly equilibrates with that derived from the stored food, until it reaches the equilibrium relative humidity (ERH); this is numerically related to the a_w of the food. Similarly, the oxygen content of the storage atmosphere influences the redox potential (*Eh*) of the contained food, although the former must usually be greatly changed before it affects the latter. The *Eh* of a food depends on its redox poising capacity, which in turn is governed by its content of reducing compounds, *e.g.* reducing enzymes, reducing sugars, thiol-containing amino acids, ascorbic acid, etc.[9] Heat-processing tends to raise the *Eh* of natural foods. The majority of osmophilic yeasts are facultative anaerobes that grow most rapidly under aerobic conditions, but they may also produce vigorous fermentation under anerobic conditions.[5] An exception is *Debary-omyces hansenii* which grows poorly in the absence of oxygen.[5] The ecological significance of this is that liquid IMF's are more susceptible to spoilage by osmophilic yeasts than by xerophilic moulds, which, being obligately aerobic, grow best near or on the surface of solid foods where the *Eh* is higher. However, some xerophilic moulds can tolerate very low partial pressures of oxygen.[5,9] Osmophilic yeasts grow faster on the surface of solid media than in liquid media; in fermenting liquids, growth is often confined to the superficial layers;[29] IMF's which possess both low *Eh* and high acidity can only be spoilt by osmophilic yeasts. In sealed containers fermentative spoilage of IMF's by yeast may yield CO_2 which is inhibitory to many aerobic organisms.[9]

Duration of storage is a most important extrinsic factor.[7] Frequently IMF's appear to be microbiologically stable when stored for, say 4 weeks, but may yet spoil after an additional, say 4 months, period. There are several reasons for this phenomenon. First, the rate of growth of osmophilic yeasts is proportional to a_w and is very slow at low a_w values.[21,3] Secondly, the lag phase of growth is inversely proportional to a_w, *e.g.* for *S. rouxii* grown in sucrose solutions, the lag phase is 20 h at a_w 0·98 and 40 h at a_w 0·90.[36] Finally, once microbial growth begins, water is released, raising the a_w locally and accelerating the rate of growth of the spoilage organism; it may even permit growth of other organisms.[7,9]

Implicit Factors

These comprise those fundamental properties of the spoilage organism which govern its competitive powers, *e.g.* specific growth rate, synergism, symbiosis and antagonism.[11,9] A detailed discussion of these factors is largely irrelevant in the case of IMF's, since spoilage is limited to xerophilic fungi. In such a selective environment the relatively slow growth rate of osmophilic yeasts ceases to be a disadvantage. Yeasts possess great metabolic activity per cell, so that fermentation and visible spoilage may become evident at relatively low population levels, *e.g.* 10^5–10^6 cells/ml.[11] Thus competitive advantages over moulds include their ability to grow anaerobically, and produce and tolerate alcohol, CO_2 and organic acids.[11] Their major competitive disadvantage compared with moulds may be the ability of the latter to penetrate and colonise solid substrates.

RECENT INCIDENCE OF SPOILAGE BY OSMOPHILIC YEASTS

Judging by the continued appearance of publications on osmophilic yeast spoilage of traditional IMF's, such problems must occur frequently and cause substantial economic losses. The extent of these spoilage outbreaks and their economic effects is difficult to assess, due to the natural reluctance of food manufacturers to disclose such information. Brief mention will be made here of recent incidents or articles on spoilage by osmophilic yeasts, not previously reviewed by Walker and Ayres.[13] In many cases the information is unpublished and is obtained either by personal experience or by personal communication with colleagues in the field.

Sugars, Syrups, Sweet Spreads and Concentrated Fruit Juices

Raw cane sugar received at the UK sugar refinery often contains osmophilic yeasts.[37] Routine microbiological checks are made on each batch as received, including the use of phase contrast microscopy to determine yeast activity.[38] Heavily infected sugar is refined immediately to avoid mixing it with other raws in the bulk store, which could spread infection and cause loss of sugar by deterioration. Bulk storage of raw sugar in the country of origin may also be a problem. In Guyana, it was estimated that growth of osmophilic yeasts resulted in sugar losses of £27 000 per annum.[21] The predominant causative organisms were identified as *S. rouxii* and *T. candida*, it was shown that they could grow in sucrose syrups of a_w values 0·65 and 0·70 respectively. More than 80% of Guyanese raw sugar samples tested had a_w values exceeding 0·65 although the sugar was almost sterile as it left the crystallisers; subsequent infection occurred by contact with contaminated sugar residues on conveyor belts, chutes and storage bins. Yeast counts of up to $10^7/g$ sugar were reached within 5 weeks of storage. 'Good housekeeping' practice was unsuccessful in preventing the infection, but control was eventually achieved by the installation of new centrifugals which produced sugar whose a_w was below 0·65.

Crystalline refined sugar is not normally susceptible to osmophilic yeast spoilage, although we have experienced one outbreak caused by *T. apicola* in a white sugar silo where moisture migration had occurred. Refined sugar syrups are susceptible to spoilage and require special handling and storage facilities, both in the refinery and at customer's premises. Syrups are sterilised by heating and filtration prior to storage in sterile tanks; special precautions are taken to prevent condensation on the surface of the syrup. Transportation takes place in steam-sterilised bulk tankers. Yeast counts of less than one per gramme sugar solids are attained, but even so, prolonged storage of syrups at customer's premises is not recommended unless scrupulous hygiene is practised. Recently we have encountered separate incidents of exploding bottles of B.P. syrup for medicinal use; in both cases the retailer had stored liquid sugar for up to six months, resulting in a slow build-up of osmophilic yeasts.

Whilst *S. rouxii* commonly occurs in impure sucrose solutions and raw sugars, invertase-producing species of yeast appear to predominate in purer sucrose solutions. Recent isolates from a variety of sugars, syrups and intermediate refinery samples include *T.*

bacillaris (= *T. apicola*); *T. globosa* (= *Cit. matritensis*); *T. lactis-condensi*; *T kestoni*; *C guilliermondii* and *S florentinus* [8] Molasses is usually microbiologically stable, but recently a case occurred in which molasses fermented in a ship's hold due to accidental dilution. The causative organisms were identified as *S. heterogenicus* and *T. holmii*.

Starch-derived glucose syrups and invert syrups have a higher solids content (75–80%) and lower a_w (0·72) than sucrose syrups; hence they are far less prone to yeast spoilage. It will be interesting to see whether any yeast problems occur with the new high-fructose corn syrups, produced by the use of glucose isomerase.

Rapid expansion has occurred recently in the home-brewing and wine-making business, resulting in increased usage of canned barley syrup, malt extract and fruit-juice concentrates. In a survey of beer-making kits, many cans of malt extract were observed to swell on

TABLE 6

Occurrence of dominant spoilage yeasts in high sugar products, Long Ashton Research Station, Bristol, 1969–1975

Organisms	Fruit concentrates (s.g. > 1305)				Sugar syrups	
	Apple	Grape	Orange	Unknown	Brown	White
Osmophilic Yeasts						
Saccharomyces rouxii	+	+	+	+	+	+
S.bisporus var. *mellis*	−	+	+	−	−	−
S.bailii var. *osmophilus*	+	+	+	+	+	+
S.cerevisiae	+	+	+	−	−	−
S.bayanus	−	−	−	+	−	−
Saccharomyces spp.	+	+	+	+	+	+
Schizosaccharomyces						
pombe	−	−	+	−	−	−
T. versatilis	−	−	+	−	−	−
Osmotolerant Yeasts						
Candida valida	+	+	−	+	+	+
H.anomala var. *anomala*	+	+	−	+	+	+
Kloeckera apiculata	+	−	−	−	−	+
Candida spp.	+	+	−	+	−	+
Torulopsis spp.	+	+	+	+	−	+
S. cerevisiae	+	+	+	+	−	+
Saccharomyces spp.	+	+	+	+	+	+

Data by courtesy of Dr R. R. Davenport.[25]

prolonged storage, due to growth of *S. rouxii*.[39] Dominant spoilage yeasts in fruit juice concentrate and sugar syrups examined routinely at Long Ashton Research Station, Bristol, over the last six years, are shown in Table 6.[25]

Sugar syrups and fruit juice concentrates are now widely used in the soft drinks industry, where spoilage problems by osmophilic yeasts have been extensively studied by Sand and others.[4,18,40,41] Sand found that fruit juice concentrates were spoilt most frequently by *S. bailii*, *S. bisporus* and *S. rouxii*, and discusses the inter-relationships between Brix, pH and spoilage potential. As a result of 12 years experience he states that concentrates of low a_w, without preservatives, are spoilt by *S. rouxii* whereas concentrates with preservative but at a higher a_w are spoilt by *S. bailii*.[18]

In the author's own laboratory, explosion of bottles of chocolate syrup at 75°Brix was caused by *T. etchellsii*, *T. versatilis* and *C. pelliculosa* (*H. anomala var. anomala*). Infection occurred post-pasteurisation prior to filling.

Jams, Fruit Concentrates and Dried Fruits

Recent spoilage problems in jams include fermentation of straw-berry and apricot jams by *T. colliculosa* and *T. cantarellii*,[42] whilst work at Chorleywood has implicated *S. bisporus*.[43] Current interest in low-calorie foods has led to the production of low-sugar jams. These are prone to spoilage by xerophilic moulds and osmophilic yeasts, as their a_w is raised from c. 0·80 to 0·94.[36]

Another 'growth-area' of business is the fruit yoghurt market. These products contain sugar and the fruit is frequently supplied to the dairy manufacturers in cans of syrup. The fruit and syrup is heat-processed, but infection appears to occur during filling into cans. Subsequent 'blowing' of the cans is reported to occur frequently, especially when stored in warm weather. In one instance of 'blown' strawberries in 40% sugar syrup, the causative yeasts were identified as *T. versatilis*, *C. pelliculosa* and *C. utilis*.[42]

Work in Australia on the spoilage of a number of fruit products has been the subject of several recent publications. Crystallised and syruped ginger was found to be contaminated and fermented by *S. rouxii*;[44] control was achieved by pasteurisation. The same authoress reports on spoilage of comminuted orange base and cordial by *S. bailii var. bailii*.[45] This organism was responsible for spoilage of fruit concentrates and other acid, liquid food products, even in the presence of preservatives.[46] In the UK, an outbreak of exploding glacé cherries was due to *S. rouxii* infection;[42] it was controlled by raising the sugar concentration in the fruit to 75% and by improvements in process hygiene.

Confectionery and Bakery Products

A useful review on microbiological deterioration of confectionery products was published by Mossel and Sand,[47] in which was stressed the importance of hygiene in prevention of infection. In a detailed study of the microbiology of marzipan and its spoilage by fermentation Windisch and Neumann[22] found that *S. rouxii* and *T. dattila* were the most sugar-tolerant osmophilic yeasts. A more recent paper[48] confirms *S. rouxii* as the principal spoilage agent of marzipan and persipan.

The equilibrium relative humidity (ERH) of baking products, with special reference to the shelf-life of cakes, was discussed by Seiler.[19] He has also published articles about yeast fermentation problems in high-sugar bakery products such as fondants, marshmallows, marzipan and almond pastes, jams, purees, fudge, etc.[49,50] Finally, one recent, dramatic and costly illustration of the unwelcome effects of osmophilic yeasts was the notorious case of the exploding soft-centred Easter eggs. This infection was caused by *S. rouxii* and occurred in the plant of a leading UK confectionery manufacturer; the result was an egg-less Easter for tens of thousands of children a few years ago!

PHYSIOLOGY OF OSMOPHILIC YEASTS IN RELATION TO IMF'S

The ability of osmophilic yeasts to tolerate extremely low a_w values and high solute concentrations has stimulated considerable interest in their physiology. Whilst a detailed discussion of research on the mechanisms of resistance to low a_w values is outside the scope of this paper, certain features are relevant to spoilage of IMF's and will be briefly mentioned.

Effects of Solutes on Growth of Osmophilic Yeasts

Whilst a_w is a useful parameter for defining the effects of high solute concentrations on growth of osmophilic yeasts, it is now clear that the effect of 'total solids' in a food is better.[7] Recent publications have shown that at equal a_w values different solutes have different effects on growth. Anand and Brown[3] showed that polyethylene glycol was more inhibitory than sucrose, whilst Horner and Anagnostopoulos[36] found that glycerol was tolerated better than sucrose. Koppensteiner and Windisch determined the limiting values of osmotic pressure for growth of both osmophilic and non-osmophilic yeasts in solutions of a range of sugars and salts.[51] The highest osmotic pressure tolerated (620 atm) occurred in fructose solutions; the salts were generally less well tolerated than the sugars. Salt tolerance increased in accordance with the Hofmeister series, *i.e.* NaCl was more inhibitory than KCl. It may be concluded that the spoilage potential of a given IMF at a particular a_w value depends on the nature of the humectant and other food ingredients, and should be determined by experiment.

A diversity of opinion exists about the existence of obligate osmophiles. Anand and Brown[3] showed that a selection of osmophilic yeasts did not have a requirement for a water activity below

TABLE 7

The effect of a_w on growth of osmophilic yeasts in sucrose/glycerol syrups after 12 weeks incubation at 27°C[21]

Organism	Water activity a_w								Min. a_w for growth
	0·800	0·750	0·725	0·700	0·675	0·650	0·625	0·600	
S. rouxii (1)	NT	4	3	2	1	t	—	—	0·650
S. rouxii (2)	4	3	NT	2	NT	1	NT	—	0·650
S. bisporus									
var. *mellis*	4	3	NT	1	NT	—	NT	—	0·700
T. candida (1)	4	3	NT	1	NT	1	NT	—	0·650
T. candida (2)	NT	3	2	1	—	—	—	—	0·700
T. versatilis	NT	4	3	2	—	—	—	—	0·700
T. etchellsii	4	3	NT	t	NT	—	NT	—	0·700
H. anomala	2	t	NT	—	NT	—	NT	—	0·750

—	less than 1·5 × original count.
t	1·5–2·0 × original count.
1	2–5 × original count.
2	5–10 × original count.
3	10–20 × original count.
4	more than 20 × original count.

NT not tested.

that of the basal medium (0·997) in order to grow; however, compared with the non-osmophilic yeasts tested, they exhibited relatively broad water activity optima and had growth rates only half as fast at their respective optimum a_w values. In contrast, Koh has recently isolated an obligate osmophilic mutant of *S. rouxii* that failed to grow at osmotic pressures corresponding to 20% w/v sucrose or less.[52,53] It was shown that the composition of the cell envelope of the mutant differed significantly from that of the parent.

More recent papers by Brown and his colleagues[54–56] have thrown some light on the mechanism of resistance of osmophilic yeasts to high solute concentrations. This work, summarised by Pitt,[5] suggests that osmophilic yeasts produce and accumulate polyols which act as 'compatible solutes' in the cell; at high concentrations these permit normal functioning of intracellular enzymes.

Minimum a_w values for growth of osmophilic yeasts from raw sugar were determined by the author,[21] using sucrose/glycerol syrups incubated for twelve weeks at 27°C. Some of the results are summarised in Table 7.

Effect of a_w on Heat Resistance of Osmophilic Yeasts

It was shown by Gibson[32] using sucrose/glucose mixtures that a reduction in a_w of the heating menstruum markedly increases the heat resistance of osmophilic yeasts. More recent work by Corry[17,33] demonstrated that at equal a_w values different solutes gave differing orders of protection, *i.e.* sucrose > sorbitol > glucose/fructose > glycerol. Some correlation was observed between the degree of plasmolysis in a solute and its degree of protectiveness. Differences in response to osmotic shock by osmophilic and non-osmophilic yeasts in several solutes were also reported by Rose.[57] Obviously the nature and concentration of solute in an IMF quantitatively affects the degree of heat-processing needed to kill osmophilic yeast contaminants.

CONTROL METHODS

Two advantages of IMF's over some other foods, are, first, that they have a long shelf-life at ambient temperature, and, secondly, they do not need heat-sterilisation by severe processes which impair flavour and colour. It has been seen that a_w values below 0·85 inhibit growth of pathogenic and spoilage bacteria, but permit spoilage by xerophilic fungi. In the absence of refrigeration and heat-sterilisation, what methods remain for control of osmophilic yeast spoilage of IMF's?

Minimise Initial Infection

It is recognised that for osmophilic yeasts the growth rate decreases and lag phase increases as the a_w of the medium is reduced below 0·85. Consequently, since visible spoilage does not occur until populations of 10^5–10^6 yeast cells/g food have been attained,[11] the shelf-life can be greatly increased by reducing the extent of the initial infection.[18,21,36,43,47] This can be achieved by good manufacturing practice, including the use of raw materials of sound quality, plant sanitation, hygienic handling, prevention of delays in processing, exclusion of insects, etc.

In the case of some liquid IMF's like sugar syrups, it is often possible to remove micro-organisms by filtration through diatomaceous earth prior to bulk handling and storage in pre-sterilised plant. In other cases, like the production of fruit juice and fruit concentrates, a mild heating step is involved which is sufficient to kill vegetative cells and ascospores of osmophilic yeasts. An example quoted by Lloyd[44] is the 'pasteurisation' of syruped ginger by dipping it into 80°Brix sucrose syrup of 93 ± 1°C for a minimum of 2 min. In such cases the heat resistance of osmophilic yeasts is greatly increased at low a_w values. Furthermore, care must be taken to prevent post-process contamination prior to packaging the product. Finally, attempts should be made to minimise temperature fluctuations leading to condensation and migration of water in the package or storage vessel, to avoid raising of a_w values beyond 'safe' limits.

Chemical and Physical Composition of the IMF

Both the nature and concentration of the solutes obviously affects the spoilage potential of IMF's and different species of osmophilic yeast have different tolerances. It is well known that at equivalent a_w's salt is more inhibitory than sugar to most organisms. However, one of the drawbacks of many traditional IMF's for human consumption is that high concentrations of salt or sugar are unpalatable. Whilst some of the novel humectants used in newer IMF's may not be so objectionable to taste, they do not completely inhibit osmophilic yeast growth at the concentration used. In some traditional IMF's like fruit-juice concentrates the inhibitory effect of low a_w is enhanced by a low pH;[18] however, many spoilage yeasts can grow in the presence of acidulants such as acetic acid at pH levels as low as 3·0–3·5.[58] Such low pH values are not widely acceptable in many foods for direct human consumption.

Chemical Preservatives

Addition of permitted food preservatives is the only feasible method of spoilage prevention in many IMF's currently under consideration. Legislation regarding both types of preservative and permitted dosage varies from country to country. At present choice is limited mainly to the following compounds: sulphurous acid (SO_2) and its salts; benzoic acid, parahydroxybenzoic acid and its salts; sorbic acid and its salts, and diethyl pyrocarbonate (DEPC).

One of the problems in the use of these organic acid preservatives is that their antimicrobial activity depends on the concentration of undissociated acid, which in turn is inversely proportional to the pH;[13] pH values of below 4·5 are needed for optimum activity. Obviously such low pH values are not acceptable in many IMF's. Even where pH values of 2·0–3·5 are practical (*e.g.* fruit juice concentrates), it has been shown that some spoilage yeasts can tolerate the maximum permissible levels of preservatives.[18,47] For example, Ingram described strains of *S. bailii* (*S. acidifaciens*) resistant to 500 ppm of benzoic acid in fruit squashes at pH 3·5, or 1000 ppm at pH 5.[59,60] More recently, Sand[18] found that all 500 strains of *S. bailii* from fruit juice concentrate could tolerate 1000 ppm of benzoic acid at pH 3·0, a_w 0·94. Lloyd obtained similar results in Australian comminuted orange products, but sorbic acid inhibited *S. bailii* var. *bailii* at concentrations between 400 and 800 ppm.[45] Use of sorbic acid, however, was precluded as it interfered with product colour; SO_2 at the maximum permitted level of 230 ppm was found to be the only acceptable preservative, provided the pH was below 3·0. The resistance of food spoilage yeasts to preservatives was also determined by Pitt.[58] Again, *S. bailii* was the most resistant species, tolerating 600 ppm of both benzoic and sorbic acids at pH 2·5, in the presence of 10% glucose. Other yeasts, including *C. krusei* and *T. holmii*, were inhibited by 300–400 ppm of these preservatives. Another investigator reported that DEPC at concentrations of 100–200 ppm was the most effective preservative against yeast spoilage of bottled table wine.[61] Use of DEPC, however, is now banned in most countries following fears of its carcinogenicity.

In the UK benzoic acid and SO_2 are the only permitted food preservatives in most foods for human consumption. Propionate and sorbate are permitted in certain bakery and confectionery products, and the latter is allowed in IMF petfoods, together with propylene glycol. There is current pressure to reduce permitted levels of SO_2, and anyway it is known that SO_2 is not very effective against yeasts, especially in the presence of large amounts of reducing substances, or where the pH is above 3·0. Since benzoate-resistant yeasts are common, it is apparent that there is no really effective antimycotic permissible in IMF's for human consumption. Hence there is an urgent need both to review legislation regarding sorbic acid, and also to find new, safe, effective and acceptable antimycotics.

METHODOLOGY

Media and Methods for Isolation and Enumeration of Osmophilic Yeasts

There are no commercially-available dehydrated selective media for osmophilic yeasts, but a number of suitable media have been described in the literature. The important features of medium composition, as discussed by Sand,[18] are its a_w, pH, redox potential and nutrient availability. Obviously a_w is the key factor which enables selection of osmophilic yeasts and inhibition of bacteria, but a relatively low pH is also useful. Ingram described a 50% glucose, citric acid Tryptone agar for isolation of osmotolerant yeasts from concentrated orange juice, but it proved tedious to prepare.[62] In our laboratory we routinely use Scarr's osmophilic agar for enumeration of osmophilic yeasts in sugar products;[63] it is simple to prepare and easy to use, but due to its relatively high a_w of c. 0·95 it occasionally permits bacterial growth; certainly it will support growth of some non-osmophilic yeasts. Van der Walt[2] recommends 50% and 60% w/w glucose agars, at a_w values of c. 0·90 and 0·845 for characterisation of osmotolerant and osmophilic yeasts respectively. Mossel[64] prefers a 60% w/w fructose peptone meat-extract agar, at an a_w of 0·84, since fructose is more soluble than glucose. Most recently,

Pitt[5] described a number of media suitable for cultivation of xerophilic fungi; one was a malt extract yeast extract agar containing 60% w/w glucose, a_w 0·845.

Techniques for enumerating osmophilic yeasts in IMF's like fruit juice concentrates were fully described by Sand.[18] Two special features warrant mention here. First, in order to avoid loss of viability of cells due to osmotic shock in preparing serial dilutions of IMF's,[10] the diluent should also be adjusted to a low a_w value;[47] 20% sterile glucose solutions are adequate for this purpose.[18] Secondly, due to the slow growth rate of osmophilic yeasts at low a_w values, plates may need incubation at 25–30°C for periods of up to 4 weeks. Hence, it is essential to prevent drying out of the medium, by use of closed boxes or desiccator jars.

Maintenance and Identification of Osmophilic Yeasts

Cultures of osmophilic yeasts are best maintained on high-sugar media, partly because some strains do not grow well on low-sugar media like malt-extract agar,[18] and also because some strains may lose their tolerance to high sugar concentrations if kept on ordinary media.[12,37] Identification of certain osmophilic yeasts, especially *S. rouxii* and *S. bisporus* var. *mellis*, is complicated by the fact that they usually exist in the haplophase and rarely produce ascospores.[25] In recognition of this fact it is easier to omit some of the morphological tests described in Lodder,[20] and use instead the shorter identification schemes of Barnett and Pankhurst[65] and Davenport.[66] Also, assimilation and fermentation patterns are best determined at sugar concentrations of 10% rather than the usual 2%.[67]

Stability and Shelf-life Tests

The rationale of such tests for confectionery products was discussed by Mossel and Sand.[47] Similar principles apply to testing of other IMF's and will be mentioned here briefly in the light of experience gained in our laboratory. First, it is important to inoculate the IMF test system with challenge organisms in an active physiological state. Ideally the inoculum should be prepared from cells actively growing in the same medium as the test system. Secondly, shelf-life tests should be extended for considerable periods of time, for reasons previously discussed. Thirdly, cycling of incubation temperatures is desirable to simulate day and night temperatures, as this may cause localised a_w changes in the food. Fourthly, adequate numbers of sub-samples should be examined, as yeast growth may be unevenly distributed in the food. Clumping of yeast cells may also lead to falsely low counts; vigorous agitation of dilutions is therefore recommended. Finally, resuscitation of damaged cells is essential prior to their enumeration; the principles were outlined by Mossel.[7]

ACKNOWLEDGEMENT

The author wishes to thank Professor A. J. Vlitos and the Directors of Tate and Lyle Limited for their kind permission to publish this paper.

REFERENCES

1. Christian, J. H. B. (1963). In: *Recent Advances in Food Science*, Vol. 3, ed. J. M. Leitch and D. N. Rhodes, Butterworths, London, p. 248.
2. van der Walt, J. P. (1970). In: *The Yeasts*, ed. J. Lodder, North-Holland, Amsterdam and London, p. 34.
3. Anand, J. C. and Brown, A. D. (1968). *J. gen. Microbiol.*, **52**, p. 205.
4. Sand, F. E. M. J. (1973). *Brauwelt.*, **113**, pp. 320 and 414.
5. Pitt, J. I. (1975). In: *Water Relations of Foods*, ed. R. B. Duckworth, Academic Press, London, p. 273.
6. Scott, W. J. (1957). *Advanc. Food Res.*, **7**, p. 83.
7. Mossel, D. A. A. (1975). In: *Water Relations of Foods*, ed. R. B. Duckworth, Academic Press, London, p. 347.
8. Scarr, M. P. and Rose, D. (1966). *J. gen. Microbiol.*, **45**, p. 9.
9. Mossel, D. A. A. (1971). *J. appl. Bact.*, **34**(1), p. 95.
10. Ingram, M. (1957). In: *Microbial Ecology, Symp. Soc. gen. Microbiol.*, Vol. 7, ed. M. R. Pollock and M. H. Richmond, University Press. Cambridge, p. 90.
11. Ingram, M. (1958). In: *The Chemistry and Biology of Yeasts*, ed. A. H. Cook, Academic Press, London, p. 603.
12. Onishi, H. (1963). *Advanc. Food Res.*, **12**, p. 53.
13. Walker, H. W. and Ayres, J. C. (1970). In: *The Yeasts*, Vol. 3, *Yeast Technology*, ed. A. H. Rose and J. S. Harrison, Academic Press, London, p. 463.
14. Kushner, D. J. (1971). In: *Inhibition and Destruction of the Microbial Cell*, ed. W. B. Hugo, Academic Press, London, p. 259.
15. Anand, J. C. (1969). Ph.D. Thesis, University of New South Wales.
16. Koh, T. Y. (1972). Ph.D. Thesis, University of Cambridge.
17. Corry, J. E. L. (1974). Ph.D. Thesis, University of Surrey.
18. Sand, F. E. M. J. (1973). In: *Technology of Fruit Juice Concentrates—Chemical Composition of Fruit Juices*, Internat. Federation of Fruit Juice Producers, Scientific-Technical Commission, Vol. 13, Vienna, p. 185.

19. Seiler, D. A. L. (1969). In: *Relative Humidity in the Food Industry*, B.F.M.I.R.A. Symposium Proceedings No. 4, p. 28.
20. Lodder, J. (Ed.) (1970). *The Yeasts*, North-Holland, Amsterdam and London.
21. Tilbury, R. H. (1967). M.Sc. Thesis, University of Bristol.
22. Windisch, S. and Neumann, I. (1965). *Süsswaren*, **7**, pp. 355, 484 and 540.
23. Davenport, R. R. (1975). Ph.D. Thesis, University of Bristol.
24. Davenport, R. R. (1976). To be published in *C.R.C. Handbook on Nutrition*.
25. Davenport, R. R. (1976). Long Ashton Research Station Advisory Notebook, Personal communication.
26. Lochead, A. G. and Farrell, L. (1930). *Can. J. Res.*, **3**, p. 51.
27. Lund, A. (1958). In: *The Chemistry and Biology of Yeasts*, ed. A. H. Cook, Academic Press, London, p. 63.
28. Tilbury, R. H. and Rose, D. (1974). Unpublished results.
29. Ingram, M. (1959). *Rev. Ferm. Ind. Alimentaires.*, **14**(1), p. 23.
30. Ingram, M., Mossel, D. A. A. and de Lange, P. (1955). *Chemy Ind.*, p. 63.
31. Acott, K. M. and Labuza, T. P. (1975). *J. Fd. Technol.*, **10**, p. 603.
32. Gibson, B. (1973). *J. appl. Bact.*, **36**, p. 365.
33. Corry, J. E. L. (1975). In: *Water Relations of Foods*, ed. R. B. Duckworth, Academic Press, London, p. 332.
34. Put, H. M. C. and Sand, F. E. M. J. (1974). *Proc, 4th Internat. Symp. on Yeasts, Vienna, Austria*, Pt. 1, p. 145.
35. Troller, J. A. (1973). *J. Milk Fd. Technol.*, **36**(5), p. 276.
36. Horner, K. J. and Anagnostopoulos, G. D. (1973). *J. appl. Bact.*, **36**, p. 427.
37. Scarr, M. P. (1954). Ph.D. Thesis, University of London.
38. Scarr, M. P. (1968). *J. appl. Bact.*, **31**, p. 525.
39. Reynolds, A. J. (1976). National Coll. Fd. Technol., Weybridge. Personal communication.
40. Mrozek, H. (1972). *Das erfrischungsgetrank, March, No.* 13/25, p. 260.
41. Sand, F. E. M. J. (1974). *Proc. 4th Internat. Symp. on Yeasts, Vienna, Austria*, Pt. I, p. 263.
42. Tilbury, R. H. (1976). Unpublished data.
43. Seiler, D. A. L. (1976). Flour Milling and Baking R.A., Chorleywood. Personal communication.
44. Lloyd, A. C. (1975). *J. Fd. Technol.*, **10**, p. 575.
45. Lloyd, A. C. (1975). *J. Fd. Technol.*, **10**, p. 565.
46. Pitt, J. I. and Richardson, K. C. (1973). *C.S.I.R.O. Fd. Res. Q.*, **33**, p. 80.
47. Mossel, D. A. A. and Sand, F. E. M. J. (1968). *Conserva.*, **17**, p. 23.
48. Blaschke-Hellmessen, R. and Teuschel, G. (1970). *Die Nahrung.*, **12**, p. 249.
49. Seiler, D. A. L. (1966). *Brit. Baking Ind. R.A. Bull., No.* 2, April, p. 49.
50. Seiler, D. A. L. (1975). *Brit. Baking Ind. R.A. Bull., No.* 2, April, p. 58.

51. Koppensteiner, G. and Windisch, S. (1971). *Arch. Mikrobiol.*, **80**, p. 300.
52. Koh, T. Y. (1975). *J. gen. Microbiol.*, **88**, p. 101.
53. Koh, T. Y. (1975). *J. gen. Microbiol.*, **88**, p. 184.
54. Brown, A. D. and Simpson, J. R. (1972). *J. gen. Microbiol.*, **72**, p. 589.
55. Brown, A. D. (1974). *J. Bacteriol.*, **118**(3), p. 769.
56. Brown, A. D. (1975). *J. gen. Microbiol.*, **86**, p. 241.
57. Rose, D. (1975). *J. appl. Bact.*, **38**, p. 169.
58. Pitt, J. I. (1974). *Fd. Technol. (Australia)*, **26**(6), p. 238.
59. Ingram, M. (1960). *Acta Microbiologica.*, **VII**/2, p. 95.
60. Ingram, M. (1960). *Ann. Inst. Pasteur.*, **11**, p. 167.
61. Rankine, B. C. and Pilone, D. A. (1974). *Australian Wine, Brewing and Spirit Rev.*, August, p. 36.
62. Ingram, M. (1959). *J. appl. Bact.*, **22**(2), p. 234.
63. Scarr, M. P. (1959). *J. Sci. Fd. Agric.*, **10**(12), p. 678.
64. Mossel, D. A. A. (1951). *Antonie van Leeuwenhoek.*, **17**, p. 146.
65. Barnett, J. A. and Pankhurst, R. J. (1974). *A New Key to the Yeasts*, North-Holland, Amsterdam and London.
66. Davenport, R. R. (1974). *J. appl. Bact.*, **37**, p. 269.
67. Scarr, M. P. and Rose, D. (1965). *Nature*, **207**, p. 887.
68. Tilbury, R. H. (1967). In: *Microbiological Deterioration in the Tropics*, S.C.I. Monograph No. 23, Soc. Chem. Ind., London, p. 63.
69. Tilbury, R. H. (1970). Ph.D. Thesis, University of Aston.

DISCUSSION

Blanchfield: Could I add one item to Dr Tilbury's black catalogue of spoilage problems? The troubles which hit the pickle and sauce industry for the first time a few years ago were elucidated by Dakin. The cause was a new micro-organism, *Moniliella aceto-abutans*, a remarkable organism which not only tolerates the acetic acid on which preservation depends, but actually metabolises it, thus reducing its amount to the level where other spoilage micro-organisms could also grow. Dakin also established that prevention could be effected by sorbic acid, which, however, was then not permitted, and is still not permitted, as a preservative in pickles and sauces.

Leistner: You mentioned as osmophilic yeasts *Candida guillermondii*, *C. parapsilosis* and *C. tropicalis*. Is there any public health concern in the UK on the occurrence of these *Candida* species in foods?

Tilbury: I haven't looked into this point, but I did note when preparing the paper that these organisms were in fact human pathogens.

Jarvis: Have you any data on the relative occurrence of yeast ascospores in foods and the environment?

Tilbury: It has been proved to be very difficult to detect ascospore formation. Davenport communicated with me to the same effect, and this is why he recommended using a shorter test.

Jarvis: Some years ago we isolated an osmophilic strain of *Saccharomyces*, which was the cause of extensive spoilage in a commercial low pH product. The organism could not possibly have survived the thermal processes applied to the product had it occurred as vegetative cells. Subsequent work at Leatherhead has shown that the isolate produces ascospores prolifically in laboratory media, although to a lesser extent in natural substrates. Under certain conditions the ascospores have a much greater thermal resistance ($>4\times$) than have the vegetative forms. It would seem important therefore to assess the effects of environmental and processing factors on ascospores of osmophilic yeasts, as well as on vegetative forms.

Tilbury: I can only speak from my own experience, but in the situations I've looked at it has been quite difficult to get ascospore production. It is speculated that some of this increased heat resistance may indeed be due to ascospores.

12

The Stability of Intermediate Moisture Foods with Respect to Mould Growth

D. A. L. SEILER

Flour Milling and Baking Research Association,
Chorleywood, Herts, England

ABSTRACT

With solid or semi-solid intermediate moisture foods with water activities within the range 0·65–0·90, mould growth is usually the most important microbiological spoilage problem and, in fact, is often the major factor limiting shelf-life.

The mould-free shelf-life of intermediate moisture foods is shown to be governed largely by the equilibrium relative humidity (ERH) of the product, which can change according to the amount of moisture loss or gain which occurs during storage, the storage temperature, the number and type of viable mould spores present, and the presence of naturally occurring or deliberately added mould inhibitors. Other factors such as the pH, nutritional value and redox potential of the food normally play a subordinate role.

An attempt is made to indicate the minimum mould-free shelf-life which can be expected from intermediate moisture foods of differing initial ERH. The effect of storage temperatures and moisture loss during storage is also discussed.

INTRODUCTION

Foodstuffs with a water activity above 0·90 are generally more subject to bacteriological spoilage than to spoilage by yeasts and moulds, but, as the water activity of the food falls below this level, problems of fermentation due to yeast and deterioration due to mould growth become more common. Fermentation problems are generally associated with liquid or semi-solid products such as brines, syrups, jams, fondants, etc., whereas mould growth can occur on all products. For the majority of intermediate moisture foods, mould growth tends to be the major problem and is often the most important factor governing shelf-life.

It is well known that the main factors governing the rate of mould growth on foods are water activity and storage temperature, and much work has been carried out to determine the effect of these factors on the rate at which specific moulds will germinate and grow on substrates of different composition.[1-4] However, much of this work has been carried out using culture media rather than foodstuffs and the criterion used to determine the effect of the various factors have been spore outgrowth, linear development of a mould colony, and, occasionally, pour plate or spread plate mould counts. Little information appears to have been published on the effect of these factors on the time taken for mould growth to become visible on foodstuffs. This is surprising, since foods are generally rejected on this basis and it is likely to be the criterion accepted by most food manufacturers for assessing the 'mould-free shelf-life' of solid and semi-solid intermediate moisture foods. What information is available on this aspect is often based on tests with the same product stored under conditions of different relative humidity rather than with products of different water activity. Moreover, the tests described are often not sufficiently detailed and the relationships established are based on only one or two results.

In this paper the results from comprehensive investigations into the factors affecting the mould-free shelf-life of cake are given and compared with results obtained with other intermediate moisture foods. The difficulties which arise in determining the mould-free shelf-life of a product are outlined.

When discussing the water relations of foods in relation to mould growth the term equilibrium relative humidity (ERH) will be used rather than water activity since it is considered this term is more meaningful in cases where growth is predominantly associated with the surface rather than the interior of the food.

FACTORS AFFECTING THE RATE OF MOULD GROWTH ON INTERMEDIATE MOISTURE FOODS

Equilibrium Relative Humidity (ERH)

It is recognised that the most important factor determining whether a mould will grow and the rate at which it will grow on a food is the relative humidity of the atmosphere surrounding the product.[1] In the case of foodstuffs wrapped in essentially moisture impermeable material or when stored under conditions where no loss or gain of moisture occurs, the relative humidity of this atmosphere is determined by the equilibrium relative humidity (ERH) of the product. The ERH, in turn, is controlled by the nature of the dissolved solids present and by the ratio of solids to moisture in the recipe.

Cake. To establish the relationships between ERH and the mould-free shelf-life of cake a large number of storage tests have been carried out at a temperature of 27°C using a variety of laboratory and commercially manufactured cakes. In each of these tests, moisture loss during storage was prevented by overwrapping the individual wrapped cakes in large polyethylene bags. Wherever possible at least 20 replicate cakes were used for each test. The mould-free shelf-life was taken as the day when visible mould growth was first noted on any of the cakes. The results from these tests are given in Fig. 1 where the ERH of the cake is plotted against the logarithm of the mould-free shelf-life in days at 27°C.

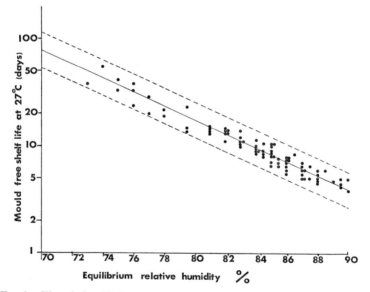

FIG. 1.   The relationship between equilibrium relative humidity and mould-free shelf-life of cake stored at 27°C.

It is apparent that there is a linear relationship between ERH and the logarithm of the mould-free shelf-life within the range 74–90 % ERH. This relationship is given by the following expression:

$$\log_{10} \text{ mould-free shelf-life (days at 27°C)}$$
$$= 6.42 - (0.0647 \times \text{ERH } \%)$$

A variation of ± 30–40 % in the average mould-free shelf-life occurs at each ERH. This variation could be due to a number of factors including inaccuracies in the method of ERH determination, difficulties in estimating mould-free shelf-life, and differences in the number and type of moulds present on the cakes in different tests. These factors will be discussed further in the second section of this paper.

It will be appreciated that the information provided in Fig. 1 is of considerable value to the baker and can enable him to estimate the minimum mould-free shelf-life which he can expect from his cakes.

Other intermediate moisture foods. The results from storage tests carried out on a range of intermediate moisture foods by various workers,[5-12] are given in Fig. 2 where the ERH of the product is plotted against the logarithm of the mould-free shelf-life in days.

Unfortunately no two sets of results are strictly comparable since differences exist between storage temperatures and methods of assessing when the product has become mouldy. It is interesting to note, however, that with the exception of Snow's results[11] with oats and beans and Barton Wright's results with flour at 20°C,[5] all workers show an approximately linear relationship between ERH and the logarithm of the mould-free shelf-life. In many cases the shape of the graph is similar to that obtained with cake (Fig. 1). It is apparent that at a given ERH the mould-free shelf-life varies considerably according to product. This variability could be due to a number of factors including the nutrient value and redox potential of the food, the presence of natural mould inhibitory substances, the method of assessing when the product has become mouldy, the storage temperature, and the method of determining ERH. No matter how far such factors are standardised, it is likely that different products will vary in the rate at which they support mould growth and for this reason it is necessary to establish a separate relationship between ERH and mould-free shelf-life for each type of product.

Moisture loss. The amount of moisture which is lost through the wrapper during storage can have a considerable effect on the ERH

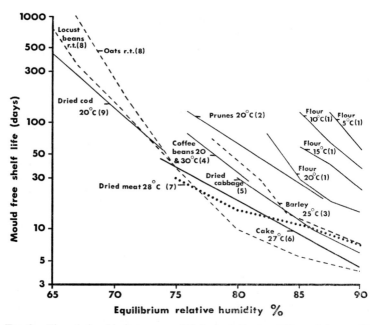

Fig. 2. The relationship between equilibrium relative humidity and the mould-free shelf-life of various foods. Sources of information are indicated by numbers in parentheses as follows: (1) Barton Wright and Tompkins;[5] (2) Tanaka and Miller;[6] (3) Burrell;[7] (4) Butt;[8] (5) Heiss and Eicher;[9] (6) Seiler (Fig. 1); (7) Macara;[10] (8) Snow *et al.*;[11] (9) Shewan.[12]

of the product as a whole and, in particular, on the ERH of the outside surfaces, which in turn affects mould-free shelf-life. The extent of this moisture loss depends on the moisture permeability of the wrapper and the integrity of the seals, the difference in relative humidity between the atmosphere inside and outside the wrapper, the storage temperature, and on the method of packing, *i.e.* products stored separately will lose more moisture than products packed close together in stacks or in cartons.

The effect of moisture loss on mould-free shelf-life can be judged from Fig. 3 which gives the results from storage tests at 27°C in which plain and fruited cakes were wrapped in M.S. grade cellulose film and the rate of moisture loss varied by the closeness of packing. It will be seen that the increase in mould-free shelf-life resulting from a given weight loss is greater the lower the ERH of the cake. In this series of tests, the lowest ERH tested was quite high at 82% but, even here, a 2 % weight loss in 14 days resulted in a 50 % increase in mould-free shelf-life. It can be appreciated that with products of lower ERH a very small moisture loss during storage could be sufficient to cause such large increases in mould-free shelf-life that mould problems may never be encountered.

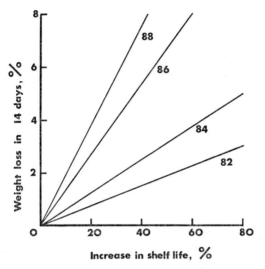

FIG. 3.   The effect of moisture loss during storage on the increase in mould-free shelf-life of cake of ERH 82%, 84%, 86% and 88% stored at 27°C.

Storage Temperature

As the storage temperature is reduced the mould-free shelf-life of the product is increased. The effect of a given reduction in storage temperature is greater with products of low ERH than with products of high ERH. This is shown in Table 1 which gives the percentage increase in mould-free shelf-life caused by a reduction in storage temperature from 27 to 21°C for cakes at different ERH.

The relationship established between the ERH and mould-free shelf-life for cake stored at 21°C is given by the following expression:

$\log_{10}$ mould-free shelf-life (days at 21°C)
$$= 7.91 - (0.081 \times \text{ERH } \%)$$

The results obtained by Burrell with barley[7] and Barton Wright with flour[5] (*see* Fig. 2) show a similar trend although the increases in mould-free shelf-life caused by a similar reduction in temperature are rather greater than those given in Table 1 for cake.

As the storage temperature is decreased the percentage increases in mould-free shelf-life for a given reduction in storage temperature become greater. For example, in a recent test in which similar cakes

TABLE 1

Effect of reduction in storage temperature on the increase in the mould-free shelf-life of cake at differing ERH

ERH of cake	Approximate % increase in mould-free shelf-life by reducing storage temperature from 27 to 21°C
90	25
85	40
80	55
75	90

were stored at different temperatures the mould-free shelf-life was increased by 40%, 86% and 110% by reducing the temperature from 27 to 21°C, 21 to 16°C and 16 to 10°C, respectively. Further work is required to obtain more exact information on the relationship between storage temperature and the mould-free shelf-life of cake.

Nature of the Mould Population

The various xerophilic fungi which cause spoilage of intermediate moisture foods have recently been described by Pitt.[13] Although the minimum water activity reported for the growth of each species is quoted, little information is provided on the time taken for the various fungi mentioned to grow and cause spoilage of food.

In the storage tests carried out to determine the effect of ERH on the mould-free shelf-life of cake (*see* Fig. 1) note was generally taken of the type of moulds present. No attempt was made to differentiate between species with the same group of fungi and the main types studied were *Wallemia sebi*, *Penicillium* sp. and *Eurotium glaucus* sp. The approximate time taken for these three types of mould to develop on cakes of different ERH is given in Fig. 4.

It is apparent that the three types of mould differ in their response to the ERH of cake, *W. sebi* and *E. glaucus* sp. showing greater tolerance of reduced ERH than *Penicillium* sp. On cakes with an

ERH of 86% or above, *E. glaucus* sp. generally appear later than the other two types of mould but, as the ERH falls below this level, this type of mould becomes predominant and largely governs mould-free shelf-life in products with an ERH below about 84%. The only mould, other than *E. glaucus* sp., which has occasionally been isolated from low ERH coatings and fillings of flour confectionery items, *e.g.* chocolate and jam, is *Monascus bisporus*.

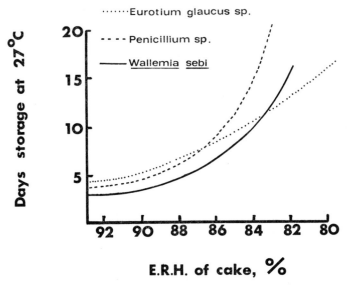

FIG. 4. The relationship between equilibrium relative humidity and the rate at which various moulds grow on cake at 27°C

Based on the results from these tests and information on the minimum ERH at which moulds will grow, it is doubtful whether the composition of the mould population will have a marked effect on the mould-free shelf-life of intermediate moisture foods with an ERH below 84% since *E. glaucus* sp. will predominate and Ayerst[2] has shown that most of the common species in this group show a similar response to reduction in ERH. However, as the ERH of the product increases above 84% the type of mould contaminant present is likely to play a more important role. For example, the results given in Fig. 4 indicate that the mould-free shelf-life of cake is likely to be reduced if *W. sebi* is present.

Level of Mould Contamination

Little detailed information appears to have been published on the relationship between mould-free shelf-life and the numbers of mould spores present in or on the product. In order to obtain information on the importance of inoculum level with respect to cake, tests were carried out where the cut surfaces of cakes of different ERH were inoculated with talc suspensions containing different numbers of mould spores. In these tests *W. sebi*, *P. notatum* and *E. amstelodami* were compared and approximately 1000 and 100 spores applied per cake cut surface. The results obtained are given in Table 2.

TABLE 2

Effect of inoculum level on the mould-free shelf-life of cakes of different ERH

Test organism	ERH of cake	Approximate no. mould spores applied per cut surface	Approximate mould-free shelf-life (days at 27°C)	% extension in mould-free shelf-life given by reducing inoculum level
Wallemia	91	1 000	3	
sebi	91	100	$3\frac{1}{2}$	17
	88	1 000	4	
	88	100	$4\frac{3}{4}$	19
Penicillium	91	1 000	4	
notatum	91	100	$4\frac{3}{4}$	19
	87	1 000	$5\frac{3}{4}$	
	87	100	$6\frac{3}{4}$	17
Eurotium	91	1 000	$5\frac{1}{4}$	
amstelodami	91	100	$5\frac{3}{4}$	10
	83	1 000	$9\frac{1}{2}$	
	83	100	$10\frac{1}{2}$	11

In all instances a longer mould-free shelf-life was obtained by reducing inoculum level but there is no indication that the extension in mould-free shelf-life is any greater for products of lower ERH. Further tests indicate that the increases caused by reducing inoculum level are also similar at different storage temperatures. It is appreciated that, even at 100 spores per cut surface, the level of inoculum was high in these tests. However, other tests comparing inoculum levels of 100 and 10 mould spores per cut surface gave comparable results. Thus, it appears that difference in level of mould contamination has a surprisingly small effect on mould-free shelf-life and is not greatly affected by the ERH of the product or storage temperature.

Other Factors Influencing Mould-free Shelf-life

It is likely that factors such as the pH, nutritional value, or redox potential of a food will have a bearing on mould-free shelf-life. However, there is little evidence to suggest that these factors will have any significant effect on the rate at which moulds will grow on the majority of intermediate moisture foods unless the product or method of packaging is deliberately adjusted with this in mind.

A more important factor, particularly for high sugar intermediate moisture foods, is the presence of natural mould inhibitory substances. Many workers[14-16] have shown that inhibitors, such as hydroxymethyl furfural, are frequently encountered in fruits and vegetables which have been heated. The effect of such natural inhibitors is demonstrated in Fig. 5 which shows the difference in the

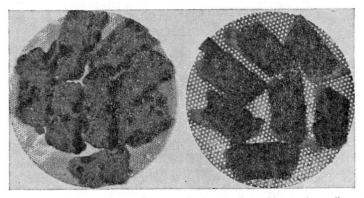

FIG. 5. The effect of steaming time on the extent of mould growth on slices of Christmas pudding stored in desiccators over water at 26°C. (Left, 3 h; right, 7 h.)

extent of mould growth on slices taken from Christmas puddings which had been steamed for 3 and 7 h. It is apparent that the inhibitory substances have been produced by prolonged steaming of the pudding. Further tests have established that the inhibitors are mainly present in the fruit. It is possible that such natural inhibitors occur quite frequently in high sugar intermediate moisture foods, particularly on caramelised outer surfaces, and that as a consequence longer mould-free shelf-life may be obtained than expected based on ERH.

DIFFICULTIES ENCOUNTERED IN PREDICTING
MOULD-FREE SHELF-LIFE

In the work described in the previous section it has been shown that the rate at which moulds will grow on intermediate moisture foods is mainly influenced by the ERH of the product. Even using a single commodity such as cake, it has been found that considerable variations in mould-free shelf-life can occur from test to test in products with the same ERH (*see* Fig. 1). Some of the factors which can give rise to such variations have already been discussed. Additional factors are considered in the remainder of this paper.

Distribution of ERH Within the Product

With many cakes and other intermediate moisture foods the ERH is not uniform throughout the product. Thus, for example the ERH of the outside crust of freshly baked cakes is usually very low in comparison with the inside crumb. Similarly, any fillings, coatings or toppings applied to the cake before or after baking may have a widely different ERH from the cake itself. If the product is stored in a completely moisture-impermeable wrapper at a constant temperature, the product will reach equilibrium, but this takes time, and, in the above examples, it is doubtful whether cake crust or fillings and coatings ever reach equilibrium within the normal shelf-life of the products. This is particularly the case if there is some moisture loss through the wrapper during storage.

The mould-free shelf-life of a product will be governed by the exposed surface of the product which has the highest ERH. Thus, a cake which has a thick crust on all surfaces will generally have a longer mould-free shelf-life than the same cake which is sliced so that the cut surface is exposed to contamination with mould spores. Again, in a filled cake, if the filling has a higher ERH than the cake, mould will first develop on the exposed surface of the filling or at the interface between the filling and the cake.

When attempting to relate ERH and mould-free shelf-life it is important that ERH determinations are carried out on the portion of the product which is most liable to support mould growth.

Variation in ERH Between Products

No matter how strictly processing conditions are controlled, it is usually found that there are slight differences between the ERH of products manufactured on the same occasion. In the case of cakes these differences may be due to variations in deposit weight, uneven oven temperatures and variable cooling losses. When establishing the mould-free shelf-life of a product it is important to take into account this inter-product variability and to carry out storage tests using sufficient randomly selected, replicate samples. We normally use at least 20 replicate products per storage test.

Batch to batch, day to day and week to week variations in the ERH of the same product may also occur under commercial conditions and it is desirable to carry out storage tests on a number of different occasions. Not only will such additional tests give greater confidence in selecting a shelf-life for the product, but it may be possible to build up a picture of the relationship between ERH, moisture content and mould-free shelf-life for that product so that it is no longer necessary to carry out routine storage tests and variations can be monitored solely on the basis of a moisture content determination.

Measurement of ERH

When assessing the mould-free shelf-life of a product in relation to ERH, it must be borne in mind that the methods used for ERH determination are unlikely to give consistent readings with an accuracy of less than $\pm 1\%$. From the results for cake given in Fig. 1 it will be seen that a 1% reduction in ERH would be expected to cause an appreciable increase in mould-free shelf-life of about 22%. Because of this inherent inaccuracy with methods of ERH determination the results from a single storage test cannot be relied upon and it is necessary to carry out several tests with the same product.

Estimation of Mould-free Shelf-life

Determining when mould growth has first commenced on a product can also give rise to inaccuracies in determining mould-free shelf-life. For example, with cake, it is often much easier to see the first stages of mould growth on a dark coloured surface than on a light coloured surface, and it is often difficult to distinguish between cake crumbs and the chocolate brown coloured colonies of *W.sebi*. Again, with low ERH products, it is often found that one replicate becomes mouldy long before the others. In this instance it is difficult to decide whether the mould-free shelf-life should be taken as the time when the first mould growth is observed or whether it should be taken as the time when mould is detected more generally. It has been found that inexperienced workers often vary in their estimation of when mould growth is first apparent on a product and that careful supervision on this aspect is required.

Despite these difficulties, it is probably easier to estimate the mould-free shelf-life of cake than it is for many other intermediate moisture foods. Much greater difficulties can be envisaged for powdered or granulated foods or for products with internal surfaces, where the first stages of mould growth are not easily visible. It is considered that the differences in mould-free shelf-lives quoted for products of the same ERH (*see* Fig. 2) are largely associated with the method used to assess when mould growth has just commenced. As in the case of variation in ERH within and between products and inaccurate ERH measurement discussed above, inconsistencies in estimating mould-free shelf-life can only be overcome by carrying out a number of storage tests with the same product.

Artificial Inoculation Techniques

It can be argued that a more accurate assessment of the mould-free shelf-life of foods can be obtained by deliberate addition of known numbers of spores of a known species of mould to the surfaces of the product prior to wrapping and storage. However, it is our experience that such techniques can give rise to misleading results. In the first place, difficulties arise in the method of applying the spores to the product, *i.e.* application of a wet suspension may encourage too rapid growth and a dry suspension may delay growth. Secondly, if large numbers of a fast growing mould, such as *W.sebi* are applied, a false impression of the mould-free shelf-life of the product may be obtained since this particular mould may not be present in the bakery or, in fact, may not be capable of growing on the product if the ERH is too low. If artificial inoculation techniques are employed, a mixed mould spore suspension in talc should preferably be used but it is considered that it is better to carry out a number of tests using products which have been allowed to become naturally contaminated by mould spores present in the atmosphere, or on surfaces with which the product has come into contact.

Moisture Loss

It has been shown that moisture loss from the product can cause large increases in the mould-free shelf-life of cakes and probably also most other intermediate moisture foods. Unfortunately moisture loss cannot be relied on as a means of increasing shelf-life since under commercial conditions, there are always situations arising where little or no moisture loss can occur. For this reason it is suggested that moisture loss considerations be discounted when establishing the mould-free shelf-life for a product. Replicate products should either be packed close together in one large stack or overwrapped in a large moisture-proof bag.

Storage Temperature

The decision on what storage temperature should be used to determine the mould-free shelf-life of products which are normally stored under ambient conditions, is not an easy one. Much will depend on the length of time that the product is likely to be stored in the factory, in depots, and in the shops, and on the temperature conditions likely to exist in these places. Most of the year in the UK, a temperature of 21°C is unlikely to be exceeded, but during hot periods in the summer the temperatures might easily rise to 27°C and above in the sites where such products are stored. For this reason, and to provide an adequate safety margin, it is considered that a storage temperature of about 27°C should be employed. If it is desired to estimate the shelf life at a lower temperature, a factor such as that given in Table 1 can be employed.

Mossel[14] has pointed out that under practical conditions fluctuations in storage temperature are likely to occur which can lead to moisture migration within a food resulting in certain portions having a higher or lower ERH than at the commencement of storage. Effects such as this could have a profound effect on mould-free shelf-life. Unfortunately, little information is available on the effects of fluctuating temperatures on the rate of mould growth in foods.

CONCLUSION

In order to estimate the mould-free shelf-life of intermediate moisture foods it is suggested that storage tests be carried out under conditions where no moisture loss occurs at the highest temperature likely to be encountered in practice. In view of the variations in ERH which are likely to occur both within and between products the inaccuracies of ERH measurement, the difficulties which occur in assessing mould-free shelf-life, and natural variations in the level of contamination with moulds, it is recommended that a number of separate storage tests be carried out using sufficient replicate samples before reaching any conclusion as to the mould-free shelf-life of the product concerned. Sufficient tests have now been carried out on cakes of differing types to enable the baker to estimate with some confidence the minimum mould-free shelf-life which he can expect from a product with a known ERH (*see* Fig. 1). It would appear, however, that there is a real need for further similar information on the relationship between ERH, storage temperature and the mould-free shelf-life of other intermediate moisture foods.

REFERENCES

1. Scott, W. J. (1957). *Adv. Fd. Res.*, **7**, p. 83.
2. Ayerst, G. (1969). *J. Stored Prod. Res.*, **5**, p. 127.
3. Horner, K. J. and Anagnostopoulos, G. D. (1973). *J. Appl. Bact.*, **36**, p. 427.
4. Pitt, J. I. and Christian, J. H. B. (1968). *Appl. Microbiol.*, **16**, p. 1853.
5. Barton Wright, E. C. and Tomkins, R. G. (1940). *Cereal Chem.*, **17**, p. 332.
6. Tanaka, H. and Miller, M. W. (1963). *Hilgardia*, **34**, p. 183.
7. Burrell, N. J. (1974). In: *Storage of Cereal Grains and their Products*, ed. C. M. Christensen, Am. Ass. Cereal Chem. Minnesota, p. 420.
8. Butt, D. J. (1966). In: *Microbial Deterioration in the Tropics*, Soc. Chem. Ind. Monog. no. 23 Soc. Chem. Ind., London, p. 80.
9. Heiss, R. and Eicher, E. (1971). *Fd. Manufacture,* May, p. 53.
10. Macara, T. J. R. (1943). *J. Soc. Chem. Ind.*, **62**, p. 104.
11. Snow, D., Crichton, M. H. G. and Wright, N. C. (1944). *Chem. App. Biol.*, **31**, pp. 102–111.
12. Shewan, J. M. (1953). *J. Hyg.*, **51**, p. 347.
13. Pitt, J. I. (1975). In: *Water Relations of Foods*, ed. R. B. Duckworth, Academic Press, London, p. 273.
14. Mossel, D. A. A. (1971). *J. appl. Bact.*, **34**, p. 95.
15. Wilson, D. C. and Brown, H. D. (1953). *Fd. Technol.*, **7**, p. 250.
16. Pitt, J. I. (1965). M.Sc. Thesis, University of New South Wales.

DISCUSSION

Tompkin: How difficult is it to obtain a uniform level of mould spore inoculum for your studies?

Seiler: It is by no means easy; it requires a considerable effort on our part to get these spore suspensions for case work. It is very difficult, too, to get the spore distribution even, you have to dilute with talc, and so on. I don't favour artificial contamination techniques because I think they lead to a wrong impression of mould-free shelf-life; I prefer natural contamination techniques.

Chairman: I believe some research was done in Germany into rye bread in which the same kind of conclusion was obtained—that artificial contamination produced misleading data. So it seems we can all agree that a high number of replicates are preferable.

Jeffery: Is your research done at a constant temperature?

Seiler: In the tests we have done we couldn't establish much difference between 27 centrigrade degrees cycling up and down, and an intermediate temperature. Not much work has been done on this type of storage condition. More research using cycling temperatures is needed.

Jeffery: Has the mechanism whereby anti-mycotic agents operate on mould been studied?

Seiler: Yes, in fact a great deal of work has been done by us on this. We have studied the use of sorbic and propionic acids (which are permitted for confectionery) for preservation. In comparing these preservatives we find that the sorbates tend to be more active. There tend to be problems with the propionic acids and their salts, particularly where products with a high pH are concerned; one can find that the volume of the product has been reduced. So one needs to be careful over the use of these in flour and confectionery items.

13

The Safety of Intermediate Moisture Foods with Respect to *Staphylococcus aureus*

ROSA PAWSEY and R. DAVIES

National College of Food Technology, University of Reading, Weybridge, Surrey, England

ABSTRACT

Enterotoxigenic strains of Staphylococcus aureus, *frequently carried on the skin and mucous membranes of healthy human beings, are fairly resistant to physical stress and thus survive and are widely distributed in the environment. Their multiplication and consequent toxin production in raw food materials or during the preparation and storage of food products constitutes a health hazard. The incidence of staphylococcal food poisoning varies with national dietary habits but can be particularly high where large quantities of commercially prepared meats and other food products are marketed and consumed. In intermediate moisture foods:* (1) *a range of factors influence the entry of toxigenic staphylococci;* (2) *environmental conditions may permit* (a) *survival or growth of* Staphylococcus aureus *and* (b) *the production of enterotoxins;* (3) *exposure to intermediate moisture conditions may injure* Staph. aureus *and analytical methods must therefore detect both injured and healthy cells.*

INTRODUCTION

Intermediate moisture foods (IMF) resemble dry foods in their resistance to microbial deterioration. The biologically available water is limited by the presence of water binding solutes to such a degree that they possess 'intermediate water activity' values, and this better describes them since between types their water contents (gramme/gramme dry weight) can vary very considerably. However they must be designed to be shelf stable not only microbiologically, but also in regard to nutritional quality, flavour, texture and colour.

Staphylococcus aureus is a ubiquitous organism whose normal habitat is the skin, skin glands and mucous membranes of warm blooded animals.[1] It is potentially pathogenic causing a wide range of infections and intoxications and some strains cause food poisoning. Its presence in IMF is of significance for two reasons: it can be an indicator of unhygienic practice in the preparation of the product, and secondly the enterotoxin which causes food poisoning may be present at levels which constitute a hazard.

In the UK staphylococcal food poisoning is responsible for only about 2 % of all reported cases. Yet in other countries, for example in the USA and Hungary,[2] it is the highest reported cause.[3] Its incidence appears to be related to national dietary habits, and it is possible that in the USA it correlates with the very high number of commercially prepared foods and communally eaten meals[4] of which IMF may continue to form an increasing proportion.

IMF fall into two categories. Traditional IMF include, for example jams, dried fruits, puddings, confectionery products, salted meat and fish. Modern IMF for human consumption are still largely at the developmental stage although many have been formulated and patented. The methods by which they are made are discussed elsewhere[5] but briefly an absorption or desorption process is used to achieve a desired water activity in the food.[6−8] Heat processes to improve microbiological quality are sometimes applied to individual constituents, to the final product or not at all. Then, after mixing, the foods are filled into flexible plastic packages, sealed and stored at ambient temperatures. The problems which arise in the manufacture and marketing of IMF with respect to *Staph. aureus* are:

(1) the possibility of the introduction of enterotoxigenic strains of *Staph. aureus* into the food;

(2) the probability and significance of their subsequent increase or survival; and

(3) the need for suitable methods of analysis for detecting viable *Staph. aureus*.

TABLE 1

Occurrence of Staphylococcus aureus

Source	Occurrence of coagulase positive staphylococci	Remarks	Ref.
I. *Man*	25–50% are healthy carriers	Nose and throat surveys reviewed	9
	80% are healthy carriers	Survey of food handlers' hands and nasal cavities	11
	15–20% carry enterotoxigenic strains		12
II. *Animals*			
Diseased cattle	23% of those examined	Liver, and lung abscesses lung pyaemia, pneumonia	13
Mastitic cows	50% of raw milk samples contained staphylococci. 119/183 of isolates were coagulase positive	1.0×10^3/ml in 67% of positive samples	14
Diseased swine	41% of those examined positive	Abscesses, nasal swabs, shoulder abscess	13
Diseased poultry	69% of those examined positive	Abscesses, arthritis, leg lesion, visceral tumour, peritonitis	13
Diseased sheep	100% of those examined positive	Prescapular lymph node, lung abscess, liver abscess	13
III. *Meat*			
Market meat	15% of samples positive	Meats from which coagulase positive staphylococci were recovered in decreasing order of frequency: chicken, pork liver, fish, spiced ham, ground beef steak, hamburger, beef liver, pork chops, veal steak, lamb chops	15
Chicken	80% of rinse water samples	$2.0–6.2 \times 10^2$/ml of rinse water	16
Hamburger	35% of samples positive	$5.0 \times 10{-}3.5 \times 10^3$/g	16
Frozen meat by-products	40% of samples positive		17

TABLE 1—*contd.*

Source	Occurrence of coagulase positive staphylococci	Remarks	Ref.
IV. *Milk and milk products*			
Raw	50% of raw milk samples contained staphylococci	1.0×10^3/ml in 67% of positive samples	14
Raw	70% of samples	Positive with 10^4/ml	18
	9% of samples	Positive with 5.0×10^5/ml	
	5% of samples	<10/ml	
Cheddar cheese	20% of samples positive	Market samples: 5.0×10–7.2×10^6/g	19
Pasteurised milk	90% of samples	Less than 10^3/g	18
Raw milk cheese (factory made)	95% of samples positive:		
	23%	5.0×10^2/g	18
	72%	10^3–10^7/g	
Cheese (from heated milk)	92% of samples positive	Less than 10^4/g	18
V. *Fish*			
Fish and crustacean shellfish	None	Generally free at harvesting except from polluted waters	20, 21
Fish—gutted and frozen at sea (cod)	99.5% of samples positive	<10^2/g	22
Fish—frozen comminuted	96.6% of samples positive	<10^2/g	22
Crab, cooked	100% of samples positive	61.3 < 10^2/g, 37.3% 10^2–10^3/g, 1.4% > 10^3/g	22

CONTAMINATION OF IMF

Staph. aureus is almost ubiquitous among man and animals. It has been estimated that 15–20% of the human population carry entero-toxigenic staphylococci.[9] In addition surveys of food products show that the organism can be widely isolated from fresh meats (chicken, pork liver, spiced ham and others), fish, frozen meat by-products, raw milk and a wide range of cooked or prepared products[10a,10b] (Table 1). Contamination of IMF is thus likely to arise primarily from human origins via the noses, hands, septic lesions of personnel within the factory[2] and from the food constituents. The risk of entry of enterotoxigenic staphylococci into IMF therefore is as great as with other manufactured foods of composite nature. The greatest single protection consequently lies in the observance of the highest standards of hygienic practice at all stages in their production,[23] with such practice being monitored by an effective system of micro-biological examination.[22] Codes of sanitary practice for the pro-duction of foods in many countries have been reviewed by Elliott and Michener[24] and also general principles for hygienic food manu-facture are detailed in the FAO/WHO Codex Alimentarius.[25]

Heat Treatment

Heat treatment may be applied to improve the microbiological quality of the ingredients, or of the mixed product. Such heat is thus applied to cells in an aqueous environment in which water binding solutes and other constituents are present. Normally the effectiveness of a heat treatment is measured in terms of D-values (time in minutes at a particular temperature $T°C$ to destroy 90% of the cells) and z-values (the increase in temperature in °C required to increase the kill ten-fold). The heat resistance of bacteria is known to depend on a number of related factors which include the strain of the organism, its growth conditions, its age, the number of cells heated and the physical and chemical composition of the heating menstruum.

$D_{60°C}$ values for *Staph. aureus* heated in buffer or in isotonic salt solutions at pH 6·5–7·2 have been found to range from 0·1 to 2·5 minutes; and z-values from 5 to 9°C.[26] If, however, the organisms are heated in a system in which solutes are present then heat resist-ance is altered. IMF characteristically have high solute levels, and it is to be expected therefore that the heat resistance of staphylococci within them will be different from cells heated in dilute systems. This alteration in resistance does not seem to be a predictable quality—an increased heat resistance has often been demonstrated in the presence of high solute concentrations but this is not always so.

Increasing heat resistance has been demonstrated in skimmed milk to which serum solids were progressively added (0 %, 9 %, 20 %, 30 %), $D_{60°C}$ values being 5·34, 6·2, 7·12 and 7·51 respectively.[27] Addition of sodium chloride to buffer to give an a_w of 0·95 was very protective to *Staph. aureus* heated to 60°C[28] and quantities of sugar (presumed to be sucrose) over 14 % added to skimmed milk progressively protected *Staph. aureus* 196E so that $D_{60°C}$ values increased—as are shown in Table 2.

TABLE 2

$D_{60°C}$ *values of* Staphylococcus aureus *heated in skimmed milk plus sugar*[27]

Heating system	$D_{60°C}$ (min)	Approx. a_w[a]
Skim milk	5·34	0·998
Skim milk plus 6 % sugar	4·11	0·994
Skim milk plus 10 % sugar	4·88	0·992
Skim milk plus 14 % sugar	5·01	0·990
Skim milk plus 25 % sugar	6·71	0·980
Skim milk plus 30 % sugar	9·11	0·974
Skim milk plus 45 % sugar	15·08	0·950
Skim milk plus 57 % sugar	22·35	0·920

[a] a_w values obtained from the sucrose/water isotherm of Norrish (1966). *J. Fd. Technol.*, **1**, 25.

However the addition of another sugar, glucose, to tryptone soy broth as heating medium, decreased the heat resistance of strain 196E thus suggesting a sensitising rather than a protective effect.[28] A similar effect was also shown for low levels of sucrose added to skimmed milk.[27] Further it has been shown more recently that for given solutes a certain concentration of each gives maximal heat protection whereas other concentrations result in greater sensitivity.[29]

Work with other organisms, especially Salmonellae and *Clostridium botulinum*, cells and spores,[30,31] in addition to *Staph. aureus* has led to the generally accepted view now that survival after heating cannot be directly related to the water activity of the heating or of the recovery medium, but that its magnitude depends to a great extent on the kinds of solutes present. It has been shown[29] for a strain of

Staph. aureus (NCTC 4135) and a strain of *Salmonella typhimurium* (B22) that some relationship exists between the demonstrated a_w for optimum heat survival and the minimum for growth, both in the same solute system; and that these values vary with solute. Horner and Anagnostopoulos[29] suggest that possibly similar relationships exist for other organisms. If this were so it could be of value to predict the effect on microbial populations of processes involving change in the solute composition of semi-preserved foods. However their work has only covered solute concentrations which give a_w in the range above 0·90. IMF are generally formulated to have a_w in a lower range (0·65–0·90). Certainly death rates in the absence of pasteurising or more rigorous heat treatments are strongly influenced by a_w and solute concentration. Whether heat survival in the IMF range can be linked to growth minima or other characteristics to aid prediction of behaviour as yet remains an open question.

Thus intermediate moisture foods may be contaminated with enterotoxigenic staphylococci during manufacture. The microbial load may be reduced by heat treatment, but it is quite possible that packaged IMF leaving the factory may carry surviving viable cells. Is it likely that these cells will lead to hazard?

GROWTH AND SURVIVAL IN INTERMEDIATE MOISTURE FOODS

If any cells of *Staph. aureus* are introduced into IMF, and if they are not subsequently destroyed by a heat treatment there is a possibility that they will grow. The statistical probability of growth is determined by the combined effects of the environmental factors on the strain type and the total number of cells initially present.

Many studies have been conducted both in foods and in model systems of the growth and survival of a range of strains of *Staph. aureus* as influenced by a_w, solute concentration, pH, temperature and degree of aerobiosis.

Staphylococci grow best at high a_w values, well above the IMF range, for example optimally at a_w 0·995.[32] Originating from Scott's work[32] it is now generally established that under otherwise optimal conditions reduction in a_w increases the lag period before exponential growth, reduces specific growth rate and reduces the maximal number of cells[33,34] (Fig. 1).

A survey[32] of the growth of 14 food poisoning strains of *Staph. aureus* both in laboratory media and in foods showed growth to be limited to a_w of 0·86 and above. Scott did not find marked differences between strains, nor between solutes used to adjust a_w. He was able to conclude that it was unlikely that in other environmental conditions in which one or more parameters were suboptimal that the a_w range for growth would be extended. In fact slow growth of some

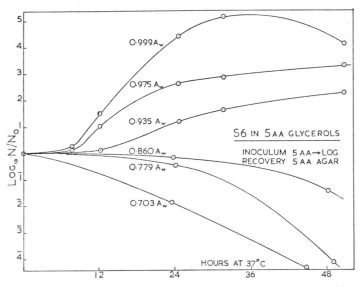

FIG. 1. Growth and survival of *Staphylococcus aureus* S6 in a defined broth containing 5 amino acids, pH 7·0 at 37°C. Water activity was adjusted with glycerol. Inoculum cells were grown to log phase in the 5 amino acid broth, inoculated into 20 ml of 5AA glycerol in 250 ml flasks and incubated in a shaking water bath at 37°C. Samples were removed and diluted in 0·1 M phosphate buffer, and plated on to 5AA agar plates incubated at 37°C.

strains of *Staph. aureus* has been demonstrated at 0·84[35] and at 0·83.[36] In addition we have been able to show for *Staph. aureus* S6 that the growth threshold in a rich fully defined medium is 0·865, yet when nutrients are limited to a defined minimal medium, growth is restricted to 0·93 and above. Thus Scott's general conclusion remains largely unchallenged. So in IMF, provided that the water activity is below 0·85 significant increases in the number of contaminating cells are unlikely to occur.

Below the growth threshold death takes place as a_w is reduced at rates increasing to a maximum after which, as a_w reduction continues cells are increasingly protected. Maximum death rates at certain a_w ranges have been observed by several groups of workers. Greatest survival of staphylococci was found at a_w 0·0–0·22 in four freeze dried foods[37] and lethality greatest at 0·53 a_w. Scott[38] obtained similar results with *Staph. aureus* freeze dried in papain broth. We have found greatest lethality at 0·68–0·73 a_w in defined broths in which the water activity is controlled by the addition of glycerol (Fig. 2). The organism, however, dies at a rate which is

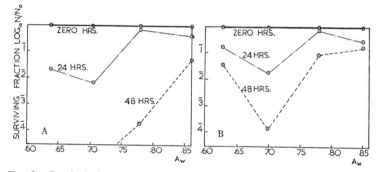

FIG. 2. Survival of *Staphylococcus aureus* S6 in 5 amino acid broth (a minimal defined growth medium) and in 18 amino acid broth, whose a_w were adjusted by the addition of glycerol. Cells were grown to log phase (A) in 5AA broth or (B) 18AA broth and inoculated into 5AA or 18AA glycerol systems respectively. Procedure was as described for Fig. 1. Cells from (A) were plated on to 5AA agar; those from (B) were plated on to 18AA agar.

determined by the combined adverse and protective effects of all the parameters describing the system. Death rate is certainly influenced by the nutrient composition of the system (Fig. 3) and in IMF survival will be longer when the range of nutrients is wide. Even where the initial number of contaminating cells is not high ($1·2–1·4 \times 10^4$/g) viable cells have been isolated from rich meat-containing IMF after a storage period at 38°C of four months[7] (Table 3).

Coagulase positive staphylococci are sensitive to acids in the environment—acetic acid being particularly effective.[39a,39b] Alteration of the pH to suboptimal values increases heat sensitivity, or if combined with a reduction in a_w has an adverse synergistic effect on growth or death.[8] This is also true for other organisms, *e.g. Cl. botulinum* vegetative cells and spores.[30,40] Riemann *et al.*[41] have

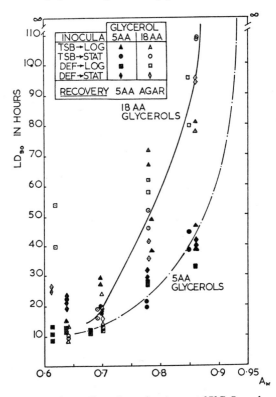

FIG. 3.   Death of S6 in nutrient glycerol systems at 37°C. Inoculum used: four types of inoculum were used as indicated. Inocula from defined media (DEF) were inoculated into the same medium plus glycerol. Log = logarithmic phase; stat = stationary phase; LD_{90} = time (h) to kill 90% of cells; TSB = tryptone soy broth. All samples were plated on to 5AA agar.

TABLE 3

Survival of staphylococci in intermediate moisture foods[7]

Food (in sealed containers at 38°C)	a_w	Viable count of Staphylococci		
		Initial count	1 month	4 months
Chicken à la King	0·85	1·2–1·4 × 10^4/g	<2·0 × 10^3/g	4·0/10 g
Ham in cream sauce	0·85	1·2–1·4 × 10^4/g	<2·0 × 10^3/g	4·0/10 g

collated data from a wide range of sources on the relationship
between pH and salt (sodium chloride) concentrations and the
growth of staphylococci. They conclude that growth can occur down
to pH 4·5 at 8–10% w/v salt or in 16% salt at pH 6·0 and above
(Fig. 4).

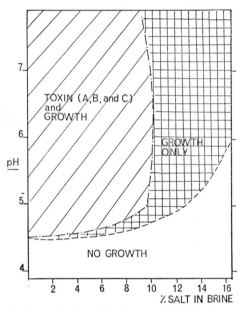

FIG. 4. Combinations of pH and NaCl concentrations which support aerobic
growth and toxin production of *Staph. aureus*. Inoculum level 1·0 × 10⁷ cells/ml.
(Adapted from Riemann *et al.*[41])

Sodium chloride is only one of a range of solutes which can be
used in IMF and the findings for one solute do not necessarily apply
to others. Plitman *et al.*[42] for example found that growth was limited
in BHI (brain, heart infusion broth) to a_w 0·865 and above when
glycerol was used to control a_w, 0·95 and above with 1,2 propanediol
and 0·97 with 1,3 butanediol. Also the latter two solutes had
bactericidal effects on *Staph. aureus* S6 which were not explained by
the water binding capacity of the solutes.

Sugars, di-, tri-, and poly-hydric alcohols, dextrins, neutral salts
and bases are all solutes which may be used in IMF. It is now established that growth is limited by the controlling solute and that a_w is
not solely responsible.[43,44]

It also seems, particularly in food systems, that in addition to a_w, solute and pH, that the water content is significant in microbiological control. Scott[32] did not find this to be so—the water content of his samples in which limiting a_w was 0·86–0·88 ranged from 16 to 375 g water/100 g dry weight. Yet subsequent work in which IMF have been prepared by both absorption and desorption processes have shown that staphylococcal growth or survival differs at the same a_w dependent on water content. This is discussed at length elsewhere.[45]

Thus many factors influence growth and survival of staphylococci in intermediate moisture conditions. Correlation of the mass of available data is very difficult because of the variability between experimental systems. For the prediction of behaviour in IMF there is a need for experimental data which can be statistically analysed. Obviously where the number of parameters is six or more the task is complex. Genigeorgis and his co-workers[46,47] have studied the initiation of aerobic growth both in laboratory media (BHI) and in meat systems in which the pH and sodium chloride concentrations have been varied. After statistical treatment of their data these workers derived equations which relate the decimal reductions of the numbers of cells of a staphylococcal population to the NaCl concentration and the pH to which the population was exposed. From these equations the probability of one cell being capable of initiating growth could be calculated. They found that as few as three cells per 1·0 g sample could initiate growth under some circumstances

e.g. beef, 3·75% NaCl, pH 5·8

yet under other conditions as many as $3·0 \times 10^6$ cells/g were needed

e.g. beef, 3·56% NaCl, pH 4·7;
     beef, 7·72% NaCl, pH 4·7;
     beef, 13·81% NaCl, pH 5·8.

The collated data of Riemann et al.,[41] previously referred to, relates to inoculum levels of approximately 1×10^7 cells/ml. Thus the stated limits of pH 4·5 and brine concentration 8–10% for staphylococcal growth would be raised when contamination levels were lower.

Such an approach, more widely applied, for example to other growth environments and to encompass other stress parameters, could facilitate the development of more meaningful standards to be applied to foods.

Enterotoxin Production

The production of enterotoxins is considered to be a function of the total growth of the organism.[23] Their production tends to be dependent on the composition of the medium and the concentration of its constituents rather than being associated with particular phases of growth.[48] Higher quantities of toxin are produced in media which afford better growth;[49] indeed Miller and Fung[50] have concluded from work in defined amino acid media that where growth and toxin production are restricted it is because of partly mutual and partly separate requirements for the biosynthesis of missing amino acids.

Staphylococci produce at least five enterotoxins—A, B, C, D, E. In a survey of foods (1974)[51] over 50 % of the strains of staphylococci isolated were shown to be enterotoxigenic (Table 4) and to be

TABLE 4

Toxigenicity of strains of Staphylococcus aureus *isolated from meat and dairy products (adapted from Payne and Wood*[51])

Product	No. of strains tested	Total producing enterotoxin (%)							Total negative for enterotoxin A, B, C, D or E (%)
		A	AC	D	CD	ACD	AD	others	
Meat products	134	34	0·75	3·7	0	0·75	9·0	12	39·5
Dairy products	48	21	6·25	10·4	8·3	8·0	4·2	14·6	27·0
Miscellaneous	18	16·6	0·0	5·5	0·0	5·5	5·5	16·6	50·0
Total	200	62·5 % enterotoxigenic							

predominantly A producers. The toxins produced by various strains tended to differ according to their source, B producers being the most infrequent. Enterotoxin A behaves as a primary metabolite[52] and is mainly released in the exponential phase of growth. When growth is depressed by the addition of up to 10 % NaCl the amount of toxin per unit of growth is unaffected. Enterotoxin B has been observed to be produced at a maximal rate after the exponential phase of growth, but when staphylococci have been grown in continuous culture enterotoxin B production occurs in steady state conditions[53] or throughout growth as a function of dissolved oxygen levels.[54] This is not consistent with the earlier view that enterotoxin B is a secondary metabolite.

However, whereas toxin production is frequently associated with growth, the latter is not essential for toxin synthesis. Jarvis *et al.*[55] have shown that non-replicating cells, initially grown in the absence of glucose, need to synthesise new protein in order to produce toxin B. They have also shown that whereas no significant amounts of toxin precursors for A, B or C were present in either log or stationary phase non-replicating cells, yet toxin could be elaborated by them.

Thus enterotoxin production can be separated as a mechanism distinct from growth and which can take place in the absence of growth. This could be of particular significance in IMF where contaminating staphylococci may be present but not replicating.

It may be expected that where staphylococci grow in IMF possessing a_w values in the higher IMF range, enterotoxin could be present. Yet it has been shown that enterotoxin production is sensitive to reduction in the a_w of the supporting medium. Work by Troller[56] in food slurries indicated that the minimal water activity for toxin production varied with the strain of organism used and with the system. 196E (an 'A' producer) produced toxin down to a_w 0·95 and C243 (a 'B' producer) produced toxin at a lower a_w, 0·93, which was a reversal of his findings in laboratory media.[33,34] Finally data collated by Riemann *et al.*[41] indicates that production of toxins A, B and C from a wide range of strains is inhibited at pH 5·0–7·0 if NaCl concentrations are in excess of 10% (Fig. 4), whereas reduction of pH to between 4·5 and 4·0 is necessary to limit toxin production in NaCl concentrations between 4 and 0% w/v.

DETECTION OF VIABLE *Staphylococcus aureus*

Intermediate moisture foods cover a wide range of foods destined to be made, stored and eaten the world over. The microbiological standards applied to their constituents, their manufacture and their final quality should be designed to ensure that they are safe to eat even after storage at ambient temperatures for several months. The standard 'safe' would have to mean that they did not contain detectable levels of toxin nor unacceptable counts of viable cells.

The presence of coagulase positive staphylococci in the IMF

would be an indicator of general processing contamination, and would demonstrate a potential to cause food poisoning if large numbers of cells were present, or if the food were treated abusively. An acceptance criterion for dry protein foods is 'not more than one sample to exceed 10 coagulase positive staphylococci per gramme (within a specified sampling plan)'.[57] The microbiological limit for 'non-thermostabilised' Skylab space foods in respect of coagulase positive staphylococci is 'none in 5 gramme'.[58] The latter standard is too high for foods manufactured for consumption by the mass market on earth! Yet the standards set will have to be based on knowledge of the likely hazards associated with IMF and the possibility of the proliferation of staphylococci and of toxin production within them during storage.

The effective operation of standards depends on the use of suitable methods of analysis. Present methods[22] for the detection of coagulase positive staphylococci use selective media:

(1) in the UK and elsewhere Baird-Parker's medium is widely used;
(2) in the USA tubes of TSB plus 10% NaCl are inoculated with serial dilutions of sample followed by the streaking of positives on to Vogel-Johnson agar (tellurite–glycine) or on to polymixin egg yolk agar;
(3) in Europe and Scandinavia egg yolk azide agar is used;
(4) in the USSR milk agar plus 6·5% NaCl is frequently used. Also if low counts are expected a pre-enrichment in 6·5% salt broth, 10% salt broth and a glucose broth may be used.

Staphylococcal growth is inhibited by intermediate moisture conditions, and cells are probably injured. If cells are injured, possibly doubly so by exposure to sublethal heating and IMF conditions, the surviving cells may lose their ability to produce colonies on selective media—such as those instanced above. Such injured cells may need a holding period in a non-stressful liquid medium to facilitate repair of injury—in much the same way as is used to resuscitate injured Salmonellae.

It has already been amply demonstrated that the staphylococci exposed to certain levels of heating,[59] to freeze drying[60] and to acids[39a] suffer injury. One method of detecting injury in staphylococci has been to use loss of normal salt (sodium chloride) tolerance as an indicator.

We have been able to show injury indicated by development of salt sensitivity in staphylococci exposed to aqueous solutions of glycerol at a_w 0·86 both in the presence and absence of nutrients (Fig. 5). We have also been able to demonstrate the repair of that injury by holding injured cells in TSB (tryptone soy broth) (Fig. 6). Further, cells which have been exposed to glycerol/water 0·86 a_w show the development of sensitivity to osmotic shock after a period of 4 h or more. When samples are removed from the stress system

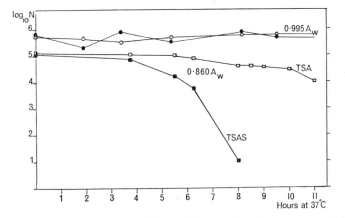

FIG. 5.   Development of salt (NaCl) sensitivity by *Staphylococcus aureus* S6 in glycerol/water systems at 37°C. Log phase cells, TSB grown were inoculated into 20 ml of glycerol-stress system, incubated in a shaking water bath at 37°C. TSA: tryptone soy agar: TSAS: tryptone soy agar plus 7·5 % salt. ○, □ recovery on TSA; ●, ■, recovery on TSAS.

and diluted in hypotonic diluent such as buffer (0·1 mol/litre in phosphate) surviving viable cells present fail to produce colonies on both TSA (tryptone soy agar) and TSAS (tryptone soy agar plus 7·5 % salt). Yet the same cells can produce colonies if they are not subjected to osmotic shock, but rather are removed from the stress system and diluted in an isotonic diluent such as glycerol/water. In addition, we have observed that injury (sensitivity to salt) develops more rapidly in lag phase cells than in log phase cells inoculated into stress systems. This could be of significance in the evaluation of the quality of IMF at production points where it would seem likely that contaminants would be in lag rather than in any other phase.

Thus if staphylococci are injured in IMF, as has been demonstrated in laboratory systems, and become sensitive to salt and liable to osmotic shock then there is a need for a re-appraisal of methods for detecting coagulase positive staphylococci in IMF. The use of salt containing media could be inappropriate as a first step. Rather the inoculation of sample into a non-stressful holding broth to permit resuscitation, as was done for the detection of staphylococci from Skylab foods,[58] could probably be recommended.

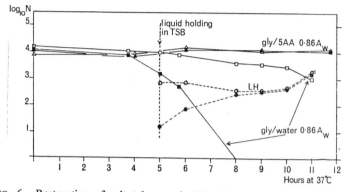

Fig. 6. Restoration of salt tolerance in S6 cells exposed to glycerol/water 0·86 a_w stress at 37°C. Log phase cells grown in tryptone soy broth (TSB) were inoculated into 20 ml of glycerol-stress system, incubated in a shaking water bath at 37°C. At 5 h a one ml sample was removed from glycerol/water 0·86 a_w and added to 19 ml TSB for liquid holding (LH). This diluted the cells 1/20. Samples were plated on TSA and TSAS. Δ, □, ○, recovery on TSA; ▲, ■, ●, recovery on TSAS.

We have also observed that where a range of media are used to recover staphylococci from glycerol/nutrient systems the best recovery was given by Baird-Parker's medium, and that other media gave lower plate counts. However, we have not carried out an exhaustive survey to evaluate recovery media for cells exposed to IMF, which must be done to ensure that standards set are being achieved.

CONCLUSIONS

The risks for the contamination of IMF by *Staph. aureus* are as great as for other manufactured foods of composite nature. In the range a_w 0·65–0·90 the risk of rapid growth of contaminants is not high, but they could either grow slowly or survive for periods of several months. Toxin production tends to be inhibited at higher a_w values than is growth—but the possibility of toxin accumulating cannot be entirely ruled out. Detection procedures should incorporate the principle of a resuscitation period for possibly injured cells before standard media are used, and avoid hypotonic diluent shock.

REFERENCES

1. *Bergey's Manual of Determinative Bacteriology* (1974). 8th edition, Williams and Wilkins.
2. Gilbert, R. J. (1974). *Postgrad. Med. J.*, **50**, p. 603.
3. Brachmann, P. S., Taylor, A., Gangarosa, E. J., Merson, M. H. and Barker, W. H. (1973). In: *The Microbiological Safety of Food*, ed. B. C. Hobbs and J. H. B. Christian, Academic Press, p. 143.
4. Angelotti, R. (1969). In: *Food Borne Infections and Intoxications*, ed. H. Riemann, Academic Press, p. 359.
5. Burrows, I. E. and Barker, D. (1976). 'Intermediate moisture petfoods', this volume, p. 43.
6. Ayerst, G. (1965). *J. Sci. Fd. Agric.*, **16**, p. 71.
7. Brockmann, M. D. (1970). *Fd. Technol.*, **24**, p. 896.
8. Scott, W. J. (1961). 'Available water and microbial growth', in: *Symp. Low Temp. Microbiol.*, Camden N.J., Campbell Soup Co., p. 89.
9. Williams, R. E. O. (1963). *Bact. Rev.*, **27**, p. 56.
10. Minor, T. E. and Marth, E. H. (1971). (a) *J. Milk Fd. Technol.*, **34**, p. 557; (b) *J. Milk Fd. Technol.*, **35**, p. 21; (c) *J. Milk Fd. Technol.*, **35**, p. 77; (d) *J. Milk Fd. Technol.*, **35**, p. 228.
11. Moore, J. M. and Bower, R. K. (1971). *H.S.M.H.A. Hlth Repts*, **86**, p. 815.
12. Untermann, F. (1973). *Zbl. Bakt. I. Orig. A.*, **222**, p. 18.
13. Ravenholt, R. T., Eelkema, R. C., Mulhern, M. and Watkins, R. B. (1961). *Pub. Hlth. Rpt.*, **76**, p. 879.
14. Hackler, J. F. (1939). *Am. J. Pub. Hlth.*, **29**, p. 1249.
15. Jay, J. M. (1962). *Appl. Microbiol.*, **10**, p. 247.
16. Messer, J. W., Peeler, J. T., Read, R. B., Campbell, J. E., Hall, H. E. and Haverland, H. (1970). *Bact. Proc.*, p. 12.
17. Chou, C. C. and Marth, E. H. (1969). *J. Milk Fd. Technol.*, **32**, p. 372.
18. Sharpe, M. E., Rewins, B. G., Reiter, B. and Cuthbert, W. A. (1975). *J. Dairy Res.*, **32**, p. 187.
19. Donnelly, C. B., Black, L. A. and Lewis, K. M. (1961). *Appl. Microbiol.*, **12**, p. 311.
20. Shewan, J. M. (1961). In: *Fish as Food*, Vol. 1, ed. G. Borgstrom, Academic Press, New York, p. 487.
21. Thatcher, F. S. (1969). In: *Technical Conf. on Fish Inspection and Control*, FAO, FE:FIC/69/R17, Rome, Italy.

22. International Commission on Microbiological Specifications for Foods (1974). *Micro-organisms in Foods*, Vol. 2, University of Toronto Press.
23. Hobbs, B. C. (1974). In: *Food Poisoning and Food Hygiene*, 3rd edition, Edward Arnold.
24. Elliott, R. P. and Michener, H. D. (1961). *Appl. Microbiol.*, **9**, p. 452.
25. FAO/WHO Codex Alimentarius Commission. *Recommended international code of practice. General principles of food hygiene*, CAC/RCP 1-1969.
26. Baird-Parker, A. C. and Holbrook, R. (1971). In: *The Inhibition and Destruction of the Microbial Cell*, ed. W. B. Hugo, Academic Press.
27. Kadan, R. S., Martin, W. H. and Mickelsen, R. M. (1963). *Appl. Microbiol.*, **11**, p. 45.
28. Calhoun, C. L. and Frazier, W. C. (1966). *Appl. Microbiol.*, **14**, p. 416.
29. Horner, K. J. and Anagnostopoulos, G. (1975). *J. Appl. Bact.*, **38**, p. 9.
30. Baird-Parker, A. C. and Freame, B. (1967). *J. Appl. Bact.*, **30**, p. 420.
31. Baird-Parker, A. C., Boothroyd, M. and Jones, E. (1970). *J. Appl. Bact.*, **33**, p. 515.
32. Scott, W. J. (1953). *Aust. J. Biol. Sci.*, **6**, p. 549.
33. Troller, J. A. (1968). *Appl. Microbiol.*, **21**, p. 435.
34. Troller, J. A. (1971). *Appl. Microbiol.*, **24**, p. 440.
35. Labuza, T. B., Cassil, S. and Sinskey, A. J. (1972). *J. Fd. Sci.*, **37**, p. 160.
36. Tatini, S. R. (1973). *J. Milk Fd. Technol.*, **36**, p. 559.
37. Christian, J. H. B. and Stewart, B. J. (1973). In: *The Microbiological Safety of Food*, ed. B. C. Hobbs and J. H. B. Christian, Academic Press.
38. Scott, W. J. (1958). *J. Gen. Microbiol.*, **19**, p. 624.
39. Minor, T. E. and Marth, E. H. (1972). (a) *J. Milk Fd. Technol.*, **35**, p. 191; (b) *J. Milk Fd. Technol.*, **35**, p. 548.
40. Tompkin, R. B., Ambrosino, J. M. and Stozek, S. K. (1973). *Appl. Microbiol.*, **26**, p. 833.
41. Riemann, H., Lee, W. H. and Genigeorgis, C. (1972). *J. Milk Fd. Technol.*, **35**, p. 514.
42. Plitman, M., Park, Y., Gomez, R. and Sinskey, A. J. (1973). *J. Fd. Sci.*, **38**, p. 1004.
43. Marshall, B. J., Ohye, D. F. and Christian, J. H. B. (1971). *Appl. Microbiol.*, **21**, p. 363.
44. Nunheimer, T. D. and Fabian, F. W. (1940). *Am. J. Pub. Hlth.*, **30**, p. 1040.
45. Sinskey, A. J. (1976). 'New developments in intermediate moisture foods humectants', this volume, p. 260.
46. Genigeorgis, C., Martin, S., Franti, C. E. and Riemann, H. (1971). *Appl. Microbiol.*, **21**, p. 934.
47. Genigeorgis, C., Savoukidis, M. and Martin, S. (1971). *Appl. Microbiol.*, **21**, p. 940.
48. Metzger, J. F., Johnson, W. S. and McGann, V. (1973). *Appl. Microbiol.*, **25**, p. 770.
49. Reis, R. F. and Weiss, K. F. (1969). *Appl. Microbiol.*, **18**, p. 1041.
50. Miller, R. D. and Fung, D. Y. C. (1973). *Appl. Microbiol.*, **25**, p. 800.

51. Payne, D. N. and Wood, J. M. (1974). *J. Appl. Bact.*, **37**, p. 319.
52. Markus, Z. and Silverman, G. J. (1970). *Appl. Microbiol.*, **20**, p. 492.
53. Jarvis, A. V., Lawrence, R. C. and Pritchard, G. C. (1975). *J. Gen. Microbiol.*, **86**, p. 75.
54. Carpenter, D. F. and Silverman, G. J. (1974). *Appl. Microbiol.*, **28**, p. 628.
55. Jarvis, A. V., Lawrence, R. C. and Pritchard, G. C. (1973). *Infect. Immunol.*, **7**, p. 847.
56. Troller, J. A. and Stinson, J. V. (1975). *J. Fd. Sci.*, **40**, p. 802.
57. PAG Bulletin (1972), **2**, p. 14.
58. Heidelbaugh, N. D., Rowley, D. B., Powers, E. M., Bourland, C. T. and McQueen, J. L. (1973). *Appl. Microbiol.*, **25**, p. 55.
59. Busta, F. F. and Jezeski, J. A. (1971). *J. Dairy Sci.*, **44**, p. 1160.
60. Fung, D. Y. C. and Vandenbosch, W. L. (1975). *J. Milk Fd.*, **38**, p. 212.

DISCUSSION

Obanu: In the reference by Tatini you mentioned, it was observed that the growth limits of *S. aureus* were slightly lower for pork than for beef. Do you have any experience of inter-species differences in meat as regards support for *S. aureus* growth?

Pawsey: I don't think I mentioned the type of food in that particular reference. In fact in the data by Tatini, he is quoting the work of Hill. They demonstrated that growth risk occurred down to 0·83, I think in a meat slurry. But I am not aware of any particular difference between meats.

Tompkin: The data you are referring to were in fact collected by someone else, and Tatini made reference to it. It was non-published data, and there is some question as to whether the data are valid. So at this point I would not use 0·83 as an action point for growth or no growth until the findings have been substantiated.

Pawsey: That is a valid point, but I think there is some risk in attaching a numerical value to growth limitation anyway.

Roberts: In the slide you showed from Riemann's paper, there is a very big difference between water activity stopping growth and water activity stopping toxin production; you quote enterotoxin A, B and C. If you go through those papers you will find there are many more on B than anything else. In our experience, using A, we never got inhibition of toxin before growth. Furthermore, whenever we got growth we always got toxin, even using $12\frac{1}{2}\%$ salts (w/v) in the particular broth we were using, plus nitrites and a reduced pH. So I think one must be very careful about the strains you're talking about. There is not enough information on enterotoxin A strains for one to be as dogmatic as one could be with B strains.

Obanu: The reason for the question I asked was that in a preliminary study in our laboratory, in which meat (both white and dark muscles) was processed in an infusion of glycerol and salt, we observed higher total plate counts and *Staph.* counts in the white muscles (pork and chicken) than in the dark muscles (mutton, beef and goat).

14

Control of Clostridia by Water Activity and Related Factors

T. A. ROBERTS and J. L. SMART

Meat Research Institute, Langford, Bristol, England

ABSTRACT

Clostridia are common contaminants of food. Their growth may be prevented by heat processing or controlled by manipulating pH, storage temperature or water activity (a_w), or by the deliberate addition of inhibitors (e.g. sodium nitrite in cured meats). These factors should not be considered in isolation, since it has been demonstrated that they interact to inhibit bacterial growth. When considering foods, published statements of 'minimum growth temperature' or 'minimum water activity for growth' are often misleading since they are commonly determined under laboratory conditions with factors other than that being studied optimal—a situation rarely pertaining in foods—and account is rarely taken of the effect of the competing microbial flora.

Intermediate moisture foods (IMF) are of sufficiently low a_w to prevent the growth of clostridia irrespective of storage temperature and pH, but growth could conceivably occur during formulation and storage prior to a_w reduction. Good hygienic and manufacturing practices, particularly with respect to temperature control, will reduce to a minimum the likelihood of such growth.

Clostridium botulinum will be present in IMF components from time to time, and it would be imprudent to pretend otherwise. Should it have grown prior to a_w reduction it is likely that the toxin will remain in the IMF. Similarly if the produce is seriously abused with respect to a_w and temperature, the clostridia initially present as spores will have remained viable, and capable of rapid growth.

Data will be presented illustrating the limiting combinations of a_w, pH and incubation temperature for Cl. botulinum.

INTRODUCTION

The remit of this paper is simply to consider the control of clostridia by water activity (a_w) and related factors—and is not intended to imply that there is necessarily a risk of their growth in intermediate moisture foods (IMF). Although it has been known for centuries that reduction of the water content of food resulted in improved microbial stability, an understanding of the phenomenon only began with the work of Scott's group.[1-3] Subsequently many publications have extended our knowledge, but surprising gaps remain, and it is intended to highlight some areas of ignorance. Most examples are drawn from low-acid foods, mainly meats, since it is here that most work has been done.

DISTRIBUTION OF CLOSTRIDIA

The most important clostridia are *Clostridium perfringens*, *Cl. botulinum* and the group comprising *Cl. sporogenes* and the 'putrefactive anaerobes'. *Cl. perfringens* is responsible for several thousand cases of food-poisoning each year in the UK[4] and is being similarly recognised as a significant cause of food-poisoning in other countries.[5,6] *Cl. botulinum* produces one of the most poisonous natural substances known to man,[7] ingestion of which causes botulism. It exists as at least six types, designated A–F, of which types A, B, E and F affect man.[8] *Cl. sporogenes* is ubiquitous, but equally common are the non-toxigenic putrefactive anerobes about which very little is known. Control of *Cl. botulinum* in any food is imperative, and it does not even require an outbreak of human botulism to precipitate commercial ruin: the mere detection of botulinal toxin in a product recently cost that area of industry millions of dollars.

The clostridia occur widely in nature, so widely that it is prudent to assume that they are always present. Bacteriological methods for the clostridia are few and unreliable, and no simple method to determine even 'total clostridia' is yet available. The most commonly used media are partially selective and rely on sulphide production by clostridia from sulphite and/or sulphate. Unhappily, many workers experience difficulties with solidified media of this type, and one can only conclude that the published data on numbers of clostridia in foods are likely to be a gross underestimate. As an example, *Cl. botulinum* has been detected relatively rarely in meats[9-11] until adequately large samples were taken.[12] In a systematic survey we have detected it relatively easily in bacon and pork, and sometimes in a surprising proportion of the samples examined.[13,14] Good selective media are now available for *Cl. perfringens*[15-17] and reliable quantitative surveys of its occurrence are to be expected. It is already known to be very common in food in many countries.[18-25] The value of further surveys would be to ascertain the serotypes which commonly occur in various foods, although the type A associated with food-poisoning would appear to be common.[24]

The clostridia form endospores which are highly resistant to heat and to desiccation and will survive in most IMF. Deliberate attempts to germinate spore populations, after which they are no more resistant than the vegetative cells, have not been successful: there seems always to be a small fraction of the spore population which fails to germinate.[26]

CONTROL OF CLOSTRIDIA

The literature on the control of food-borne bacterial pathogens by a_w has been reviewed by Troller,[27] and it is plain that within the a_w values normally regarded as the range for IMF (0·7–0·85)[28] *Cl. botulinum* and *Cl. perfringens* are unable to grow irrespective of pH and storage temperature. For the sake of completeness, however, the literature will be reviewed briefly with reference to the stages of development of the clostridia from the dormant (resting) spore, through germination, swelling and outgrowth, to cell division.

Although evidence is lacking, clostridia are generally assumed to exist in nature as dormant spores. Future surveys might clarify this, but to some extent studies on conditions to prevent germination and outgrowth are irrelevant since both can occur without damage to a food or danger if it is consumed. Metabolic activity at these stages is insufficient to affect the product, and no significant toxin is produced by *Cl. botulinum* until the cells multiply. Both however are pre-requisite to cell multiplication.

Control of Germination

The minimum a_w at which germination of spores of *Cl. botulinum* types A, B and E occurred in a laboratory medium varied with the solute used to control it, for example, at lower a_w with glycerol (0·89) than NaCl (0·93).[29] Germination was inhibited, however, by similar a_w in curing brines[30] and cured meats[31] but the additional presence of nitrate or nitrite (156 ppm) rendered spores less liable to germinate.[31]

Although germination may be reduced by lowering a_w, caution should be expressed because germination inhibition is an 'absolute' requirement. Germination may occur at very low rates and laboratory experiments rarely simulate the time available for incubation which obtains in commercial practice.

Control of Spore Outgrowth

Glycerol is again less effective than NaCl in preventing spore outgrowth and additionally both germination and outgrowth occurred at lower a_w at 30°C than at 20°C.[29] Salt concentrations with little inhibitory effect at optimal incubation temperatures significantly delayed outgrowth at lower temperatures.[32,33] From these studies it is also plain that *Cl. botulinum* type E strains, mainly associated with fish and marine mammals, are more sensitive to NaCl than are types A and B.

Control of Growth

Several groups of workers have studied the effects of the solute on the limiting a_w for growth of *Cl. botulinum*, and results agree reasonably well. Emodi and Lechowich[34] reported the effects on *Cl. botulinum* type E of sodium formate, sodium chloride, potassium chloride, sucrose and glucose and reported inhibitory a_w's of the order reported previously by Baird-Parker and Freame[29] using sodium chloride. Growth occurred at lower a_w's when adjusted by glycerol.[29,35] Reduced incubation temperature increased the limiting a_w for growth of *Cl. botulinum* type E,[36] and the combined effect of temperature and pH on the a_w for growth of *Cl. botulinum* types A, B and E has also been reported.[37]

The inhibitory factors in pasteurised cured meats have been investigated over many years, and are now under detailed scrutiny with the intention of reducing the level of nitrite to the minimum. It has long been established that complex interactions of pH, NaCl, $NaNO_2$, $NaNO_3$ and F_0 were significant in the bacterial stability of such products,[38] but the extent and significance of particular interactions is only now being revealed, *e.g.* NaCl × pH,[39] NaNO$_2$ × NaCl.[40] The triple interaction of pH × NaCl × NaNO$_2$ has been quantitated in a laboratory medium using *Cl. botulinum* types A, B, E and F,[41] but the data have not yet been extended to reduced incubation temperatures. Similar studies in a minced defatted pasteurised pork slurry containing 1·8% or 3·5% NaCl (on the water) on growth or toxin production by *Cl. botulinum* types A and B show clearly the additional effects of increasing concentrations of NaNO$_2$ and of reducing the incubation temperature.[42]

One obvious limitation of such laboratory studies is the possibility that the growth medium in which the studies are made may not be representative of the foods in question. In studies on *Cl. perfringens*, growth in fluid thioglycollate medium adjusted with glycerol occurred at lower a_w (0·93) than in that adjusted with sucrose (0·97) or sodium chloride (0·95),[43] and there was some loss of viability of the vegetative inoculum at a_w values below 0·95 in NaCl and sucrose-adjusted media. In a superficially similar study[44] glucose was found to be less inhibitory (growth at $a_w = 0·96$) than NaCl or KCl (no growth at 0·965) but growth was only determined optically, and the choice of fluid thioglycollate medium can be criticised for studies of spore germination and outgrowth since thioglycollate is inhibitory to clostridia in certain media.[45] In these studies on *Cl. perfringens* insufficient attention has been paid to the effects of pH and reduced incubation temperature and in most cases the duration of incubation is unrealistically short in industrial terms. Difficulties in measuring redox-potential (*Eh*) deter many workers, but the possible effect of *Eh* on the limiting a_w for growth should not be overlooked.[46] The significant problems with most of the above studies, however, are the relatively small number of strains of *Cl. botulinum* and *Cl. perfringens* which have been examined, and the question of whether the properties of these 'laboratory' strains are representative of those of strains occurring naturally.

The obvious conclusion from the above is that control of clostridial growth is a complex interaction of many factors including pH, incubation temperature and a_w (dependent on the solute used). It may also be important whether the a_w is achieved by adsorption or desorption.[47] Further investigations in this area should not disregard the clostridia, particularly since the study reporting different growth-limiting a_w's by adsorption and desorption used chicken muscle which is an excellent growth medium for *Cl. perfringens*[48] and, in our experience, *Cl. botulinum*. Superimposed on the pH × temperature × a_w interaction is the additional effect of other chemical additives (*e.g.* nitrite).[42]

Loss of Viability at Low a_{ws}, and the Effects of Damage

The loss of viability of a range of microbes at low a_w is well established,[47] but information on the clostridia is inadequate. Labuza *et al.*[49] quote a report where numbers of *Cl. perfringens* in chicken à la King (a_w 0·85) fell substantially over 3–4 months' storage but they express reservations concerning the adequacy of the data. There was no information on whether *Cl. perfringens* was present as spores or vegetative cells, though the loss of spore viability in such a manner would not be expected.

The recovery of microbes may be affected greatly by damage received during drying[50,51] but detailed investigations of drying damage to clostridia have not been carried out. Clostridial spores damaged by gamma-radiation[52] or by heat[53,54] are known to be more sensitive than undamaged spores to inhibition by NaCl (*i.e.* reduced a_w) but despite extensive investigations, the recovery of clostridial spores, particularly those which have been injured, is poorly understood.[55] The effects of similar damage on the recovery of vegetative cells of *Clostridium* spp. has rarely been examined. A somewhat surprising example was the discovery of 'cold-shock', thought previously only to occur in Gram negative bacteria, in vegetative cells of *Cl. perfringens*.[56,57] Clearly the effects of drying on vegetative cell viability warrant detailed investigation, but care will be necessary in the choice of method and medium for recovery[58] since the recovery of spores of *Cl. perfringens* damaged by heat was reduced by some of the inhibitors used in selective media[59] which have been used to determine numbers of (undamaged?) *Cl. perfringens* in foods.

Possible Abuse

The occurrence of abuse before or after processing is rarely admitted; nevertheless on occasions it happens. Clostridia are likely to be present in all meats, and able to grow unless refrigerated.[60] Storage below 10°C generally suffices to prevent growth of clostridia, including *Cl. perfringens* and *Cl. botulinum* types A and B[61] but growth and toxin production by *Cl. botulinum* type E has been reported below 5°C.[33,62,63] Non-proteolytic strains of *Cl. botulinum* types B and F are also able to produce toxin below 5°C.[64]

Some food components also carry large numbers of clostridia, *e.g.* mushrooms, many vegetables and notably various spices and onion. Should these be incorporated and the mix not dried at once it must obviously be refrigerated. Should *Cl. botulinum* have grown before dehydration, its toxin could be preserved by dehydration. The toxin is sensitive to heat in aqueous systems particularly at acid pH values, but may be protected by food components.[65] In addition spores may contain as much as 500 molecules of toxin per spore, which is more heat resistant than sporangium or released toxin.[66] Titres of toxin often show little or no fall upon storage,[67] hence production of toxin must be consciously avoided.

REFERENCES

1. Scott, W. J. (1953). *Austr. J. biol. Sci.*, **6**, p. 549.
2. Scott, W. J. (1957). *Adv. Fd Res.*, **7**, p. 84.
3. Christian, J. H. B. (1963). *Recent Adv. Fd Sci.*, **3**, p. 248.
4. Vernon, E. and Tillett, H. E. (1974). *Publ. Hlth., Lond.*, **88**, p. 225.
5. Mikkelsen, H. D., Petersen, P. J. and Skovgaard, N. (1962). *Nord. VetMed.*, **14**, p. 200.
6. Genigeorgis, C. (1975). *J. Amer. vet. med. Ass.*, **167**, p. 821.
7. Lamanna, C. (1959). *Science, N.Y.*, **130**, p. 763.
8. Dolman, C. E. and Murakami, L. (1961). *J. inf. Dis.*, **109**, p. 107.
9. Greenberg, R., Tompkin, R. B., Bladel, B. O., Kittaka, R. S. and Anellis, A. (1966). *Appl. Microbiol.*, **14**, p. 789.
10. Taclindo, C., Midura, T., Nygaard, G. S. and Bodily, H. L. (1967). *Appl. Microbiol.*, **15**, p. 426.
11. Insalata, N. F., Witzeman, S. J., Fredericks, G. J. and Sungo, F. C. A. (1969). *Appl. Microbiol.*, **17**, p. 542.
12. Abrahamsson, K. and Riemann, H. (1971). *Appl. Microbiol.*, **21**, p. 543.
13. Roberts, T. A. and Smart, J. L. (1976). *J. Fd Technol.*, in press.
14. Roberts, T. A. and Smart, J. L. (1976). In: *Spores 1976*, ed. J. Wolf, A. N. Barker, D. J. Ellar, G. J. Dring and G. W. Gould, in press.
15. Harmon, S. M., Kautter, D. A. and Peeler, J. T. (1971). *Appl. Microbiol.*, **22**, p. 688.
16. Hauschild, A. H. W. and Hilsheimer, R. (1974). *Appl. Microbiol.*, **27**, p. 521.
17. Handford, P. M. (1974). *J. appl. Bact.*, **37**, p. 559.
18. Matches, J. R., Liston, J. and Curran, D. (1974). *Appl. Microbiol.*, **28**, p. 655.
19. McKillop, E. (1959). *J. Hyg. Camb.*, **57**, p. 30.
20. Hall, H. E. and Angelotti, R. (1965). *Appl. Microbiol.*, **13**, p. 352.
21. Seligman, R. (1973). *Refauh vet.*, **30**, p. 4.
22. Keoseyan, S. A. (1971). *J.A.O.A.C.*, **54**, p. 106.

23. Strong, D. H., Canada, J. C. and Griffiths, B. B. (1963). *Appl. Microbiol.*, **11**, p. 42.
24. Sidorenko, G. I. (1967). *J. Hyg. Epidemiol. Microbiol. Immunol.*, **11**, p. 171.
25. Nakamura, M. and Kelly, K. D. (1968). *J. Fd Sci.*, **33**, p. 424.
26. Gould, G. W., Jones, A. and Wrighton, C. (1968). *J. appl. Bact.*, **31**, p. 357.
27. Troller, J. A. (1973). *J. Milk Fd Technol.*, **36**, p. 276.
28. Brockman, M. (1970). *Fd Technol.*, **24**, p. 896.
29. Baird-Parker, A. C. and Freame, B. (1967). *J. appl. Bact.*, **30**, p. 420.
30. Pedersen, H. O. (1957). *Proc. 2nd Int. Symp. Fd Microbiol.*, Cambridge, England, HMSO, p. 289.
31. Yesair, J. and Cameron, E. J. (1942). *Canner*, **94**, p. 89.
32. Schmidt, C. F. and Segner, W. P. (1964). *Proc. 16th Res. Conf. Amer. Meat Inst. Foundation*, University of Chicago, p. 13.
33. Segner, W. P., Schmidt, C. F. and Boltz, J. K. (1966). *Appl. Microbiol.*, **14**, p. 49.
34. Emodi, A. S. and Lechowich, R. V. (1969). *J. Fd Sci.*, **34**, p. 82.
35. Marshall, B. J., Ohye, D. F. and Christian, J. H. B. (1971). *Appl. Microbiol.*, **21**, p. 363.
36. Ohye, D. F., Christian, J. H. B. and Scott, W. J. (1967). In: 'Botulism 1966', *Proc. 5th Int. Symp. Fd Microbiol.*, Moscow, July 1966, ed. M. Ingram and T. A. Roberts, Chapman & Hall, London, p. 136.
37. Ohye, D. F. and Christian, J. H. B. (1967). In: 'Botulism 1966', *Proc. 5th Int. Symp. Fd Microbiol.*, Moscow, July 1966, ed. M. Ingram and T. A. Roberts, Chapman & Hall, London, p. 217.
38. Riemann, H. (1963). *Fd Technol., Champaign*, **17**, p. 39.
39. Riemann, H., Lee, W. H. and Genegeorgis, C. (1972). *J. Milk Fd Technol.*, **35**, p. 514.
40. Pivnick, H., Barnett, H. W., Nordin, H. R. and Rubin, L. J. (1969). *Can. Inst. Fd. Technol. J.*, **2**, p. 41
41. Roberts, T. A. and Ingram, M. (1973). *J. Fd Technol.*, **8**, p. 467.
42. Roberts, T. A., Jarvis, B. and Rhodes, A. C. (1976). *J. Fd Technol.*, **11**, p. 25.
43. Kang, C. K., Woodburn, M., Pagenkopf, A. and Cheney, R. (1969). *Appl. Microbiol.*, **18**, p. 789.
44. Strong, D. H., Foster, E. M. and Duncan, C. L. (1970). *Appl. Microbiol.*, **19**, p. 980.
45. Hibbert, H. R. and Spencer, R. (1970). *J. Hyg. Camb.*, **68**, p. 131.
46. Mead, G. C. (1969). *J. appl. Bact.*, **32**, p. 468.
47. Acott, K. M. and Labuza, T. P. (1975). *J. Fd Technol.*, **10**, p. 603.
48. Mead, G. C. (1969). *J. appl. Bact.*, **32**, p. 86.
49. Labuza, T. P., Cassil, S. and Sinskey, A. J. (1972). *J. Fd Sci.*, **37**, p. 160.
50. Lewicki, P. P. and Silverman, G. J. (1969). In: 'The Microbiology of Dried Foods', *Proc. 6th Int. Symp. Fd Microbiol.*, Bilthoven, The Netherlands, June, 1968, ed. E. H. Kampelmacher, M. Ingram and D. A. Mossel, Int. Assoc. Microbiological Socs., p. 106.

51. Ray, B., Jezeski, J. J. and Busta, F. F. (1971). *Appl. Microbiol.*, **22**, p. 184.
52. Roberts, T. A., Ditchett, P. J. and Ingram, M. (1965). *J. appl. Bact.*, **28**, p. 336.
53. Roberts, T. A. and Ingram, M. (1966). *J. Fd Technol.*, **1**, p. 147.
54. Roberts, T. A., Gilbert, R. J. and Ingram, M. (1966). *J. appl. Bact.*, **29**, p. 549.
55. Roberts, T. A. (1970). *J. appl. Bact.*, **33**, p. 74.
56. Traci, P. A. and Duncan, C. L. (1974). *Appl. Microbiol.*, **28**, p. 815.
57. El Sanousi, S. M. (1975). Ph.D. Thesis, University of Bristol.
58. Sutton, R. G. A. and Hobbs, B. C. (1969). In: 'The Microbiology of Dried Foods', *Proc. 6th Int. Symp. Fd Microbiol.*, Bilthoven, The Netherlands, June, 1968, ed. E. H. Kampelmacher, M. Ingram and D. A. A. Mossel, Int. Assoc. Microbiological Socs., p. 243.
59. Barach, J. T., Adams, D. M. and Speck, M. L. (1974). *Appl. Microbiol.*, **28**, p. 793.
60. Roberts, T. A. and Hobbs, G. (1968). *J. appl. Bact.*, **31**, p. 75.
61. Ohye, D. J. and Scott, W. J. (1953). *Austr. J. biol. Sci.*, **6**, p. 178.
62. Schmidt, C. F., Lechowich, R. V. and Folinazzo, J. F. (1961). *J. Fd Sci.*, **26**, p. 626.
63. Abrahamsson, K., Gullmar, B. and Molin, N. (1966). *Can. J. Microbiol.*, **12**, p. 385.
64. Eklund, M. W., Wieler, D. I. and Poysky, F. T. (1967). *J. Bact.*, **93**, p. 1461.
65. Riemann, H. (1969). In: *Food-borne Infections and Intoxications*, ed. H. Riemann, Academic Press, p. 291.
66. Grecz, N. and Lin, C. A. (1967). In: *Botulism 1966*, ed. M. Ingram and T. A. Roberts, Chapman & Hall, London, p. 302.
67. Wagenaar, R. O. and Dack, G. M. (1958). *J. Dairy Sci.*, **41**, 1182.

DISCUSSION

Chairman: What is in fact happening in a situation like this where you have a combination of preservative agents which do not allow growth for a period as long as 6 months?

Roberts: Where you are putting in a large number of spores, you could argue that the germination times are distributed in some fashion, and those that germinate easily will germinate first. Initially a few will germinate, and then the majority, and you start getting an occasional positive result. It is extremely difficult to know when to stop. In fact, you could argue that 6 months isn't long enough. But I really think 6 months is unworkable when you start doing as many experiments as we are doing now, and I'm thinking very seriously of cutting it down to 3 months.

Jarvis: There are vast differences between the results you get in 3 months and the results you get in 6 months, so I would be very unhappy about cutting down from 6 to 3; if anything, I would prefer to extend from 6 to 12, but we just haven't got the space or the facilities to do this.

Roberts: We are both making a case for bigger laboratories and more staff!

How to control the temperature can be a very serious problem. We've now got very carefully-controlled constant temperature rooms, in which the temperature is monitored constantly through a computer, and if the temperature in the sample bottle varies more than $\pm 0.3°C$, the computer makes noises. Of course, if this happens on a Friday night, you could ruin a lot of work by Monday morning.

Chairman: The important commercial situation here is that cans can stay in a distribution chain, or in someone's shop, for well over a year. Can one predict from the shorter time what would happen over a longer time?

Roberts: We are hoping in the end to be able to do this. We have got some idea, but the answer's not quite right.

Covell: Can you comment on what is the effect of inoculum size on the recent studies you have carried out?

Roberts: We have deliberately chosen small inoculum levels. We are using two different levels in these experiments; we initially did some work using very high levels because we wanted some rough answers quickly. But at present we put in 1000, or 10 per bottle (which isn't very many because that is 10 cells in 28 grammes of slurry). I don't really think we can get much lower than this without running into problems.

Covell: This would still be a considerably higher level than one would get in a commercial situation.

Roberts: Yes. But out of many thousands of cans of ham, there will be quite a number that will contain a few *Cl. botulinum* spores. In fact, if one really studied this, the results could be surprising.

Jarvis: Some of the work we've been doing recently using this meat system inoculated with botulinum, and looking at different fat levels, but keeping the salt-on-water content constant, has shown apparent effects of fat in reducing the incidence of toxigenicity. We can't explain this.

Roberts: You could argue that the more rancid the fat the better, because a lot of the compounds in rancid fat will inhibit germination!

We are just mentioning more and more factors that should be taken into account. In any model we take, we have a formula which is pH by water activity by nitrite (in a ham situation), and we've literally had a formula from the first diagram I showed you. At various values if the answer comes up positive it means that *Cl. botulinum* would grow, and if the answer comes up negative it means that it wouldn't. The same sort of thing can be done with the other data; you can choose an arbitrary incubation time like 3 months; take fat into account, if you like—ours has been standardised at 5% fat. As people do more work, so the formulae will get bigger and bigger, and this is what I mean by a model which will predict whether or not microbes will grow.

Davies: Since we're concerned here with IMF which are expected to have a very long shelf life, and therefore will be around for years possibly before being consumed, I wonder about the currently quoted a_w limitations on botulinum and on perfringens, and whether those original experiments took time-scale into account?

Roberts: The short answer is that that is most unlikely. Most of those experiments were for a very short incubation period, a fortnight probably being the longest. But now people are beginning to do these experiments.

While I am not mistrusting the early work, it is very difficult to simulate the conditions in which they did their experiments, and one sometimes questions exactly what they had in their system. But nevertheless the new data coincide rather well with the old data.

Jarvis: We have some work under way at the present time on the interaction of pH and water activity in a food system with botulinum. Certainly the critical levels of water activity, after the best part of a year's incubation, appear to be very similar to the levels which have been published previously.

Roberts: I'm not by any means an expert on IMF, nor on long-term stability and storage conditions in industry, but I think one must be very careful about 'abuse'. First of all one's got to have the proper sort of starting material—for example, it would be unwise to use prime grade beef, chicken or whatever, and then mix in onion. I can literally use onion powder as a source of spores. I can get powdered onion that contains 10^8 spores per gramme. So if you've got a product which contains 99% prime beef, and then you add 1% onion, you are really just pouring in spores.

Then at the end of this, you have a product which is undoubtedly very stable but what about abusive storage conditions or surface condensation? The spores will have survived—no doubt at all about this, and if a toxin producer has grown during preparation, *e.g.* if there hasn't been much heat processing that toxin will also be preserved.

Sinskey: Are the effects of water activity on germination irreversible or reversible? That is, if I have spores that are inhibited from germination at 0·937 water activity, and I stop germination, but I then take these out and put them in a water activity of 0·98, will they germinate?

Roberts: Yes, you can have spores that are inhibited in one system, and if you take them out and put them in a system where they will germinate, then they will germinate.

Sinskey: Is this also true for the glycerol situation?

Roberts: Yes. These spores do not die if you inhibit germination, they just sit there, viable but not germinating.

Sinskey: Is this also true for growth?

Roberts: I don't know that anyone has looked at this detail, to be honest. If you ask me about the vegetative cells, I'm not quite sure what I would say, because it would depend on something other than water activity. I don't think the water activity itself is lethal to vegetative cells, but they may be in a condition where something else is lethal to them. I can't answer that part of the question.

15

The Safety of Intermediate Moisture Foods with Respect to Salmonella

JANET E. L. CORRY

Metropolitan Police Forensic Science Laboratory,
109 Lambeth Road, London, England

ABSTRACT

Salmonellae have been isolated from many of the ingredients of intermediate moisture foods and confectionery. The moisture relations of these foods are such that multiplication of salmonellae cannot occur, but their resistance to heating is greatly increased, and they may persist in dry and intermediate moisture foods for long periods, and cause outbreaks of food poisoning.

The problem of eliminating salmonellae from the individual ingredients and from final products, and possible modifications of formulae for intermediate moisture foods that would minimise salmonella heat resistance, are discussed.

INTRODUCTION

A great deal of attention has been paid during the last 35 years by food microbiologists, veterinarians and epidemiologists to the problem of food-borne salmonellosis. Many measures have been taken to control their spread, epidemiological studies are legion, and the numbers of suggested methods for their detection and isolation must exceed those for any other group of micro-organisms. Yet in spite of this the problem seems to loom as large as ever. The latest published figures for England and Wales[1] (Table 1) show no reduction in the numbers of food poisoning cases due to salmonellae. For the years 1969–1973 approximately 80% of all food poisoning cases of bacterial origin were caused by salmonellae, and about one third of these were due to *Salmonella typhimurium*. In fact the picture may not be quite as gloomy as it appears, since the figures depend on the numbers of *reported* cases for which a causative organism has been found, and may well reflect improved reporting and detection rather than increased incidence. The appearance in the

TABLE 1

Total cases according to year and causal agent (1969–73) (From Vernon and Tillett 1974.[1])

Causal agent	1969	1970	1971	1972	1973[a]
Salmonella typhimurium	1 892	2 396	2 691	2 043	2 367
	(23·1%)	(27·8%)	(33·3%)	(33·9%)	(27·6%)
Other salmonellas	4 384	4 452	4 093	2 806	4 506
	(53·4%)	(51·6%)	(50·7%)	(46·6%)	(52·6%)
Staphylococci	397	523	302	116	168
	(4·8%)	(6·1%)	(3·7%)	(1·9%)	(2·0%)
Clostridium welchii	1 534	1 263	978	1 026	1 311
	(18·7%)	(14·6%)	(12·1%)	(17·0%)	(15·3%)
Bacillus cereus	—	—	15	16	61
			(0·2%)	(0·3%)	(0·7%)
Escherichia coli	—	—	—	—	141
					(1·6%)
Vibrio parahaemolyticus	—	—	—	13	17
				(0·2%)	(0·2%)
Total	8 207	8 634	8 079	6 020	8 571
	(100%)	(100%)	(100%)	(100%)	(100%)

[a] Provisional returns.

figures for 1971–1973 of groups of organisms not previously implicated as causes of food poisoning (*Bacillus cereus*, *Escherichia coli* and *Vibrio parahaemolyticus*) is another indication of the improved methods of detection and reporting. However, there are undoubtedly still many cases of salmonella infection every year that are not reported. On the other hand, more widespread application of intensive rearing techniques tends to encourage the spread of infections due to the more species-specific serotypes, such as *Salmonella dublin* and *S. typhimurium* in cattle and *S. typhimurium* in poultry, and the spread of more exotic serotypes from imported animal feeds, all of which tend to be reflected in human infections.[2,3]

The purpose of this contribution is to discuss salmonellae with particular reference to intermediate moisture foods (IMF). Little has been published specifically on IMF, but problems in the elimination of salmonellae from the ingredients of IMF, and in particular the effects of the water relations of IMF, and the solutes that may be present, will be discussed.

CHARACTERISTICS OF INTERMEDIATE MOISTURE FOODS

No doubt many other better-qualified contributors to this symposium will discuss the concept of IMF in detail, but a brief definition seems necessary before their relations with salmonellae can be adequately discussed.

Water Activity

A survey of the literature has shown considerable divergence of opinion as to the water activity (a_w) range of IMF. It has been defined as: 0·70–0·85,[4] 0·60–0·85,[5] 0·70–0·90,[6] 0·60–0·90[7] and even 0·20–0·75.[8] The last definition would exclude almost all foods generally considered to be IMF and include almost all dried foods. The range of 0·70–0·90 seems a reasonable definition since below a_w 0·70 foods are stable for considerable lengths of time with respect to microbial spoilage and can essentially be classified as 'dry', while an a_w of 0·90 or below inhibits growth and toxin production by the majority of bacteria.[9–13] However, this a_w range is not sufficient to prevent the growth, and perhaps mycotoxin production by a number of microfungi unless antifungal agents are incorporated.[14,15] Halophilic bacteria may grow in salt-containing IMF. Salmonellae have not been observed to multiply between any of the a_w limits mentioned above. The lower a_w limit for growth of salmonellae falls between a_w 0·95 and a_w 0·92, depending on the strain and the method of controlling the a_w level, *e.g.* the solute added to the growth medium.[16–19] When temperature or pH are not optimum, or in the presence of inhibitors such as lactic or fatty acids or NaCl, the limiting a_w for growth may be even higher.[20]

Types of Foods and Ingredients

Traditional IMF include jams and some confectionery and cakes, some sausages and cheeses, and dried and salted meat and fish.

The newly-developed IMF usually contain a number of different ingredients (meat or meat products, dried skimmed milk, cereal, etc., with relatively high concentrations of sugars (sucrose, glucose, fructose) and polyols such as glycerol and sorbitol, and lower concentrations of NaCl, antimycotics such as sorbate and propylene glycol, and sometimes antioxidants). There is no reason why a wide variety of other ingredients should not be used, however. New IMF usually have an a_w value in the range 0·75–0·85[21,22,6] and are intended, as are many traditional IMF, to be consumed without further cooking, so that any salmonellae present will be consumed, and salmonellae have been detected in many of their ingredients (*see* next section).

The problem of salmonellae in IMF can be seen from the above to be primarily one of survival and persistence rather than growth, although there is a possibility of multiplication during drying processes, for instance in the early stages of cheese-making or during the fermentation of sausage or the drying of meat or fish, if the temperature and other factors are favourable.

PRINCIPAL SOURCES OF SALMONELLAE

These include all substances of animal origin such as egg, meat and milk products or by-products, but vegetable-derived foods cannot be assumed to be free of salmonellae either. Desiccated coconut,[23] copra,[24] cocoa beans[25] (and cocoa powder) and even oil seeds[24] can harbour salmonellae. In these cases contamination occurs because of unhygienic conditions during harvesting, processing or storage—usually due to contamination from the faeces of humans, farm animals, birds or rodents. The problem is made worse if salmonellae are able to multiply in the food, as can happen with coconuts before drying,[26] or if processing machinery becomes contaminated and continuously inoculates fresh batches of product. Fortunately contamination of grains and flour is rare.[23,27,28] Fish (and fish products) are not considered to be natural reservoirs of salmonellae, but may be contaminated if caught in sewage-polluted water, or may become contaminated during processing, as with foods of vegetable origin. Imported fish meal for animal feeds has frequently been found to contain salmonellae.[29,30]

MINIMAL INFECTIOUS DOSE

Although one or a few typhoid organisms are thought to be sufficient to cause illness in man, it is generally believed that much higher numbers of other salmonella serotypes are required to cause food poisoning. McCullough and Eisele in 1951[31-33] found that the numbers of cells required to cause symptoms in prisoners varied from 0·59 to 44·5 million, depending on the strain of salmonella and the individual, although as few as 12 000 could result in temporary excretion of salmonellae. Investigations of a recent outbreak of food poisoning due to salmonellae from chocolate balls has indicated that comparatively low numbers of *S. eastbourne* were probably present (2–9 per ball).[34] Almost half the affected individuals in this outbreak were children aged 1–4 years,[34] which may reflect their lower resistance to infection with small numbers of salmonellae. Also there is evidence that when taken on an empty stomach, low numbers of salmonellae can be infective.[35] Chocolate is frequently consumed between meals, when the stomach is empty, and IMF 'snack' foods would probably have a similar consumption pattern.

The risk of infection of other foods and subsequent multiplication remains, even when the food in question (IMF or dried food) is unable to support the growth of salmonellae. It is therefore undesirable for any salmonellae to be present in a food, both because other foods may be contaminated and because even low numbers may cause illness (either directly by ingestion, or via another person who may be subclinically infected and merely excrete the organisms temporarily).

METHODS OF DETECTING SALMONELLAE

A wide variety of methods for the detection and isolation of salmonellae from foods have been developed, many from media originally intended to isolate salmonellae from faeces (*e.g. see* Corry[36]). Acceptable methods for the examination of foods are those drafted by the International Standardisation Organisation (*see* Schothorst and Leusden[37]) and those of Thatcher and Clark.[38] The advantages of one combination of isolation media over another will not be discussed here; many factors influence the numbers of salmonellae isolated: the use of more than one method, the temperature of incubation, the time(s) of subculture, the size of sample, the numbers of replicates and the skill of the operator.

Use of a non-selective 'pre-enrichment' medium (*e.g.* lactose broth) when isolating salmonellae from dried foods was recommended some years ago by several workers.[39-42] Pre-enrichment of suitable foods can even be carried out by incubation of a suspension of the food in distilled water.[42] After incubation the pre-enrichment medium is normally subcultured into a selective liquid enrichment medium and sometimes directly on to a solid selective medium. 'Pre-enrichment' is something of a misnomer since numbers of salmonellae in non-selective liquid media often increase during growth relative to other organisms.[43] Another benefit of 'pre-enrichment', which has been more wisely appreciated in the last few years is that sublethally-damaged cells survive better in media without selective agents.[44-48] Brilliant green, selenite, tetrathionate, bile salts and deoxycholate can all be lethal to damaged salmonellae. Incubation at 43° frequently increases lethality.[44] Cells may be sublethally damaged by many different agents, including drying, heating, radiation, chemicals and even senescence.

Media designed specifically to resuscitate differ from non-selective pre-enrichment media in that they are designed to allow repair rather than multiplication. The time required for repair to be completed (assessed by comparison of numbers of viable organisms counted on a selective and a non-selective solid medium, neither of which are inhibitory to undamaged cells) depends to some extent on the selective medium employed—for instance salmonellae recover the ability to grow on violet red bile agar more quickly than on brilliant green agar.[45,48]

There is also evidence from the work of Gomez and co-workers[49] and Wilson and Davies[50] that some non-essential nutrients can have a lethal effect on heat-damaged salmonellae, and that a 'minimal medium' rather than one rich in nutrients should be used for resuscitation. Similar effects may occur with cells damaged by other factors.

A related factor which may be important in the isolation of damaged salmonellae from IMF and dried foods is the effect of osmotic shock. I obtained higher recoveries of heat-damaged salmonellae from high osmotic-pressure substrates using a diluent and plating medium containing 20% (w/v) sucrose than in media without added sucrose, although recovery of unheated cells from the same substrate was unaffected.[51] Slow rehydration of freeze-dried cells has been found to increase viability.[52] Further studies, particularly with naturally-contaminated IMF and dried foods, are needed. (The effect of osmotic shock on salmonellae should also be borne in mind when inoculating salmonellae experimentally into high osmotic pressure media—particularly if the media are also hot (when carrying out heat resistance tests.) There is some evidence that salmonellae (and yeasts) subjected to rapid increases in temperature and osmotic pressure simultaneously are less heat resistant than those where the cells are placed in high osmotic pressure media prior to heating (cf. studies of Corry[53,51] and Gibson[54]).

Finally, it should not be forgotten that an effective method of sampling is required if salmonellae are to be detected, because they are frequently very unevenly distributed within a consignment—*see* Ingram *et al.*[55] and Mossel and Shennan.[56]

MEASURES FOR THE ERADICATION OF SALMONELLAE FROM FOODS

Heating and other methods of eliminating salmonellae from human foods should be the second and not the first line of defence. Much can still be done to control numbers of salmonellae in foods by taking measures to break the cycle of salmonella infection. Compulsory monitoring and, if necessary, sterilisation of animal feeds in Denmark has markedly reduced the incidence in pigs of the exotic serotypes of *Salmonella* associated with these feeds,[24,57] and similar measures in Britain would be beneficial. A step in this direction was taken when it was made obligatory to sterilise all meat not fit for human consumption.[58] The Zoonoses Order (1975)[59] which made salmonella isolations from a wide variety of animals notifiable and authorised investigation and, if necessary, measures to protect human health, should help combat the spread of infection between animals, and hence to humans. The effectiveness of legislation depends, however, on the effectiveness of its enforcement. Also animals (and humans) are frequently treated for their symptoms, without any isolation of causative organisms, salmonellae or otherwise, being attempted.

Elimination of Salmonellae from High a_w Foods

When treatment of foods is necessary this should be carried out wherever possible before foods are dried or incorporated into IMF. This is because salmonellae, in common with other micro-organisms, have a much greater resistance (particularly to heat) in dry situations. At high a_w levels (*e.g.* in fresh meat) cooking should be sufficient to kill salmonellae. These organisms are more sensitive than many other groups of organisms to heating.

Regulations in this country requiring pasteurisation of liquid egg[60] have undoubtedly reduced numbers of food poisoning cases due to consumption of commercially-produced egg-containing foods.[3] Treatment of whole liquid egg at 64·4° (Shrimpton *et al.*[61]) or of egg albumen at 57·2° (Corry and Barnes[62]) for 2·5 min appears to be effective in eliminating salmonellae. Pasteurisation of milk (60° for 30 min) is more than sufficient to eliminate salmonellae, and forbidding completely the sale of unpasteurised milk and cream would prevent outbreaks of salmonella infection caused by milk from cows that can be symptomless excretors of salmonellae.[2]

In spite of the ease with which salmonellae are killed during cooking, a high proportion of cases of salmonella food poisoning have been attributed to poultry. (52% of the identified sources of salmonellae outbreaks in England and Wales from 1969 to 1972 were poultry or poultry products.[1]) This appears to be caused by contamination from the raw to the cooked product (post-process contamination) rather than survival of the cooking process, although this also can occur, particularly in catering-size turkeys or in-adequately-thawed birds.[3]

An effective alternative to heating would be to use gamma radiation pasteurisation to eliminate salmonellae. The advantages of this method are that it can be used on frozen products without prior thawing, and the relatively low doses required to eliminate sal-monellae have little organoleptic effect (particularly with frozen products).[63-66] The necessity of applying for exemption as laid down by the Statutory Instrument of 1969,[67] which depends on the demonstration that the irradiated food contains no mutagenic or cytotoxic agents, and perhaps the cost, may explain why this method has not yet been employed commercially for the pasteurisation of food. Irradiation of food before it reached the kitchen would also have the advantage of reducing the risks of cross contamination during preparation.

Death of Salmonellae During Drying

Since salmonellae are relatively sensitive organisms (Gram positive cocci, bacterial spores and a number of other organisms are much more resistant) it might be thought that the drying process and the heat applied during the drying of egg, milk or other products would be sufficient to eliminate them. Unfortunately, this does not appear to be the case. Salmonellae have frequently been isolated from spray-dried milk and egg (*e.g.* Report, 1947;[68] Collins *et al.*[69]), and although spray drying does reduce numbers of contaminating salmonellae substantially, it cannot be relied upon to eliminate them completely, even when post-process contamination is prevented.[68, 70–72] Similar results were obtained when survival of salmonellae in freeze-dried chicken was studied.[73] This demonstrates the advantage of pasteurisation prior to drying. Freezing, similarly, kills some but not all salmonellae. It is significant that Enkiri and Alford[74] observed that salmonellae which were more resistant to drying and freezing were also more frequently the cause of food poisoning.

Elimination of Salmonellae from Dried Foods

In spite of all precautions salmonellae may be found in dry products and they have been known to persist for as long as 3 years.[75] Usually they die off slowly during storage, but this mechanism cannot be relied upon to make feeds safe.[76,77] Storage at elevated temperature results in a higher death rate, although this may result in unacceptable changes in organoleptic or functional properties in some products.[78,79] Practical investigations on survival of salmonellae in heated dried foods and animal feeds have indicated that the death rate increases as the moisture level (or a_w) is increased.[80–83] The upper limit of a_w for treatment is about 0·95 when the temperature is below about 50°, since the salmonellae would be able to multiply at higher a_w levels. Observations on heat resistance in dried foods agree quite well with those obtained for salmonellae freeze-dried and equilibrated to a range of relative humidities,[84] as well as bacterial spores similarly treated.[85] Heat resistance in these systems increases as a_w level is reduced, reaching a maximum between a_w 0·0 and 0·4. The time required to eliminate salmonellae from dried foods depends on the temperature of storage and probably on the nature of the food itself, as well as its water relations, so that investigations may be necessary to determine the treatment required for each product. Heating and pelleting techniques for dried animal feeds

appear to be effective in eliminating salmonellae in most circumstances,[56,57,86] although high numbers of salmonellae might not all
be killed, and high fat-containing feeds have been found to require
greater heat treatment.[87,88] Cane *et al.*[88] stated that 'expansion
extruded' pelleted feed was freed of salmonellae when treated at
93–121° for 45–60 s at 25–35% moisture, but not when 'pelleted
extruded' at 71–100° for 2–16 s at 11–19% moisture. Riemann[80]
found a 10-fold reduction after heating bone meal at a_w 0·99 (13%
w/v water) at 55° for 40 min, and the same heating time at a_w 0·77
(7% w/v water) required a temperature of 75° to achieve the same kill.

Contamination of cocoa beans with salmonellae has been implicated as the original source of infection in chocolate that caused
widespread food-poisoning during 1974 in North America.[25,34,89]
Even the heat during the 'conching' process does not destroy
salmonellae in cocoa beans.[90] Salmonellae in milk chocolate have *D*
values (decimal reduction times: time to reduce the population to
one tenth of its original numbers) of 12–20 h at 71°.[91,92] The a_w
level of chocolate is in the region 0·3–0·4,[93] and the *D*-value at 71°
at $a_w \simeq 1·0$ would be only a few fractions of a second. It may be that
the high levels of fat in chocolate also contribute to the increased
heat resistance.[94] As well as being extraordinarily heat resistant,
salmonellae can persist in chocolate for many months.[34,93] The
exceptional problems caused by salmonellae in chocolate illustrate
again the advantage of taking measures to remove these organisms
before the beans are used in production. This might be achieved by
steam treatment, or preferably by improved hygienic measures in the
country of origin.

Resistance of vegetative organisms to radiation in dried food is
increased, but the increase does not appear to be as great as with heat
resistance. The effect of drying cells of *E. coli* or *Pseudomonas
aeruginosa* in nutrient broth has been shown to increase radiation
resistance by about 4-fold;[95] frozen cells have a similarly increased
radiation resistance. There is disagreement as to whether drying
per se increases radiation resistance. Studies with *E. coli* have
indicated maximum X-ray damage to cells with no additives present,
between 70 and 80% relative humidity,[96] while another study
indicated that a variety of sporing and vegetative organisms were not
protected by drying in the absence of solutes.[97] Gamma radiation
doses of the order 1 Mrad have been recommended for the treatment
of dry animal feeds to eliminate salmonellae.[98,99]

Survival of Salmonellae in Traditional IMF

The literature reviewed by Mossel in 1963[100] indicated that salmonellae were able to persist in many of the traditional IMF, as they do in dried foods, and publications since have confirmed these conclusions. A number of studies during production of cheese[101-103] and fermented sausages[104-106] have shown that numbers of salmonellae usually decline during fermentation and subsequently. The rate of death depends on a complex interaction of temperature (as with dried foods the death rate increases as the temperature of storage is increased),[103] pH (and type of acid),[107,108] a_w, NaCl concentration,[109] and other factors such as competing flora,[103,106] smoking[106] and salmonella serotype.[105] These effects cannot be relied upon to eliminate salmonellae, although outbreaks of salmonella food poisoning from matured cheese and fermented sausages are rare.

The Survival of Salmonellae in New IMF

Most of the new IMF differ from the traditional types because they contain high concentrations of non-ionic solutes at neutral pH, in combination with ingredients that can be frequently contaminated with salmonellae. As with the dried foods, the salmonellae would not multiply, but there is evidence that they could persist for long periods. They have been shown to survive for over a year at 5° in concentrated solutions of sucrose (up to 66% w/w) and in solutions of other sugars and polyols,[51] and in 20% NaCl in nutrient broth for over 70 days at 5° and for up to 30 days at 20°.[110] No studies have been reported on salmonella survival during storage of high-solute containing IMF. Heating fermented sausages or cheese is not a practicable procedure, but might be used to free new IMF of contaminating salmonellae.

Heat Resistance of Salmonellae in the Presence of High Levels of Solutes

Results of determinations of heat resistance in dried foods indicated that a_w was the most important factor in determining survival.[80-83] Growth studies had also indicated that the a_w level, rather that the solute present was the most important factor in determining whether or not micro-organisms would be able to grow.[9,10] However, studies of heat resistance of salmonellae and other micro-organisms showed that very big differences in heat resistance existed when cells were heated in different solutes at the same a_w level.[50,111-113]

Results of studies at Leatherhead[50,114] on salmonellae showed that heat resistance at 65° was increased in concentrated solute solutions in the order sucrose > glucose > sorbitol > fructose > glycerol, and that this relationship held whether resistance at equivalent a_w or % (w/w) concentration was compared. There was a straight line relationship between log $D_{65°C}$ and % w/w concentration for all solutes except perhaps glycerol (Fig. 1). Studies by Baird-Parker *et al.*[111] showed that the effect of NaCl in broth on the heat

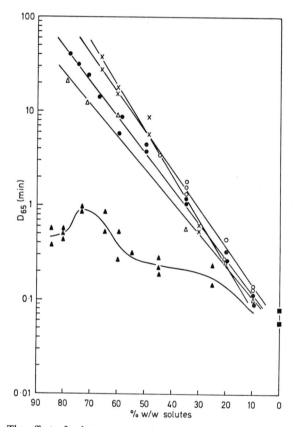

FIG. 1. The effect of solute concentration on the heat resistance of *S. typhimurium* 7M 4987 in 0·1 M phosphate buffer at pH 6·5 with ×, sucrose; ○, glucose; △, fructose; ●, sorbitol; ▲, glycerol; ▣, no added sugar. (From Corry;[51] reproduced by permission of the Society of Applied Bacteriology.)

resistance of salmonellae at a_w levels between 0·98 and 0·85 depended to some extent on strain, but was approximately equivalent to glycerol. Equivalent concentrations (up to 10% w/w) in egg yolk have shown that NaCl is more protective than sucrose.[115] Mould spores have been shown to be more resistant in NaCl than sucrose or glucose.[116]

The increase in heat resistance observed at high solute levels for salmonellae is considerable ($D_{65°C}$ at $a_w \simeq 1·0$ for *S. typhimurium* is about 0·06 min, while in saturated sucrose ($a_w \simeq 0·86$) it is increased to about 30 min, and in 78% (w/w) sorbitol ($a_w \simeq 0·65$) the $D_{65°C}$ approaches 40 min (*see* Table 2)).[51] The heat resistance of strains

TABLE 2

$D_{65°C}$ *values in minutes of salmonellae in various solutes at* 70% *and* 30% (w/w) *concentration in* 0·1M *phosphate buffer pH* 6·5. (*Extrapolated or interpolated where necessary*) (From Corry, 1974[51])

Solute		*Salm. typhimurium* 7M 4987	*Salm. typhimurium* 39H	*Salm. senftenberg* 775W
Sucrose	70%	53	54	43
	30%	0·7	0·8	1·4
Glucose	70%	42	48	17
	30%	0·9	1·1	2·0
Sorbitol	70%	20	NT	17
	30%	0·7	NT	2·1
Fructose	70%	12	NT	8·5
	30%	0·5	NT	1·1
Glycerol	70%	0·9	1	0·7
	30%	0·2	0·3	0·95

NT = Not tested.

with very high heat resistance at high a_w (*e.g. S. senftenberg* 775W) is fortunately not increased in proportion, and they may even be less resistant than other strains at reduced a_w.[51,111]

The differences in heat resistance in solutions of different sugars and polyols can be correlated with the differing degrees of plasmolysis they cause,[51,114] but not with the ability to utilise the solutes.[51,114,117] Preliminary studies using freeze-etch electron microscopy showed that salmonellae in sucrose, glucose, sorbitol and fructose were plasmolysed, while those in glycerol at equivalent a_w were not (*see* Fig. 2(a–c)).[51] Further studies using optical density measurements to

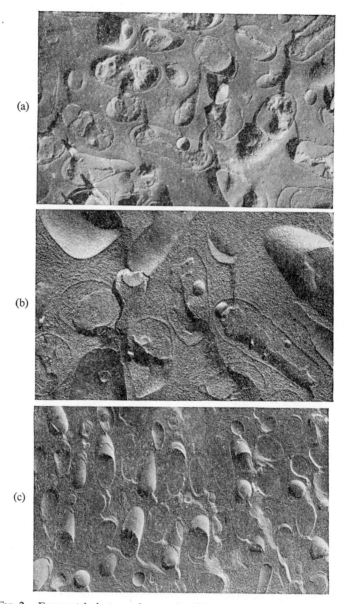

Fig. 2. Freeze-etch electron micrographs of *S. typhimurium* 7 M 4987 in (a) 0·1 M phosphate buffer, pH 6·5 with 48% sucrose ($a_w \simeq 0.95$) ($\times$ 13 500); (b) in buffer with 35% glucose ($a_w \simeq 0.95$) ($\times$ 37 500); (c) in buffer with 30% glycerol ($a_w \simeq 0.92$) ($\times$ 15 000). (Reproduced by permission of Leatherhead Food R.A.)

monitor shrinkage showed that shrinkage (increase in optical density when allowance had been made for the increasing refractive indices of the solutions) could be correlated with the increased heat resistance previously observed (Fig. 3).[114] Heat resistance thus appeared to be increased most when water was removed, and less when it was replaced, or partially replaced by solutes.

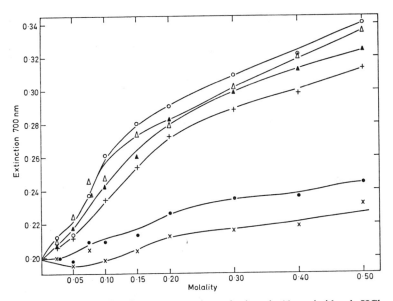

FIG. 3. The effect of various concentrations of solutes in 10 mM imidazole HCl buffer pH 6·5 on the extinction at 700 nm of suspensions of *S. typhimurium* 7 M 4987. ○, sucrose; △, glucose; ▲, fructose; +, sorbitol; ×, glycerol; ●, polyethylene glycol m.w. 200. (From Corry,[114] reproduced by permission of the Society for Applied Bacteriology.)

Reduction of the percent (w/w) solute concentration in IMF (*e.g.* replacing sucrose by glycerol) while keeping a_w level constant would reduce the heat resistance of contaminating salmonellae (provided other serotypes behave in the same way as those so far studied— *S. typhimurium* and *S. senftenberg*). Figure 4 shows the effect of adding increasing proportions of glucose or glycerol to sucrose solutions, while maintaining a constant a_w level. Although the effect of the solutes present is important, there is also an effect of a_w.

Preliminary experiments have indicated that potassium sorbate and propylene glycol (common IMF additives) have a small effect in

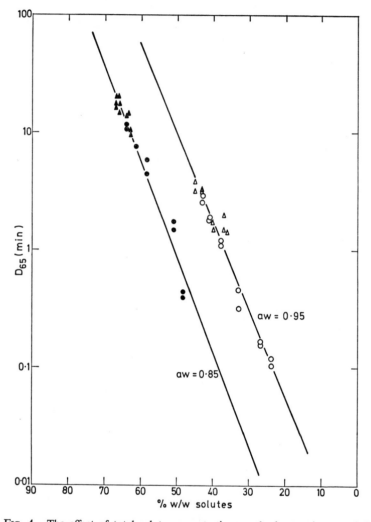

FIG. 4. The effect of total solute concentration on the heat resistance of *S. typhimurium* 7 M 4987 in sucrose/glycerol mixtures at a_w 0·85 (●); a_w 0·95 (○); or in sucrose/glucose mixtures at a_w 0·85 (▲); a_w 0·95 (△). (From Corry,[51] reproduced by permission of the Society for Applied Bacteriology.)

reducing salmonella heat resistance in sucrose solutions (Table 3).[117] One method of increasing heat sensitivity might be to add substances capable of increasing membrane permeability (reducing plasmolysis or shrinkage). However, verification of these results in a practical situation is needed, *e.g.* an IMF containing meat and skimmed milk powder.

TABLE 3

Heat resistance of Salmonella typhimurium 7M 4987 *in* 48% *w/w sucrose solution with* 0·1M *phosphate buffer, pH* 6·5 *with various additions of propylene glycol and potassium sorbate.* (From Corry, 1974[117])

Additions (w/v)		$D_{65°C}$ (min)	Mean $D_{65°C}$ (min)
Propylene glycol	K sorbate		
1. —	—	6·78, 8·33, 5·57	6·89
2. 0·5%	—	4·22, 5·27	4·75
3. 5·0%	—	3·47, 1·38	2·42
4. —	0·3%	5·83	5·83[a]
5. 0·5%	0·3%	4·29, 4·05	4·17
6. 5·0%	0·3%	1·85	1·85[a]

[a] Not a mean, only one $D_{65°C}$ value determined.

The suitability of gamma radiation of new IMF has not been studied, but there is evidence that non-penetrating solutes would be less protective than those, such as glycerol, that permeate the cytoplasm.[96,97] If these effects hold for salmonellae it might be that in low a_w situations, when salmonellae have the greatest heat resistance, their radiation resistance would be increased to a lesser extent, and *vice versa*. In view of the generally smaller effect of drying on radiation resistance, irradiating may be better than heating for ridding low a_w systems of salmonellae. However, radiation may have other undesirable effects, particularly in IMF, such as degrading sugars and polyols to possibly cytotoxic products[118-121] and increasing non-enzymic browning.[122,123]

CONCLUSIONS

The drying process cannot be relied upon to render dried foods free of salmonellae but heat or radiation pasteurisation prior to drying is effective and requires relatively low doses of heat or radiation. Pelleting of dried animal feeds, provided the initial contamination load is low, appears to be successful, although there seems to be a fairly small margin of safety. Care should be taken to ensure that the a_w level is not allowed to fall.

Fermented sausages and hard cheeses are rarely reported as sources of salmonellae, but if the milk or meat is not pasteurised initially the processing and subsequent storage cannot be considered sufficient to kill all salmonellae.

Salmonellae in high levels of sucrose have an especially high heat resistance, and other sugars and polyols have similar, though lesser, effects. It would be difficult to remove salmonellae from high sugar foods (including many new IMF) by heating the final product, and although it may be possible to reduce the resistance of contaminating salmonellae by modifying the IMF formula, it would be preferable to be sure that salmonellae were absent before mixing the ingredients.

REFERENCES

1. Vernon, E. and Tillet, H. E. (1974). *Publ. Hlth, Lond.*, **88**, p. 225.
2. Osborne, A. D. (1976). *Roy. Soc. Hlth J.*, **96**, p. 30.
3. McCoy, J. M. (1976). *Roy. Soc. Hlth J.*, **96**, p. 25.
4. Brockmann, M. C. (1970). *Fd Technol.*, **24**, p. 896.
5. Plitman, M., Park, Y., Gomez, R. and Sinskey, A. J. (1973). *J. Fd Sci.*, **38**, p. 1004.
6. Karel, M. (1973). *CRC Crit. Rev. Fd Technol.*, **3**, p. 329.
7. Collins, J. L., Chen, C. C., Park, J. R., Mundt, J. O., McCarty, I. E. and Johnston, M. R. (1972). *J. Fd Sci.*, **37**, p. 189.
8. Smith, M. C., Huber, C. S. and Heidelbaugh, N. D. (1971). *Aerospace Med.*, **42**, p. 1185.
9. Scott, W. J. (1957). *Adv. Fd Res.*, **7**, p. 83.
10. Corry, J. E. L. (1973). *Adv. Ind. Microbiol.*, **12**, p. 73.
11. Scott, W. J. (1953). *Aust. J. biol. Sci.*, **6**, p. 549.
12. Troller, J. A. (1971). *Appl. Microbiol.*, **21**, p. 345.
13. Troller, J. A. (1972). *Appl. Microbiol.*, **24**, p. 440.
14. Pitt, J. I. (1975). In: *Water Relations of Foods*, ed. R. B. Duckworth, Academic Press, London, p. 273.
15. Corry, J. E. L. (1976). In: *Food and Beverage Mycology*, ed. L. R. Beuchat, AVI, Westport, Connecticut, in press.
16. Christian, J. H. B. and Scott, W. J. (1953). *Aust. J. biol. Sci.*, **6**, p. 565.
17. Christian, J. H. B. (1955). *Aust. J. biol. Sci.*, **8**, p. 490.
18. Clayson, D. H. F. and Blood, R. M. (1957). *J. Sci. Fd Agric.*, **8**, p. 404.

19. Marshall, B. J., Ohye, D. F. and Christian, J. H. B. (1971). *Appl. Microbiol.*, **21**, p. 363.
20. Leistner, L. and Rödel, W. (1975). In: *Water Relations of Foods*, ed. R. B. Duckworth, Academic Press, London, p. 309.
21. Potter, N. N. (1970). *Fd Prod. Dev.*, **4**(7), p. 38.
22. Kaplow, M. (1970). *Fd Technol.*, **24**, p. 889.
23. Blood, R. M. (1969). *Salmonellae in Foods*. BFMIRA Scientific and Technical Surveys no. 60.
24. Watson, W. A. (1976). *Roy. Soc. Hlth J.*, **69**, p. 21.
25. Craven, P. C., Mackel, D. C., Baine, W. B., Barker, W. H., Gangarosa, E. J., Goldfield, M., Rosenfeld, H., Altman, R., Lachapelle, G., Davies, J. W. and Swanson, R. C. (1975). *Lancet*, **1**, p. 788.
26. Meediniya, K. (1969). *J. Hyg.*, *Camb.*, **67**, p. 719.
27. Bothast, R. J., Rogers, R. F. and Hesseltine, C. W. (1974). *Cereal Chem.*, **51**, p. 829.
28. Patterson, J. T. (1972). *Rec. Agric. Res.*, **20**, p. 27.
29. Jacobs, J., Guinee, P. A. M., Kampelmacher, E. H. and van Keulen, A. (1963). *Zentbl. VetMed.*, **10**, p. 452.
30. Report (1961). *Mon. Bull. Minist. Hlth*, **20**, p. 73.
31. McCullough, N. B. and Eisele, G. W. (1951). *J. infect. Dis.*, **88**, p. 278.
32. McCullough, N. B. and Eisele, G. W. (1951). *J. infect. Dis.*, **89**, p. 209.
33. McCullough, N. B. and Eisele, G. W. (1951). *J. infect. Dis.*, **89**, p. 259.
34. D'Aoust, J. Y., Aris, B. J., Thisdele, P., Durante, A., Brisson, N., Dragon, D., Lachapelle, G., Johnson, M. and Laidley, R. (1975). *Can. Inst. Fd Sci. Technol. J.*, **8**, p. 181.
35. Mossel, D. A. A. and Oei, H. V. (1975). *Lancet*, **1**, p. 751.
36. Corry, J. E. L. (1970). Resistance and recovery of Salmonellae. M.Sc. Thesis, University of Bristol.
37. Schothorst, M. van and Leusden, F. M. van (1975). *Can. J. Microbiol.*, **21**, p. 1041.
38. Thatcher, F. S. and Clark, D. S. (Eds.) (1968). *Microorganisms in Foods: their Significance and Methods of Enumeration*, University of Toronto Press, Toronto, Ontario.
39. North, W. R. (1961). *Appl. Microbiol.*, **9**, p. 188.
40. McCoy, J. H. (1961). *J. appl. Bact.*, **25**, p. 213.
41. Hobbs, B. C. (1963). *Annls Inst. Pasteur, Paris*, **104**, p. 621.
42. McCoy, J. M. and Spain, G. E. (1969). In: *Isolation Methods for Microbiologists*, ed. D. A. Shapton and G. W. Gould, Society for Applied Bacteriology, Technical Series No. 3, Academic Press, London, p. 17.
43. Thomson, S. (1955). *J. Hyg.*, *Camb.*, **53**, p. 217.
44. Corry, J. E. L., Kitchell, A. G. and Roberts, T. A. (1969). *J. appl. Bact.*, **32**, p. 415.
45. Mossel, D. A. A. and Ratto, M. A. (1970). *Appl. Microbiol.*, **20**, p. 273.
46. Schothorst, M. van and Leusden, F. M. van (1972). *Zentbl. Bakt. Parasitkde Abt. I Orig. A*, **221**, p. 19.
47. Silliker, J. H. and Gabis, D. A. (1973). *Can. J. Microbiol.*, **19**, p. 475.

48. Schothorst, M. van and Leusden, F. M. van (1975). *Zentbl. Bakt. Parasitkde Abt. I Orig. A*, **230**, p. 186.
49. Gomez, R. F., Sinskey, A. J., Davies, R. and Labuza, T. P. (1973). *J. gen. Microbiol.*, **74**, p. 267.
50. Wilson, J. M. and Davies, R. (1976). *J. appl. Bact.*, **40**, p. 365.
51. Corry, J. E. L. (1974). *J. appl. Bact.*, **37**, p. 31.
52. Leach, R. H. and Scott, W. J. (1959). *J. gen. Microbiol.*, **21**, p. 295.
53. Corry, J. E. L. (1976). *J. appl. Bact.*, **40**, p. 277.
54. Gibson, B. (1973). *J. appl. Bact.*, **36**, p. 365.
55. Ingram, M., Bray, D. F., Clark, D. S., Dolman, C. E., Elliot, R. R. and Thatcher, F. S. (Eds.) (1974). *Microorganisms in Foods. II Sampling for Microbiological Analysis*, University of Toronto Press, Toronto, Ontario.
56. Mossel, D. A. A. and Shennan, J. L. (1976). *J. Fd Technol.*, **11**, p. 205.
57. Public Health Laboratory Service Working Group, Skovgaard, N. and Nielsen, B. B. (1972). *J. Hyg., Camb.*, **70**, p. 127.
58. Statutory Instrument no. 871 (1969). *Food and Drugs, Food Hygiene*, The Meat (Sterilisation) Regulations 1969, HMSO, London.
59. Statutory Instrument no. 1030 (1975). *Animals, Diseases of Animals*, The Zoonoses Order 1975, HMSO, London.
60. Statutory Instrument no. 1503 (1963). *Food and Drugs*, The liquid Egg (Pasteurisation) Regulations 1963, HMSO, London.
61. Shrimpton, D. H., Monsey, J. B., Hobbs, B. C. and Smith, M. E. (1962). *J. Hyg., Camb.*, **60**, p. 153.
62. Corry, J. E. L. and Barnes, E. M. (1968). *Brit. Poult. Sci.*, **9**, p. 253.
63. Brooks, J., Hannan, R. S. and Hobbs, B. C. (1959). *Int. J. appl. Radiat. Isotopes*, **6**, p. 149.
64. Comer, A. G., Anderson, G. W. and Garrard, E. H. (1963). *Can. J. Microbiol.*, **9**, p. 321.
65. Ley, F. J., Freeman, B. M. and Hobbs, B. C. (1963). *J. Hyg., Camb.*, **61**, p. 515.
66. Ley, F. J., Kennedy, T. S., Kawashima, K., Roberts, D. and Hobbs, B. C. (1970). *J. Hyg., Camb.*, **68**, p. 293.
67. Statutory Instrument no. 385 (1967). *Food and Drugs Composition*, The Food (Control of Irradiation) Regulations 1967, HMSO, London.
68. Report (1947). 'The bacteriology of spray dried egg with particular reference to food poisoning', *Spec. Rep. Ser. med. Res. Coun.* No. 260, HMSO, London.
69. Collins, R. N., Treger, M. D., Goldsby, J. B., Boring, J. R., Coohon, D. B. and Barr, R. N. (1968). *J. Am. med. Ass.*, **203**, p. 838.
70. Gibbons, N. E. and Moore, R. L. (1944). *Can. J. Res.*, **22**, p. 58.
71. Ingram, M. and Brooks, J. (1952). *J. Roy. sanit. Inst.*, **72**, p. 411.
72. Licari, J. J. and Potter, N. N. (1970). *J. Dairy Sci.*, **53**, p. 865.
73. May, K. N. and Kelly, L. E. (1965). *Appl. Microbiol.*, **13**, p. 340.
74. Enkiri, N. C. and Alford, J. A. (1971). *Appl. Microbiol.*, **21**, p. 381.
75. Miura, S., Sata, G. and Miyamae, T. (1964). *Avian Dis.*, **8**, p. 546.
76. Ribiero, A. M. (1970). *Ann. Inst. Pasteur, Lille*, **21**, p. 255.

77. Ray, B., Jezeski, J. J. and Busta, F. F. (1971). *J. Milk Fd Technol.*, **34**, p. 423.
78. Banwart, G. J. and Ayres, J. C. (1956). *Fd Technol.*, **10**, p. 68.
79. Licari, J. J. and Potter, N. N. (1970). *J. Dairy Sci.*, **53**, p. 871.
80. Riemann, H. (1968). *Appl. Microbiol.*, **16**, p. 1621.
81. Liu, R., Snoeyenbos, G. H. and Carlson, V. L. (1969). *Poult. Sci.*, **48**, p. 1628.
82. Carlson, V. L. and Snoeyenbos, G. H. (1970). *Poult. Sci.*, **49**, p. 71.
83. Christian, J. H. B. and Stewart, B. J. (1973). In: *Microbiological Safety of Food*, ed. B. C. Hobbs and J. H. B. Christian, Academic Press, London.
84. Alderton, G. and Halbrook, W. U. (1973). *Abstr. ann. Meet. Am. Soc. Microbiol.*, **E95**, p. 16.
85. Murrell, W. G. and Scott, W. J. (1966). *J. gen. Microbiol.*, **43**, p. 411.
86. Mossel, D. A. A., Schothorst, M. van and Kampelmacher, E. H. (1967). *J. Sci. Fd Agric.*, **18**, p. 362.
87. Rasmussen *et al.* (1964) op. cit. Cane *et al.* (1973) (Ref. 88).
88. Cane, F. M., Hansen, M., Yoder, R., Lepley, K. and Cox, P. (1973). *Milling*, **155**(1), p. 21.
89. Gershman, M. (1975). *Publ. Hlth Lab.*, **33**, p. 145.
90. Rieschel, H. and Schenkel, J. (1971). *Alimenta*, **10**, p. 57.
91. Goepfert, J. M. and Biggie, R. A. (1968). *Appl. Microbiol.*, **16**, p. 1939.
92. Barrile, J. C. and Cone, J. F. (1970). *Appl. Microbiol.*, **19**, p. 177.
93. Tamminga, S. K., Beumer, R. R., Kampelmacher, E. H. and Leusden, F. M. van (1976). *J. Hyg.*, *Camb.*, **76**, p. 41.
94. Senhaji, A. F. (1973). Protection des micro-organismes par les matières grasses au cours des traitements thermiques. Thése de Docteur-Ingenieur, Université, Paris.
95. Moos, W. S. (1952). *J. Bact.*, **63**, p. 688.
96. Webb, S. J. and Dumasia, M. D. (1964). *Can. J. Microbiol.*, **10**, p. 877.
97. Webb, R. B. (1963). *Radiat. Res.*, **18**, p. 607.
98. Mossel, D. A. A. (1967). In: *Microbiological Problems in Food Preservation*, IAEA, Vienna, p. 15.
99. Epps, N. A. and Idziak, E. S. (1972). *Poult. Sci.*, **51**, p. 277.
100. Mossel, D. A. A. (1963). *Ann. Inst. Pasteur, Paris*, **104**, p. 551.
101. McDonough, F. E., Hargrove, R. E. and Tittsler, R. P. (1967). *J. Milk Fd Technol.*, **30**, p. 354.
102. Goepfert, J. M., Olson, N. F. and Marth, E. H. (1968). *Appl. Microbiol.*, **16**, p. 862.
103. Hargrove, R. E., McDonough, F. E. and Mattingly, W. A. (1969). *J. Milk Fd Technol.*, **32**, p. 480.
104. Goepfert, J. M. and Chung, K. C. (1970). *J. Milk Fd Technol.*, **33**, p. 185.
105. Baran, W. L. and Stevenson, K. E. (1975). *J. Fd Sci.*, **40**, p. 618.
106. Smith, J. L., Palumbo, S. A., Kissinger, J. C. and Huhtanen, C. N. (1975). *J. Milk Fd Technol.*, **38**, p. 150.
107. Goepfert, J. M. and Hicks, R. (1969). *J. Bact.*, **97**, p. 596.
108. Chung, K. C. and Goepfert, J. M. (1970). *J. Fd Sci.*, **35**, p. 326.

236   *Janet E. L. Corry*

109. Alford, J. A. and Palumbo, S. A. (1969). *Appl. Microbiol.*, **17**, p. 528.
110. Blanche Koelensmid, W. A. A. and Rhee, R. van (1964). *Ann. Inst. Pasteur, Lille*, **15**, p. 85.
111. Baird-Parker, A. C., Boothroyd, M. and Jones, E. (1970). *J. appl. Bact.*, **33**, p. 515.
112. Goepfert, J. M., Iskander, I. K. and Amundsen, C. H. (1970). *Appl. Microbiol.*, **19**, p. 429.
113. Härnulv, B. G. and Snygg, B. G. (1972). *J. appl. Bact.*, **35**, p. 615.
114. Corry, J. E. L. (1976). *J. appl. Bact.*, **40**, p. 277.
115. Cotterill, O. J. and Glauert, J. (1969). *Poult. Sci.*, **48**, p. 1156.
116. Doyle, M. P. and Marth, E. H. (1975). *J. Milk Fd Technol.*, **38**, p. 750.
117. Corry, J. E. L. (1974). The effect of sugars and polyols on the heat resistance of Salmonella and osmophilic yeasts. Ph.D. Thesis, University of Surrey.
118. Karel, M. and Proctor, B. E. (1957). *Modern Packaging*, **30**(5), p. 141.
119. Berry, R. J., Hills, P. R. and Trillwood, A. (1965). *Int. J. Radiat. Res.*, **6**, p. 302.
120. De, A. K., Aiyar, A. S. and Sreenivasan, A. (1973). In: *Radiation Preservation of Food*, Symposium, IAEA, Vienna, p. 715.
121. Kawakishi, S., Kito, Y. and Namiki, M. (1973). *Carbohydrate Res.*, **30**, p. 220.
122. Binkley, W. W., Altenburg, M. E. and Wolfrom, M. L. (1972). *Sugar J.*, **34**(12), p. 25.
123. Baraldi, D. (1973). *J. Fd Sci.*, **38**, p. 108.

DISCUSSION

Leistner: Do you think it might be feasible to influence the survival of salmonellae and of *Staph.* at the end of the production of IMF, by holding the products for, let's say, 12 h at 50°C?

Corry: Yes, I think it might be feasible. I don't know what the effect would be on other properties of the food. I would think it might not be desirable.

Roberts: I think this was done for scrambled egg, where they in fact used a rather low temperature for several days, extrapolating your idea even further. It seems to be a process which can work.

Corry: Certainly with egg whites it affected the functional properties. Perhaps with dog food this wouldn't matter very much, but I think with some things it's not a very good idea. Storage at higher temperatures will mean that some organisms may die off more quickly, but not sufficiently reliably to say that if we keep a product for a month, then it will be safe after that. There are all sorts of imponderables.

There have been examples in chick fluff of salmonellae living for 3 years after the original contamination, so I think one needs to be very cautious about this. Of course it may be that the temperature which kills off the salmonellae will allow some other more tolerant organism to grow.

Tompkin: Actually the use of a low temperature for a long time has been used rather extensively in the United States; 140°F for 14 days has been used on dried eggs. There is one product—a dry blend of cornflour and soy flour—that is shipped overseas as part of the aid programme. The USDA monitors that particular product, and if they find salmonellae in it, it states in the regulations that you are to place it at 140° for x number of days and then re-examine it.

Corry: I think this could be a very useful secondary defence, but I think it is more practicable to sterilise the egg—pasteurise it—before it is dried.

Tompkin: It has gone one step further, too. Some companies, which have experience of environmental contamination of equipment, in cases where they have had problems with a recontaminated product, close off a particular room and put heaters in the room, and then let it sit for a day or two till you get 140° or 150°F.

Gardner: One of your slides mentioned carriers of salmonellae. What information do you have regarding frequency of occurrence and the length of time this state may persist?

Corry: I don't know for humans. Perhaps Professor Mossel has some information on this.

Mossel: In humans this may last for years unless properly treated. This is a terrible problem with staff employed in catering. They may contract salmonellosis on their holidays, and come back as carriers. It is a very unpleasant situation both for staff and for employers.

It has been estimated that the frequency varies with individuals and with gastro-intestinal systems, but it is somewhere between 5 and 10% who are at risk, if not actually contaminated.

Jeffery: How pH sensitive are salmonellae?

Corry: They are inhibited somewhere around the region of pH 4·5. It depends on the acid used to govern the pH, and on the temperature at which you store them. Again you get this effect, that if you store them at a higher temperature, they will die off more quickly. They have been found, for instance, in frozen orange juice, which has a very much lower pH, so the lower the temperature you keep them, the more resistant they are to the effect of pH.

Jeffery: This depends on the solutes with them, presumably?

Corry: I should think it probably does, but I haven't come across any work on this. If you had more sodium chloride, yes, but I don't know about other solutes.

16

Do Mycotoxins Present a Potential Hazard for Intermediate Moisture Foods?

B. JARVIS

*Chief Microbiologist, Leatherhead Food R.A.,
Randalls Road, Leatherhead, Surrey, England*

ABSTRACT

At the present time about 200 *microfungi are known to be capable of producing mycotoxins although many species have not been implicated in outbreaks of clinical mycotoxicosis. Although some mycotoxinogenic strains are hygrophilic, most are mesoxerophilic or xerophilic and are therefore able to grow in conditions of reduced water activity* (a_w).
Control of growth of such organisms is dependent in part on the interactions between a_w *and the other physical, chemical and biotic parameters of the microenvironment. In a similar way, mycotoxin production is affected by environmental conditions. This paper explores briefly the factors affecting growth and toxin production by a few mycotoxinogenic fungi and considers the implications for manufactured intermediate moisture foods. Suggestions are made of areas in which research is needed before a definitive answer can be given regarding the potential mycotoxin hazard for such foods.*

INTRODUCTION

The term 'Intermediate Moisture Foods' (IMF) covers a diverse range of stored primary agricultural commodities and manufactured food products in which the water activity (a_w) is restricted by chemical or physical dehydration to lie within the range of a_w 0·60–0·85. Such foods have greater microbiological stability than do fresh perishable foods but, unlike dried foods, they may still be

239

subject to microbiological deterioration. Since the a_w of the products lies below that at which bacterial proliferation will occur (with the exception of a few extreme halophiles) microbial spoilage will be associated with growth of osmophilic yeasts[1] and/or xerophilic microfungi.[2,3]

The growth of many microfungi is now known to be accompanied by the production of metabolites which produce diverse toxic effects in susceptible animal species, including man.[4-8] Such metabolites, known collectively as mycotoxins, range from relatively simple organic molecules (*e.g.* kojic acid) to substituted coumarins (*e.g.* aflatoxins, ochratoxins), scirpenes (*e.g.* fusarenon-X, T-2 toxin), phenolic macrolides (*e.g.* zearalenone (F-2 toxin)) and many other chemical forms.[4] At the present time about 200 microfungi are known to be capable of producing mycotoxins[6,9] although not all myco-toxinogenic organisms have been implicated as aetiological agents of disease other than in laboratory animals. Equally, many fungi long believed to be harmless are now known to be mycotoxinogenic and in the years to come many more will doubtless be shown to produce toxins. The present state of knowledge of the role of mycotoxins in clinical diseases of man, domestic animals and farm livestock has recently been the subject of several excellent appraisals.[5,8]

Since IMF are potentially subject to fungal spoilage and since many common spoilage fungi are potentially mycotoxinogenic it is pertinent to consider whether, and if so to what extent, mycotoxins may present a problem for the development of IMF. The routes by which mycotoxins may contaminate foods have been discussed recently.[6,7] In the present paper consideration will be given only to the consequences of mycotoxin production directly associated with fungal growth on various substrates. Since there is little published information on mycotoxin production on manufactured IMF, examples will be drawn from stored natural products and traditional IMF.

FACTORS AFFECTING GROWTH OF MYCOTOXINOGENIC FUNGI

The growth of any micro-organism is affected by the various physical, chemical and biotic factors associated with the microenvironment, including storage temperature, water activity, solute concentration and type, pH value, nature and concentration of atmospheric gases.[10] Mycotoxinogenic fungi include strains with xerophilic (*i.e.* capable of growth at $a_w < 0.80$), mesoxerophilic (grow at a_w 0.80–0.90) and hygrophilic (minimum $a_w > 0.90$) characteristics[11] of growth. For IMF produced and subsequently stored at a_w values of 0.85 and below, growth of hygrophilic species can be discounted and attention can be directed to the so-called 'storage fungi' capable of growth at reduced a_w values. Examples of such organisms, together

TABLE 1

Xerophilic and mesoxerophilic fungi—their toxins and limiting a_w *levels*
(Data collated from various sources, expecially References 3–5, 9, 11, 12, 14, 30, 31)

Organism	Mycotoxin(s) produced	Limiting a_w level for: Growth	Limiting a_w level for: Toxin production
Aspergillus amstelodami	Unknown	0·70	—
A. chevalieri[a]	Xanthocillin X	0·65	—
A. flavus	{ Aflatoxins	0·78	0·83–0·87
	{ Aspergillic acid		—
A. fumigatus	{ Fumagillin	0·82	—
	{ Gliotoxin		—
A. nidulans[b]	{ Kojic acid	0·78	—
	{ Nidulline		—
A. niger	Oxalic acid	0·88	—
A. ochraceus	{ Ochratoxins	0·76	0·85
	{ Penicillic acid		0·81
A. rubrum	Anthraquinones	0·70	—
A. versicolor	Sterigmatocystin	0·75	—
Penicillium citrinum	Citrinin	0·80	—
P. cyclopium	Penicillic acid	0·81	—
P. expansum	Patulin	0·82	—
P. islandicum	{ Luteoskyrine	0·83	—
	{ Islanditoxin		—
P. martensii	Penicillic acid	0·79	—
P. palitans	Penicillic acid	0·83	—
P. patulans	Patulin	0·81	—
P. puberulum	Penicillic acid	0·81	—
P. viridicatum	{ Ochratoxin	0·81	—
	{ Citrinin		—

— = limiting a_w for toxin production not known.
[a] Ascosporogenic forms properly belong to the genus *Eurotium*.[3]
[b] Ascosporogenic forms properly belong to the genus *Emericella*.[3]

with their associated toxins and the limiting a_w values for growth are presented in Table 1.

As one growth-controlling factor is changed from the optimum, the limits for growth with respect to other factors will also change. This is shown diagrammatically (Fig. 1) with respect to temperature–a_w interactions for *Aspergillus flavus* and *A. chevalieri* growing on a laboratory medium equilibrated to various a_w values.[12] At the

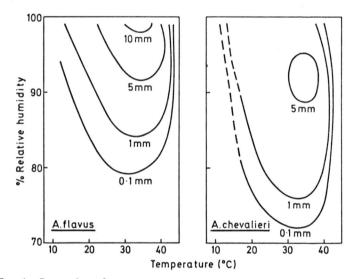

FIG. 1. Interaction of temperature and a_w on rate of growth (mm/day) of *Aspergillus Flavus* and *Aspergillus chevalieri* on laboratory media. (From Ayerst.[12])

optimum temperature of 33°C growth of *A. flavus* occurs at a_w values down to 0·78 but at a lower temperature (*e.g.* 20°C) the growth-limiting a_w is increased to about 0·83. The limiting a_w for germination of conidia or ascospores may be above that for growth, as also may the a_w levels at which spore formation will occur. Similar interactions occur for most micro-organisms and the range of factors which may affect growth in this manner is wide.[10,12−15]

Recent studies of preservative-free IMF model systems[16,17] have shown that growth of mesoxerophilic fungi such as *Aspergillus niger* occurs at a lower a_w level in IMF prepared by desorption than in similar systems produced by freeze drying followed by rehydration to the required a_w level. Since *A. niger* is not xerophilic, these studies might have been better undertaken with a xerophile such as *A. chevalieri.* However, the phenomenon confirms the opinion expressed by Mossel[18] that the term a_w may be misleading and is better replaced by the symbol p_w which takes account of the a_w *per se* and of the nature and concentration of solute.

One factor which affects the growth of microfungi is the presence of mycostatic agents in foods. Most model IMF studied[16] and commercial semi-moist petfoods[19,20] contain sorbic acid (or sorbates) at levels up to 5000 ppm. Other mycostatic agents known to inhibit mycotoxin production include pimaricin[21] and natural inhibitors (*e.g.* cinnamon extract).[22] The use of chemical preservatives in foods is subject to legislative control and may in some instances be undesirable.[15]

OCCURRENCE OF POTENTIAL MYCOTOXINOGENIC FUNGI AND PRODUCTION OF MYCOTOXINS IN LOW a_w FOODS

Many fungi are capable of producing mycotoxins in stored cereals, pulses, staples, oilseeds and nuts.[6,7,10] The predominant mycotoxinogenic storage fungi are strains of *Aspergillus* (and the ascosporogenic forms properly included in the genus *Eurotium*[3]) and *Penicillium*. Important species include members of the *Aspergillus glaucus* group (*e.g. A. chevalieri* and *A. amstelodami*), the *Aspergillus flavus-oryzae* group, *A. ochraceus, Penicillium viridicatum, P. patulum,* etc. Such organisms occur widely on natural products and in soil, air and other environmental samples. Members of the *A. glaucus* group are the most common causes of spoilage in preservative-free IM petfoods and traditional products such as jams, marmalades, sugar confectionery, rich fruit cakes and Christmas puddings. However, at the present time there is no evidence for the production of mycotoxins by these organisms in these products, although many of the strains isolated produce mycotoxins on laboratory media. Organisms such as *Monascus bisporus* (*Xeromyces bisporus*) and *Wallemia sebi* (*Sporendonema sebi*) occur commonly on dried fruits, salted fish products and sweetened condensed milk but are not generally regarded as mycotoxigenic. Indeed, one strain of *W. sebi* isolated from a salt fish product has been shown to be atoxinogenic on laboratory media.[23]

Traditional low a_w fermented meat products such as Cracower and salami, and country-cured hams frequently contain mycotoxinogenic organisms amongst their natural fungal flora.[24-27] Although some mycotoxins are reputedly inactivated by chemical reaction with available sulphydryl groups,[25] other mycotoxins have been detected at various levels in both naturally-contaminated and laboratory-inoculated samples of such meat products.

Modern technological improvements in processing may adversely affect the mycological stability of the products. Such an effect has been observed for continental sausages in which condensation on the surface led to enhanced fungal growth.[28] This was overcome by careful control of both temperature and humidity during the initial ripening process. A similar effect has been observed with certain sugar confectionery products. Drums of the product were traditionally packed in cardboard outers which permitted escape of migrating moisture during initial storage of the product. Introduction of shrink-wrapping in plastic prevented moisture migration from the product and led to a rapid increase in surface a_w with consequent rapid growth of *Aspergillus amstelodami*, *A. chevalieri* and related organisms.

The limiting a_w level for mycotoxin production is frequently above that for growth of fungi[10] and will be further affected by other environmental factors (*vide supra*). There are only limited published data on the limiting a_w values for mycotoxin production, most reports relating growth only to percentage moisture (often on a wet weight basis!). Production of aflatoxin on groundnuts occurs at a_w levels down to 0·83 at about 30°C but the limiting a_w is increased to 0·85–0·87 if competitive fungi are also present.[29] In similar studies using pistachio nuts aflatoxin production occurred only at a_w levels of 0·87 and above.[30] The differences observed in these two studies may reflect the different chemical composition of the two substrates or the differences in the competing mycoflora. On pistachio nuts rapid growth of *Aspergillus amstelodami* occurred at a_w levels of 0·80–0·86 and effectively suppressed growth of inoculated *A. flavus* conidia. Growth of the *A. flavus* occurred to a limited extent at a_w 0·87 but pronounced growth and aflatoxin production occurred only at a_w 0·88 and above. However, in nuts equilibrated to a_w 0·85 and sealed into flasks, metabolic water produced by the growth of *A. amstelodami* raised the a_w, and growth of *A. flavus* ensued with delayed aflatoxin production. By this stage fungal growth was so extensive that the nuts were obviously unfit for consumption.

The interaction of temperature and a_w on the production of penicillic acid and ochratoxin A by *Aspergillus ochraceus* in an animal feed have been reported by Bacon and co-workers.[31] It is noteworthy that at low temperatures penicillic acid was produced at lower a_w levels than was ochratoxin (Table 2). Changes in the microenvironmental conditions may cause changes in metabolic activity which may

TABLE 2

Interaction of a_w *and temperature on growth of* A. ochraceus *and production of penicillic acid and ochratoxin* A (modified from Bacon *et al.*[31])

| Temperature (°C) | Minimum a_w for | | | Optimum a_w for production of | |
| | Growth | Production of | | | |
		Penicillic acid	Ochratoxin A	Penicillic acid	Ochratoxin A
15	0·85	0·85	0·95	>0·99	>0·99
22	0·76	0·81	0·90	0·90	0·95
30	≤0·76[a]	0·81	0·85	0·90	0·95

[a] Lowest a_w value tested.

result in the production of toxins other than that expected from particular strains of fungus. Such a possibility demonstrates the necessity to produce and store IMF in conditions where any fungal growth will be inhibited rather than to rely on marginal inhibition conditions.

WHAT IS THE LIKELIHOOD FOR MYCOTOXIN PRODUCTION IN INTERMEDIATE MOISTURE FOODS?

Although many potentially mycotoxinogenic fungi are capable of growth at the a_w levels of IMF, growth will not necessarily be accompanied by mycotoxin production, especially at the lower a_w levels. By appropriate formulation of foods at low a_w levels, with control of pH value, methods of packaging, etc., and by the use of good quality raw materials with a low incidence of fungal propagules, it should be possible to produce IMF with a low propensity to fungal spoilage. Further control can be achieved by the use of appropriate mycostatic agents although total reliance on chemical inhibitors at relatively high a_w levels may lead to problems of product stability. So far as is known at the present time, mycotoxin production always accompanies overt fungal growth which can therefore serve as an index of both product acceptability and safety. Unfortunately several problems still remain unanswered at the present time. Little is known about the limiting a_w values for production of the majority of mycotoxins and it is conceivable that some may be produced at lower a_w levels than are aflatoxin, ochratoxin or penicillic acid. Studies of the growth of mycotoxinogenic organisms should be integrated with investigations of toxin production using both chemical and biological assays, in order to cover the possibility for production of unexpected toxic metabolites at low a_w levels. Such studies should be undertaken both in laboratory media and on model IMF inoculated with appropriate xerophilic organisms. Such studies should not neglect the interaction of other parameters such as temperature, pH value, gas phase of packaging, etc., and should have the objective of producing background information which is essential for any food manufacturer wishing to produce both shelf-stable and safe IMF.

REFERENCES

1. Tilbury, R. (1976). 'The microbial stability of intermediate moisture foods with respect to yeasts', this volume, p. 138.
2. Seiler, D. (1976). 'The stability of intermediate moisture foods with respect to mould growth', this volume, p. 166.
3. Pitt, J. I. (1975). In: *Water Relations of Foods*, ed. R. B. Duckworth, Academic Press, London, p. 273.
4. Austwick, P. K. C. (1975). *Brit. Med. Bull.*, **31**, p. 222.
5. Jarvis, B. (1972). In: *Health and Food*, ed. G. G. Birch, L. F. Green and L. G. Plaskett, Applied Science Publishers, London, p. 64.
6. Jarvis, B. (1975). In: *Recent Trends in Agriculture, Fisheries and Food*, ed. F. A. Skinner and J. G. Carr, Academic Press, London, p. 251.
7. Jarvis, B. (1975). *Inter. J. environmental Studies*, **8**, p. 187.
8. Moss, M. O. (1975). *Inter. J. environmental Studies*, **8**, p. 165.
9. Moreau, C. (1974). *Moisissures Toxiques dans L'Alimentation*, 2nd edition, Masson et Cie, Paris.
10. Jarvis, B. (1971). *J. appl. Bact.*, **34**, p. 199.
11. Apinis, A. E. (1972). In: *Biodeterioration of Materials*, Vol. 2, ed. A. H. Walters and E. H. Hueck-Van Der Plas, Applied Science Publishers, London, p. 493.

12. Ayerst, G. (1969). *J. stored Prod. Res.*, **5**, p. 127.
13. Mossel, D. A. A. (1971). *J. appl. Bact.*, **34**, p. 95.
14. Heintzeler, I. (1939). *Arch. Mikrobiol.*, **10**, p. 92.
15. Jarvis, B. and Burke, C. S. (1976). In: *Inhibition and Inactivation of Vegetative Microbes*, ed. F. S. Skinner and W. Hugo, Academic Press, London (in press).
16. Labuza, T. P., Cassil, S. and Sinskey, A. J. (1972). *J. Fd. Sci.*, **37**, p. 160.
17. Acott, K. M. and Labuza, T. P. (1975). *J. Fd Technol.*, **10**, p. 603.
18. Mossel, D. A. A. (1976). *Gordian*, **76**, p. 10.
19. Brockmann, M. C. (1970). *Proc. Meat Ind. Res. Conference* 1970, p. 57.
20. Obanu, Z. A., Ledward, D. A. and Lawrie, R. A. (1975). *J. Fd Technol.*, **10**, p. 657.
21. Shahani, K. M. (1974). *Abstracts, 2nd IUPAC Symposium on Mycotoxins, Poland*, p. 38.
22. Bullermann, L. B. (1974). *J. Fd Sci.*, **39**, p. 1163.
23. Jarvis, B. and Moss, M. O. (1974). In: *The Microbiological Safety of Food*, ed. B. C. Hobbs and J. H. B. Christian, Academic Press, London, p. 293.
24. Leistner, L. and Ayres, J. C. (1968). *Fleischwirtschaft*, **48**, p. 62.
25. Ciegler, A., Mintzlaff, H. J., Weisleder, D. and Leistner, L. (1972). *Appl. Microbiol.*, **24**, p. 114.
26. Strzelecki, E. L., Lillard, H. S. and Ayres, J. C. (1969). *Appl. Microbiol.*, **18**, p. 938.
27. Strzelecki, E. L. (1972). *Acta microbiol. pol. Ser. B*, **4**, p. 155.
28. Leistner, L. and Rödel, W. (1975). In: *Water Relations of Foods*, ed. R. B. Duckworth, Academic Press, London, p. 309.
29. Diener, U. L. and Davis, N. D. (1969). In: *Aflatoxin*, ed. L. A. Goldblatt, Academic Press, New York, p. 13.
30. Denizel, T., Rolfe, E. J. and Jarvis, B. (1976). In preparation.
31. Bacon, C. W., Sweeney, J. G., Robbins, J. D. and Burdick, D. (1973). *Appl. Microbiol.*, **26**, p. 155.

DISCUSSION

Sinskey: With regard to the relationship between water activity and toxin production, do you mean by this that there is no toxin in the growth environment and hence the toxin accumulated inside the cell is not released?

Jarvis: The short answer is, we don't know. Certainly some of the metabolic products of the organism are changed by changing factors. I think it's quite possible that they don't in fact produce any significant quantities, but I'm not sure if anyone has actually looked to see if it's there in small quantities.

17

Microbiological Specifications for Intermediate Moisture Foods with Special Reference to Methodology used for the Assessment of Compliance

D. A. A. MOSSEL

*Chair of Food Microbiology, Faculty of Veterinary Medicine,
The University, Utrecht, The Netherlands*

ABSTRACT

Microbiological specifications per se *are of very limited value in controlling the microbiological quality of foods. This is best achieved by adherence to strict Codes of Good Manufacturing Practices (GMPs). However, specifications aid the assessment of quality and are therefore a valuable part of GMPs.*

The expression 'microbiological reference values' is preferred over the more ambiguous term 'specifications'. Considerations involved in drafting such reference values appropriate to intermediate moisture foods (IMF) are discussed in relation to rationale, important microorganisms and enumeration procedures. In the latter, account is invariably taken of the need to resuscitate cells which may be injured after exposure to sublethal stress, resulting from their presence in IMF.

Methods found useful for the selective enumeration of moulds and yeasts, Staphylococcus aureus, *Lancefield Group D streptococci, clostridia and* Enterobacteriaceae *in IMF are recommended. An essential element of the monitoring of IMF is the repetition of such examinations after exposure of the samples to a cyclic challenge test of e.g. 2 weeks at $16 \pm 2°C$ overnight and at $24 \pm 2°C$ during daytime, allowing an assessment of the intrinsic stability of IM commodities.*

THE ROLE OF SPECIFICATIONS IN QUALITY ASSURANCE

It is generally recognised that microbiological specifications *per se* are of almost no value to control the microbiological quality of foods for at least two reasons. Unless unattainable massive sampling is applied, the sensitivity of this approach is inevitably inadequate. In addition, results invariably become available at a time when very little consequent action can be taken.[1] Hence microbiological quality assurance has rather to be achieved by laying down and adhering to strict Codes of Good Manufacturing and Distribution practices, often indicated as: 'GMP'. However, specifications are valuable as a part of such GMPs, *i.e.* in assessing, rather than in attaining good microbiological quality of marketed end products.[1]

The drafting of microbiological specifications for intermediate moisture foods requires, as always, a preliminary estimation of microbiological risks with regard to: (i) safety for consumers ('wholesomeness'); and (ii) maintenance of hedonic rating ('quality'). Two classes of potentially harmful organisms have emerged from such studies on intermediate moisture foods:

(i) Those which can proliferate at the highest, locally occurring p_w ('a_w') value[2] to be expected. This p_w is not well defined,[3-9] but according to our experience is approximately 0·90. At these levels yeasts, moulds[10-17] and staphylococci[18-23] will be able to grow, unless inhibited by other intrinsic factors, such as pH or added preservatives.[24]

(ii) Less osmotolerant organisms, of which numbers of colony forming units ('cfu') are reduced upon storage, as is the case in dried foods,[25] *e.g. Salmonella* species.[26-41]

The number of criteria to be used in the estimation of safety and quality has always (and hence also in the case of intermediate moisture foods) to be strictly limited, for two reasons.[1] First, unnecessary specifications degrade microbiological quality assurance to at least a non-scientific, perhaps an irrelevant and possibly even a ridiculous sort of activity. Also, by reducing the numbers of tests more samples can be examined at a given laboratory capacity, thus reducing the uncertainty of results due to heterogeneous distribution of contaminants.[25]

AN APPROACH TO SUGGESTED SPECIFICATIONS FOR IMF

Choice of Criteria

The minimum set of specifications for all intermediate moisture foods should, at any rate, comprise the following assessments.

(i) The determination of cfu of moulds, yeasts and *Staphylococcus aureus*, at receipt of the samples;

(ii) As (i), subsequent to a challenge test, aiming to study the fate of these organisms. 'Cyclic' incubation for 2 weeks, overnight at $16 \pm 2°C$ and at $24 \pm 2°C$ during daytime, is suggested for this purpose.

A similar examination for initial values and rate of decrease subsequent to storage of Enterobacteriaceae is required for commodities (a) of pH over 4·5; (b) containing ingredients of animal or other origin that are more or less frequently contaminated with enteric pathogens.[1] A short justification of the use of these index organisms may be appropriate.

First the question may be raised whether at present, with more or less reliable methodology available for the detection of most pathogenic enteric organisms, including viruses, there is a place for the use of indicator bacteria. The answer is definitely in the affirmative sense for at least five reasons: (i) failure to detect a pathogen in a sample is not identical with its absence; (ii) absence of a pathogen in a sample is no proof at all of its absence in a consignment; (iii) freedom from a pathogen in a given consignment does not guarantee its absence in the next one; (iv) a rather broad spectrum of pathogenic Enterobacteriaceae has often to be taken into account; (v) customary methods are frequently rather complicated and sometimes, in addition, only partly developed. Any of these problems can be resolved by the proper choice and use of index organisms.[1]

Secondly, whereas the 'coli-aerogenes' group of bacteria was formerly used as the index organisms *par excellence*, this seems no longer advisable in the light of evidence obtained since about 1950. The taxonomic position of the coli-aerogenes group is equivocal, if not chaotic,[42-44] leading to appalling differences, *i.e.* of the order 10^3, between results obtained from different laboratories.[45] In addition tests for the lactose positive 'coli-aerogenes' group of the Enterobacteriaceae are less sensitive than methods of enumeration of the entire class.[1] Finally, from the ecological point of view, it makes little sense to concentrate on lactose positive bacteria when the lactose negative or 'late' biotypes are at least as relevant.[42]

For some products assessment of additional criteria merits consideration. This pertains to studying the fate of clostridia in some particular intermediate moisture foods.[46] In addition, in some instances an enumeration of Lancefield group D streptococci may be useful to assess the microbiological quality of the main ingredients of intermediate moisture foods and hence allow the barring of less satisfactory components.[1]

The Need for Standard Values

Microbiological examination of intermediate moisture foods along the lines developed in the previous section requires, obviously, that standard values should be available for comparison. 'Standard values of attainable quality', in this sense, should be distinguished from 'microbiological standards' which term is mostly used to express that such limit values are part of a Law, or at least of an Administrative Regulation. To avoid all ambiguity the expression *reference values* will be used in this paper, as is generally done in biomedical sciences.[47]

To assess such reference values, acceptable levels for all groups of organisms considered significant are derived from surveys on sufficient numbers of samples drawn from production lines which have previously been checked for GMP and corrected if required.[1] From these surveys sets of reference values are calculated as illustrated by Fig. 1. The parameter to be computed first is the 95th percentile from which, as a rule, two further criteria are derived, *viz.* the value aimed at (n) and the maximum which should never be exceeded (N). This system of so-called 'tolerances' implies that the fraction of samples (v/d) which may be encountered in the range $n \rightarrow N$ should be accurately defined. All pertinent values are determined by the parameters of the distribution curve,[1] as shown in Fig. 1.

RECOMMENDED METHODOLOGY

General Aspects

Satisfactorily accurate methods for the selective enumeration of the organisms mentioned and for the assessment of their fate upon

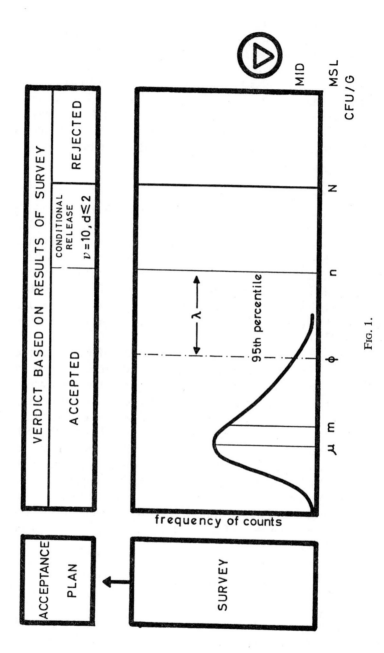

Fig. 1.

storage are available. They will always have to include a resuscitation step, allowing cells that have been sublethally injured by the exposure to reduced p_w and often rather high pO_2 values to be repaired to the extent that they will develop into colonies in or on the customarily used selective media.[1,48,49]

For theoretical reasons the required repair treatments cannot be expected to be uniform or even similar, because they depend on many factors. The most important of these are: (i) type of organism; (ii) condition of the cells (log phase, stationary phase, *etc.*) when the stressing occurred; (iii) character and severity of injury; (iv) composition of diluent used for preparing the first decimal dilution and particularly (v) properties of the selective medium used ultimately for their enumeration.[50,51,48,49] Nevertheless it has appeared empirically that, generally, 2 h exposure of suspensions of the food under examination in a buffered infusion broth at 20–25°C will suffice for most practical purposes.[52,50,48] In some cases, such a restoration treatment has been shown to be 'inadequate' in the sense that full recovery is not attained even when using the least intrinsically toxic, selective medium.[53–55] When this applies, primary culturing on a non-selective medium, followed by replication onto the conventional selective media is the procedure of choice.[56]

Specific Selective Techniques Recommended for the Examination of IMFs

Quantitative microbiological examination of foods is a relatively young branch of the biomedical sciences; the first fundamental studies in this area virtually date from the 1950s.[1] Therefore it is not surprising that no agreement has yet been reached on optimal procedures. In part this is also due to an essential fact, *viz.* that a given medium, *e.g.* one containing particular antibacterial antibiotics allowing the selective enumeration of mould propagules, may lead to quite satisfactory results when applied to a given food, because of its particular bacterial association,[24] whereas when examining another commodity with a quite different bacterial 'background' flora, the antibiotics used may partially fail resulting in unsatisfactory results.[57] Pending considerable progress in this area, every competent food bacteriologist should choose the methods that give the most satisfactory results when applied to the intermediate moisture commodities in his field of studies—and in the hands of his technicians!

With these reservations in mind, the following procedures are recommended for the enumeration of pertinent organisms, once sublethally stressed cells having been restored to full vitality.

Mould propagules and yeasts. The medium of choice is oxytetracycline gentamicin agar,[58-61,57] used as poured plates. In cases where copious aerial mycelial growth might obscure readings, 35 mcg/ml rose bengal[62] should be added to control interference by a few of such colonies spreading over the entire plates. In this instance yeast counts obtained may be erroneously low and should not be taken into account without further verification.[57]

Staph. aureus. The generally accepted procedure is based on spread drop-plates of Baird-Parker's tellurite glycine pyruvate egg yolk agar.[63] Three of these should be used to absorb a total of one ml of the 10^{-1} dilution, thus allowing improved sensitivity.[64] Incubation for *c.* 30 h at 37°C should be applied. Subsequently, egg yolk (EY) positive (and when required also EY-negative colonies)[65-67] are examined for growth in brain, heart infusion broth at 43°C,[1] discarding negative isolates and testing positive cultures for: (i) their behaviour in so-called Gram-positive diagnostic tubes,[68] allowing the assessment of the mode of attack on glucose and the catalase reaction thus eliminating micrococci and Lancefield D streptococci among EY-negative isolates; and (ii) the anerobic mode of dissimilation of mannitol thus eliminating *Staph. epidermidis.*[68] Isolates showing the properties of *Staph. aureus* are finally examined for coagulase activity.

Where Baird-Parker's medium cannot be used, for reasons of its relatively low stability, Vogel and Johnson's tellurite mannitol agar[69] is a satisfactory substitute.

Enterobacteriaceae. Poured plates of violet red bile glucose agar[70] are customarily used for the enumeration of the Enterobacteriaceae group. The medium should be of previously verified performance, because properties of the bile preparation used may interfere with optimal functioning.[71] Plates should be covered with an overlayer of the same medium to suppress the growth of pseudomonads, acinetobacters and moraxellas[72] and be incubated for *c.* 18 h at 30°C. Where required a representative selection of colonies can be tested for typical behaviour in so-called Gram-negative diagnostic tubes, allowing the determination of mode of attack on glucose, oxidase reaction, motility and the formation of indole and H_2S.[68]

Lancefield group D streptococci. The recommended medium is a modified Colobert agar,[73] containing aesculin, azide[74] and kanamycin.[75] This medium is to be used as spread drop plates and after 18 h incubation at 37°C typical colonies show black halos. They can be tested for identity with Lancefield group D streptococci by culturing, first of all, in brain heart infusion broth at 45°C.[1] Positive cultures are subsequently examined for morphology, catalase reaction and typical behaviour in Gram-positive diagnostic tubes (*vide supra*).[68]

Clostridia. Because virtually all species of the genus Clostridium reduce sulphite,[76] use of suitable anaerobic sulphite iron media allowing enumeration of colonies with black halos remains the method of choice for the assessment of numbers of clostridia. Sulphite iron polymyxin agar, incubated in Miller-Prickett oval tubes or plastic pouches[77] is recommended for the enumeration of all types of clostridia and sulphite iron cycloserine agar, to be incubated at 46°C, for the selective enumeration of *Cl. perfringens*.[78] Estimation of numbers of *Cl. botulinum* requires the use of more complicated techniques.[77]

ACKNOWLEDGEMENT

The author wishes to express his sincerest gratitude to Dr R. Davies, National College of Food Technology, Weybridge, Surrey, who has kindly reviewed the first draft of this paper.

REFERENCES

1. Mossel, D. A. A. (1975). *Crit. Revs. Environm. Control*, **5**, p. 1.
2. Mossel, D. A. A. (1975). In: *Water Relations of Foods*, ed. R. B. Duckworth, Academic Press, London, p. 347.
3. Chordash, R. A. and Potter, N. N. (1972). *J. Milk Food Technol.*, **35**, p. 395.
4. Collins, J. L., Chen, C. C., Park, J. R., Mundt, J. O., McCarthy, I. E. and Johnston, M. R. (1972). *J. Food Sci.*, **37**, p. 189.
5. Labuza, T. P., Cassil, S. and Sinskey, A. J. (1972). *J. Food Sci.*, **37**, p. 160.
6. Bone, D. (1973). *Food Technol.*, **27**, no. 4, p. 71.
7. Collins, J. L. and Yu, A. K. (1975). *J. Food Sci.*, **40**, p. 858.
8. Hagenmaier, R. D., Cater, C. M. and Mattil, K. F. (1975). *J. Food Sci.*, **40**, p. 717.

9. Acott, K. M. and Labuza, T. P. (1975). *J. Food Technol.*, **10**, p. 603.
10. Grover, D. W. (1947). *J. Soc. Chem. Ind.*, **66**, p. 201.
11. Snow, D. (1949). *Ann. Applied Biol.*, **36**, p. 1.
12. Miller, M. W. and Tanaka, H. (1963). *Hilgardia*, **34**, p. 183.
13. Ayerst, G. (1969). *J. Stored Prod. Research*, **5**, p. 127.
14. Schultheiss, J. and Spicher, G. (1974). *Getreide, Mehl u. Brot*, **28**, p. 288.
15. Jarvis, B. (1976). 'Do mycotoxins present a potential hazard for intermediate moisture foods?', this volume, p. 239.
16. Seiler, D. A. L. (1976). 'The stability of intermediate moisture foods with respect to mould growth', this volume, p. 166.
17. Tilbury, R. (1976). 'The microbial stability of intermediate moisture foods with respect to yeasts', this volume, p. 138.
18. Henneberg, W. and Kniefall, H. (1935/1936). *Milchwirtsch. Forsch.*, **17**, p. 146.
19. Bem, Z. and Leistner, L. (1970). *Fleischwirtschaft*, **50**, p. 1412.
20. Troller, J. A. (1971). *Applied Microbiol.*, **21**, p. 435.
21. Troller, J. A. (1972). *Applied Microbiol.*, **24**, p. 440.
22. Troller, J. A. and Stinson, J. V. (1975). *J. Food Sci.*, **40**, p. 802.
23. Leistner, L. and Rödel, W. (1976). 'The stability of intermediate moisture foods with respect to micro-organisms', this volume, p. 120.
24. Mossel, D. A. A. (1971). *J. Appl. Bacteriol.*, **34**, p. 95.
25. Mossel, D. A. A. and Shennan, J. L. (1976). *J. Food Technol.*, **11**, in press.
26. Monk, G. W., Elbert, M. L., Stevens, C. L. and McGaffrey, P. A. (1956). *J. Bacteriol.*, **72**, p. 368.
27. Bateman, J. B. and White, F. E. (1963). *J. Bacteriol.*, **85**, p. 918.
28. McDade, J. J. and Hall, L. B. (1964). *Amer. J. Hygiene*, **80**, p. 192.
29. Mossel, D. A. A. and Koopman, M. J. (1965). *Poultry Sci.*, **44**, p. 890.
30. Cox, C. S. (1968). *J. Gen. Microbiol.*, **54**, p. 169.
31. Cox, C. S. (1969). *J. Gen. Microbiol.*, **57**, p. 77.
32. Crumrine, M. H. and Foltz, V. D. (1969). *Applied Microbiol.*, **18**, p. 911.
33. Liu, T. S., Snoeyenbos, G. H. and Carlson, V. L. (1969). *Poultry Sci.*, **48**, p. 1628.
34. Carlson, V. L. and Snoeyenbos, G. H. (1970). *Poultry Sci.*, **49**, p. 717.
35. Li Cari, J. J. and Potter, N. N. (1970). *J. Dairy Sci.*, **53**, p. 877.
36. Doesburg, J. J., Lamprecht, E. C. and Elliott, M. (1970). *J. Sci. Food Agriculture*, **21**, p. 632.
37. Ray, B., Jezeski, J. J. and Busta, F. F. (1971). *J. Milk Food Technol.*, **34**, p. 423.
38. Christian, J. H. B. and Stewart, B. J. (1973). In: *The Microbiological Safety of Food*, ed. B. C. Hobbs and J. H. B. Christian, Academic Press, London, p. 107.
39. Turner, A. G. and Salmonsen, P. A. (1973). *J. Appl. Bacteriol.*, **36**, p. 497.
40. Marshall, B. J., Ohye, D. F. and Christian, J. H. B. (1971). *Applied Microbiol.*, **21**, p. 363.

41. Corry, J. E. L. (1976). 'The safety of intermediate moisture food products with respect to Salmonella', this volume, p. 215.
42. Mossel, D. A. A. (1967). *J. Assoc. Offic. Anal. Chem.*, **50**, p. 91.
43. Carney, J. F., Carty, C. E. and Colwell, R. R. (1975). *Applied Microbiol.*, **30**, p. 771.
44. Sayler, G. S., Nelson, J. D., Justice, A. and Colwell, R. R. (1975). *Applied Microbiol.*, **30**, p. 625.
45. Baird-Parker, A. C. (1976). *Fleischwirtschaft*, **56**, p. 96.
46. Roberts, T. A. and Smart, T. L. (1976). 'Control of Clostridia by water activity and related factors', this volume, p. 203.
47. Gräsbeck, R. (1976). *Lancet*, **I**, p. 244.
48. Busta, F. F. (1976). *J. Milk Food Technol.*, **39**, p. 138.
49. Pawsey, R. and Davies, R. (1976). 'The safety of intermediate moisture foods with respect to *Staph. aureus*', this volume, p. 182.
50. Roth, L. A., Stiles, M. E. and Clegg, L. F. L. (1973). *Canad. Inst. Food Sci. Technol. J.*, **6**, pp. 227; 235.
51. Stiles, M. E. and Clark, P. C. (1974). *Canad. J. Microbiol.*, **20**, p. 1735.
52. Mossel, D. A. A. and Ratto, M. A. (1970). *Applied Microbiol.*, **20**, p. 273.
53. Mossel, D. A. A. and Harrewijn, G. A. (1972). *Alimenta*, **11**, p. 29.
54. Schothorst, M. van and Leusden, F. M. van (1975). *Zbl. Bakt. I, Orig.*, A, **230**, p. 186.
55. Stevenson, K. E. and Richards, L. J. (1976). *J. Food Sci.*, **41**, p. 136.
56. Mossel, D. A. A., Jongerius, E. and Koopman, M. J. (1965). *Annls Inst. Pasteur Lille*, **16**, p. 119.
57. Mossel, D. A. A., Vega, C. L. and Put, H. M. C. (1975). *J. Appl. Bacteriol.*, **39**, p. 15.
58. Smith, G. N. and Worrel, C. S. (1950). *Arch. Biochem.*, **28**, p. 232.
59. Holt, R. (1967). *Lancet*, **I**, p. 1259.
60. Mossel, D. A. A., Kleynen-Semmeling, A. M. C., Vincentie, H. M., Beerens, H. and Catsaras, M. (1970). *J. Appl. Bacteriol.*, **33**, p. 454.
61. Ingram, J. M. and Hassan, H. M. (1975). *Canad. J. Microbiol.*, **21**, p. 1185.
62. Jarvis, B. (1973). *J. Appl. Bact.*, **36**, p. 723.
63. Baird-Parker, A. C. (1962). *J. Appl. Bact.*, **25**, p. 12.
64. Baer, E. F., Messer, J. W., Leslie, J. E. and Peeler, J. T. (1975). *J. Assoc. Offic. Anal. Chem.*, **58**, p. 1154.
65. Grün, L. and Pulverer, G. (1966). *Z. Medizin. Mikrobiol. Immunol.*, **153**, p. 1.
66. Koskitalo, L. D. (1971). *Canad. Inst. Food Sci. Technol. J.*, **4**, p. 137.
67. Mayer, S. (1975). *Milchwissenschaft*, **30**, p. 607.
68. Mossel, D. A. A., Eelderink, I. and Sutherland, J. P. (1976). *J. Gen. Microbiol.*, in press.
69. Vogel, R. A. and Johnson, M. A. (1960). *Public Health Lab.*, **18**, p. 131.
70. Mossel, D. A. A., Mengerink, W. H. J. and Scholts, H. H. (1962). *J. Bacteriol.*, **84**, p. 381.
71. Mossel, D. A. A., Harrewijn, G. A. and Nesselrooy-van Zadelhoff, C. F. M. (1974). *Health Lab. Sci.*, **11**, p. 260.

72. Holtzapfel, D. and Mossel, D. A. A. (1968). *J. Food Technol.*, **3**, p. 223.
73. Colobert, L. and Morélis, P. (1958). *Annls Inst. Pasteur*, **94**, p. 120.
74. Facklam, R. R., Padula, J. F., Thacker, L. G., Wortham, E. C. and Sconyers, B. J. (1974). *Applied Microbiol.*, **27**, p. 107.
75. Mossel, D. A. A., Bijker, P. G. H., Spreekens, K. A. van, Shennan, J. L. and Eelderink, I. (1976). *J. Appl. Bact.*, in press.
76. Prévot, A. R. (1948). *Annls Inst. Pasteur*, **75**, p. 571.
77. Mossel, D. A. A. and de Waart, J. (1968). *Annls Inst. Pasteur Lille*, **19**, p. 13.
78. Mossel, D. A. A. and Pouw, H. (1973). *Zbl. Bakt. I, Orig.*, A, **223**, p. 559.

DISCUSSION

Sinskey: Have any surveys been done that you know of on the microbiology of intermediate moisture foods?

Mossel: As Professor Leistner has shown, we have a lot of experience with conventional IMF, and as far as the non-conventional ones are concerned we have a host of petfoods. But for humans, I wouldn't know of any yet. But for conventional, traditional IMF, such as meat products, we have plenty of data.

On petfoods I must say in all honesty that I was surprised at the excellent bacteriological quality—this has been said before by several speakers. We have now examined, I would say, perhaps 2 thousand examples of 3 brands, and 3 or 4 different items (for dogs, cats, hamsters or whatever), and I was always surprised at the excellent microbiological condition which I do not normally encounter in cooked sausages and the like. We had our chemists look at them, and we couldn't detect any illegal preservatives, and the amount of sorbates which we uncovered at least were not excessive. So I take it that these formulae have been very carefully devised. I have been impressed by the very low counts of these products, and by their excellent shelf-life. We have done cyclic incubation, and not one single sample so far has turned mouldy.

Of course the subsidiaries concerned belong to multi-nationals of very high standing, and notably of high scientific standing. But I was impressed, after so many years of analytical food bacteriology, by the excellent bacteriological and microbial condition of the product.

Dehnel: How serious do you think is the possibility, with the increasing use of IMF type foods preserved under the a_w, pH, and preservative conditions we have been hearing about, that new strains of organism may develop which will become much more tolerant of such conditions?

Mossel: This is the common fear whenever new preservation methods are applied. We encountered it in radiation, and in using new preservatives; we encountered it at the time the use of antibiotics was being considered (I think they are still used in agriculture, though not in food). We have looked for this, and any new organisms we have harvested we have studied in the well-known way—gradient plates for enhanced resistance to the external factors deliberately used for their suppression. So far we haven't found any but we are keeping an eye on this, because during my career I have been asked this question in at least 4 main fields of research. Thus, in the hundred strains that we have studied, we haven't discovered any adaptation that might be a hazard to the process in the future. But your question is very much to the point.

Lift: Are the tests you are conducting to assess the contamination of your IMF designed to control the numbers of bacteria and other micro-organisms in the foodstuffs, or are they designed to eliminate them from the foodstuffs?

Mossel: The conventional procedure follows the counts as a function of time in these incubation tests of ours, taking all possible precautions for the resuscitation of injured cells. The second procedure is the artificial inoculation of samples with well-known foci of contamination, for instance minced meat, or sausage meat. This is still conventional, because you are counting cells that you can recover. In addition we have a modern approach whereby we follow the phase-by-phase picotrophy, if we can, which is more unconventional. The last and most fascinating procedure is to check chemically, by chromatography, for microbial metabolites. We have done all that and, as the computer says, 'the evidence for any instability was negative'. So with the limited number of IMF we were in a position to study, we used all the parameters of modern microbial ecology.

18

New Developments in Intermediate Moisture Foods: Humectants

ANTHONY J. SINSKEY

Department of Nutrition and Food Science,
Massachusetts Institute of Technology, Cambridge,
Massachusetts, USA

ABSTRACT

Humectants are usually assumed to control microbial proliferation in intermediate moisture foods by their ability to lower water activity (a_w). *Recent work has, however, shown that they probably act by three mechanisms. One mechanism concerns their ability to lower water activity* (a_w), *the second involves lowering the available moisture content, and the third is due to a microbial effect independent of* a_w *or moisture.*

Concerning the first two mechanisms, intermediate pork dices at the same a_w *(0·88) but with different moisture contents showed different biological responses when* Staphylococcus aureus *was the test organism according to the method of preparation, i.e. desorption or adsorption. With samples prepared by desorption, using glycerol as the humectant, growth of* S. aureus *occurred during storage. However, in samples prepared via adsorption, death occurred. On the other hand, with samples prepared at equal moisture contents by either method, no difference was observed in the behaviour of* S. aureus.

The antimicrobial mechanisms of a variety of aliphatic diol humectants have been investigated. Inhibition of growth of Bacillus subtilis *was found to depend on the chain length and position of hydroxyl groups. 1,2 Diols were more effective than 1,3 diols. Esterification also affects antimicrobial activity. Studies with membrane vesicles prepared from* B. subtilis *indicate that inhibition of amino acid transport is a primary antimicrobial effect of diols and their esters.*

INTRODUCTION

The current status and the numerous technical problems of intermediate moisture foods (IMF) have been discussed thoroughly by Karel.[1] Studies have been reported regarding the growth of microorganisms as a function of water activity. Microbial growth has been reported at a_w ranging from very close to 1·0 to about 0·62. Within its particular range, each micro-organism exhibits an optimum a_w for growth, which in the great majority of cases lies between 0·99 and 0·90. As a_w is increased above the optimum, the rate of growth falls steeply; as it is reduced below the optimum a_w, the decrease in growth rate is usually less abrupt. Reduction in a_w leads also to an increase in the lag phase, a decrease in the growth rate and cell yield and for spores, an increase in the time required for germination.[2,3] It was postulated that the biological response to a particular a_w was largely independent of the type of solutes and the total moisture content of the substrate. Limiting values of water activity, below which certain types of micro-organisms will not grow have been established, as described by Mossel and Ingram,[4] Mossel,[5] and Leistner and Rödel.[6]

The lower limits of water activity at which micro-organisms can grow are influenced by environmental conditions such as temperature, pH, nutrient supply and availability of oxygen. Many examples that illustrate the effects of environmental conditions on water requirements are presented in reviews by Scott,[2] Christian,[3] Kushner,[7] Troller[8] and Mossel.[5] Of great importance to IMF is to distinguish between the effects of lowered water activity and specific effects of different solutes that can be used as water-binding agents. For example, Baird-Parker and Freame[9] found that with spores of *Clostridium botulinum* in media adjusted to different water activities by the addition of NaCl or glycerol, initiation of growth does not depend solely on the a_w of the medium; the minimum a_w at which spores could initiate growth being higher in the media containing NaCl. Calhoun and Frazier[10] compared the effects of glucose and NaCl (at concentrations giving the same a_w values) on the growth of *Escherichia coli, Pseudomonas fluorescens* and *Staphylococcus aureus*. The two solutes had the same effect on the growth of *S. aureus*, but NaCl inhibited the growth of the other bacteria more than glucose. Marshall *et al.*[11] compared the inhibitory effects of NaCl and glycerol on 16 species of bacteria. Only 3 species responded identically to both solutes. When compared at similar levels of water activity, glycerol was more inhibitory than NaCl to relatively salt-tolerant bacteria and less inhibitory than NaCl to salt-sensitive species. These results indicate that the microbial inhibitory effects of different humectants cannot be ascribed entirely to reduced water activity. Thus, for specific intermediate moisture foods, experiments have to be made to determine how the microbial stability is influenced by a given humectant.

MICROBIOLOGICAL STUDIES WITH IMF

Several studies have been made on the microbiological stability of intermediate moisture foods. Hollis *et al.*[12,13] studied the viability of several pathogenic bacteria in IMF-chicken à la King casserole (a_w: 0·85). They reported that *S. aureus* decreased by one log cycle in 1 month and by more than 5 log cycles in 4 months. *E. coli*, *Salmonella sp.* and *Cl. perfringens* decreased by more than 3 log cycles in 4 months. Similar results were found for a ham in cream sauce casserole (a_w: 0·85). Sahoo[14] studied the microbiological stability of intermediate moisture pork. It was reported that the viable count in raw intermediate moisture pork declined during storage when the water activity was 0·83 or less. At this a_w level, the decline in viable count was greater during 37°C storage than at 21° or 4°C. Water activity of 0·85 was marginal with respect to microbial stability. At this level, low a_w resistant strains of micro-organisms (not identified) grew unless the pH of the samples was reduced with 0·014% lactic acid. He stated that lactic acid in heat-processed intermediate pork acted synergistically with potassium sorbate (0·35%) in providing mycotic stability to the product at an a_w of 0·855. Without the lactic acid, intermediate moisture pork was stable at 0·835 a_w but required 0·43% potassium sorbate. Chordash and Potter[15] prepared several IMF by dehydration and inoculated them with *P. aeruginosa* and *S. aureus*. Growth of *P. aeruginosa* was inhibited at a_w below 0·99, 0·98 and 0·96 in custard, pea and beef products respectively; growth of *S. aureus* did not occur below 0·94 and 0·96 a_w in custard and ham products, respectively. Collins *et al.*,[16] prepared intermediate moisture deep-fried fish fillets at a_w of 0·83 and 0·86. They reported that no bacteria, mould or staphylococci were found in the product with the exception of one sample stored for one week which had a total bacterial count of 70 cells/g of product.

EFFECT OF IMF PREPARATION METHOD

Labuza *et al.*,[17] prepared intermediate moisture pork and banana systems by desorption and adsorption methods to different a_w. Large hysteresis effects were reported in the sorption isotherms of the IMF systems. Samples with and without potassium sorbate were inoculated with *Aspergillus niger*, *Candida utilis*, *P. fragi* and *S. aureus*. They found that with respect to desorption systems the minimum a_w for growth of micro-organisms as reported in the literature could be used as guidelines in determining the microbial stability of intermediate moisture foods. However, in adsorption samples the minimum a_w for growth of micro-organisms was much higher (>0.90) under conditions where stress was eliminated.

A similar study with *S. aureus* in intermediate moisture meats was undertaken by Plitman *et al.*[18] Although the original study by Plitman *et al.*[18] reported on the viability of *S. aureus* in strained chicken and commercial lean pork loin intermediate moisture preparations, this paper only addresses the research findings with the pork IMF system. The intermediate moisture pork dices were prepared by desorption or adsorption procedures as described by Plitman *et al.*,[18] using glycerol, 1,2 propanediol and 1,3 butanediol

TABLE 1

Equilibrating solutions for the preparation of pork dices—IMF systems

Run No.	Composition of equilibrating solution (% wt)[a]					Equilibrating temperature (°C)[b]
	Water	Glycerol	1,2-Propanediol	1,3-Butanediol	NaCl	
B-1	48·75	48·75	—	—	2·5	4
B-2	24·4	73·1	—	—	2·5	4
B-3	—	97·5	—	—	2·5	4
B-4	58·5	39·0	—	—	2·5	25
B-5	58·5	—	—	39·0	2·5	25
B-6	58·5	—	39·0	—	2·5	25
B-7	39·0	58·5	—	—	2·5	25
B-8	39·0	45·5	—	13·0	2·5	25
B-9	39·0	45·5	13·0	—	2·5	25

[a] The weight ratio pork/infusion solution was kept constant at 1:3. In every run the fresh pork was distributed in portions of about 10 cubes each.
[b] The samples soaked in the infusion solution were heated for 15 min at 96°C and incubated for 24 h at the equilibrating temperature.

TABLE 2

Parameters of pork dices—IMF systems

Run No.	Humectant	Desorption samples			Saturated salt solution	Adsorption samples		
		Water activity (at 25°C)	Moisture content (g H_2O/g solids)	Humectant (% wt)[a]		Water activity (at 25°C)	Moisture content (g H_2O/g solids)	Humectant (% wt)[a]
B-1	Glycerol	0·880	0·932	26·5	KCl	0·860	0·772	28·9
B-2	Glycerol	0·805	0·710	36·8	$CdCl_2$	0·820	0·675	37·6
B-3	Glycerol	0·730	0·640	51·7	NaCl	0·750	0·585	53·5
B-4	Glycerol	0·915	1·130	20·1	KNO_3	0·920	1·110	20·3
B-5	1,3-Butanediol	0·925	1·180	18·2	KNO_3	0·920	1·060	19·3
B-6	1,2-Propanediol	0·915	1·080	20·2	KNO_3	0·920	1·090	20·1
B-7	Glycerol	0·865	0·871	26·8	K_2CrO_4	0·880	0·860	27·0
B-8	Glycerol-butanediol ratio 3·5:1	0·875	0·903	28·1	K_2CrO_4	0·880	0·845	29·0
B-9	Glycerol-propanediol ratio 3·5:1	0·865	0·858	26·9	K_2CrO_4	0·880	0·852	27·0

[a] Estimated from the water activity lowering capacity of the various humectants.

as humectants. The composition of the equilibrating solutions for the preparation of the IM-pork dices is presented in Table 1 and the various parameters of the desorption and adsorption samples summarised in Table 2. The sorption isotherm of IM-pork cubes prepared with glycerol at 25°C is shown in Fig. 1. Please note that the

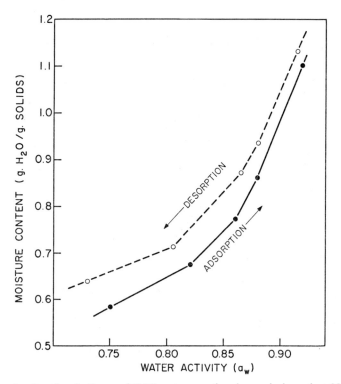

FIG. 1.   Sorption isotherm of IMF system: pork cubes and glycerol at 25°C.

hysteresis loop is much less than that commonly depicted by several eminent scientists in the field. Hysteresis makes it possible to prepare IMF at the same a_w with different moisture contents and vice versa.

These IM-pork dices were inoculated with *S. aureus* S-6 which had been propagated in Brain, Heart Infusion broth at 37°C, washed and suspended in a water–glycerol solution at the same water activity as the food for 1–2 h at 25°C. IM-pork cubes were inoculated by pipetting 0·1 ml of the water–glycerol suspension of cells over the surface of the meat piece to a final concentration of $4\text{--}8 \times 10^5$ bacteria/g. The desorption and adsorption samples of each run were inoculated in the same way and at the same time.

In Fig. 2 the viability of *S. aureus* in IM-pork cubes at 25°C prepared with glycerol is presented as a function of storage time. Brain, Heart Infusion plate count agar was employed for viability determinations.

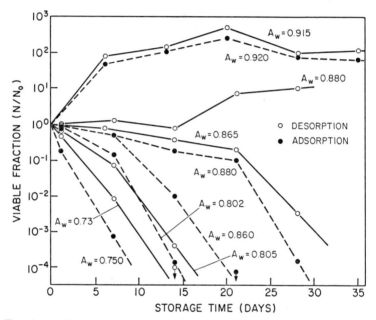

FIG. 2   Viability of *Staphylococcus aureus* in IMF systems: pork cubes and glycerol at 25°C.

At an a_w greater than 0·88 in desorption samples microbial proliferation occurred. With the desorption sample at 0·88, an extended lag time is noticed, *i.e.* no net increase in viable cells was observed until after the 15th day. In addition, the total number of cells produced at an a_w of 0·88 is much less than at 0·915. With desorption samples at a_w less than 0·88 death occurred during storage. It appears that the exponential decay rates are similar, but the time at which exponential death occurs is controlled by the a_w. Thus a_w affects the shoulder of the survival curve. On the other hand, with adsorption samples at similar a_w we observe that no net microbial growth occurs at an a_w of 0·88 during a storage period of 25 days after which time a net decrease in viable cells is noted. When one determines and examines the moisture content it is established (Table 3) that regardless of the preparation method

TABLE 3

Effect of total moisture content on viability of Staphylococcus Aureus *in intermediate moisture pork as a function of the preparation method. Humectant: Glycerol only*

Total moisture content g H_2O/ g solids	Preparation method			
	Desorption		Adsorption	
	Initial biological response	F (days)	Initial biological response	F (days)
1·130	Growth	8	—	—
1·110	—	—	Growth	12
0·932	Growth	>30	—	—
0·871	Death	26	—	—
0·860	—	—	Death	24
0·722	—	—	Death	14
0·710	Death	10	—	—
0·675	—	—	Death	10
0·640	Death	7	—	—
0·585	—	—	Death	4

F: time to change the viable population by 99% (a 2 log cycle change).

(desorption or adsorption, with glycerol as the humectant) at moisture contents of 0·932 g H_2O/g solids or above, the viable counts increased at higher rates with increasing moisture contents; conversely at moisture contents of 0·871 g H_2O/g solids or below, the viable counts decreased at higher rates with decreasing moisture contents.

Similar results have been reported by Haas *et al.*[19] In their study, freeze-dried meat solids were adjusted to different moisture contents (15, 25 and 40%) at a constant a_w of 0·83 and inoculated with *Aspergillus glaucus* as a test organism. Growth was slower in the food samples with 15% water than in an environment with 40% water. The use of sorbate as on antimycotic was also evaluated at a constant a_w of 0·83 as a function of water content. At the 0·1% sorbate level at 15% H_2O mould growth was observed in 45 days as compared to 25 days without sorbate. At 40 % H_2O and 0·1 % sorbate mould growth occurred in 24 days and without 0·1 % sorbate in 17 days.

To date, we have not been able to explain the fundamental reasons why these phenomena are observed. The concepts and use of water activity are not as simple as previously thought. Obviously, more fundamental information of a physical-chemical nature is needed to explain how water interacts with micro-organisms in complex biological systems.

EFFECTS OF DIFFERENT HUMECTANTS

Next 1,3 butanediol and 1,2 propanediol were employed as humectants in IM-pork. For samples prepared by adsorption (Fig. 3) two observations were made. At an a_w of 0·92 both 1,3 butanediol and 1,2 propanediol were bactericidal. When both propanediol and

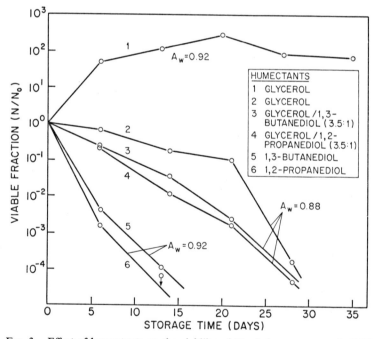

FIG. 3.   Effect of humectants on the viability of *Staphylococcus aureus* in IMF pork cubes prepared by adsorption.

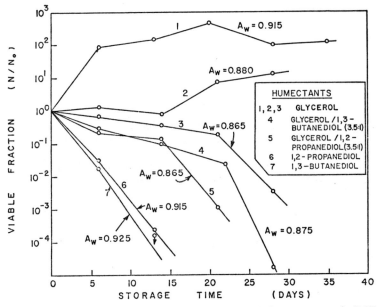

FIG. 4. Effect of humectants on the viability of *Staphylococcus aureus* in IMF pork cubes prepared by desorption.

butanediol were used in combination with glycerol at a ratio of 3·5:1, some bactericidal activity was noted.

For samples prepared by desorption (Fig. 4) similar results were observed. Again, outgrowth occurred at an a_w of around 0·88 when glycerol was the only humectant. Outgrowth could be prevented when butanediol was used in combination with the glycerol.

BIOLOGICAL EFFECTS OF HUMECTANTS

A literature review indicated that *S. aureus* is one of the most resistant micro-organisms to the bactericidal effects of various polyhydric alcohols.[20,21] Robertson *et al.*[20] reported that the lowest concentrations found inhibitory for *S. aureus* were 15 % for 1,3 butanediol and 20 % for 1,2 propanediol (Table 4). Our values are in close agreement.

We then initiated studies designed to determine the antimicrobial mode of action of humectants. Employing *S. aureus* as a test organism, several observations were made with the humectants. For example, the humectants were more inhibitory at 25°C than at 37°C Also, pH was found to be important and results similar to those reported by Labuza[22] were found—namely, as one lowers the pH at a constant a_w less humectant is needed to inhibit the growth of *Staphylococcus aureus* (Table 4).

TABLE 4

Effect of pH on inhibitor concentration required to prevent growth of Staphylococcus Aureus *at* $a_w = 0.88$ (from Labuza[22])

Inhibitor	Inhibitory concentration (% w/w) at	
	pH = 5·2	pH = 5·6
1,3 Butylene glycol	3·0	5·0
Propylene glycol	—	7·0

— = not tested.

As these studies were in progress a report by Freese *et al.*[23] appeared describing the mode of action of lipophilic acids commonly used as antimicrobial food additives. Also since previous studies had indicated that diols and diol esters, which have been investigated for use as humectants, have antimicrobial properties[24] a more fundamental study was undertaken to determine how humectants such as glycerol and diols may in fact inhibit microbial growth.

Bacillus subtilis was employed as the test organism in the manner described by Freese *et al.*[23] A flow sheet describing the experimental protocol is given in Fig. 5. The formulas for the inhibition indices for both *in vitro* and *in vivo* experiments are also given. A value of zero means no inhibition and a value of 1·0 means complete inhibition.

INHIBITION OF MICROBIAL GROWTH BY DIOLS

First the growth inhibitory concentrations of diols were determined (Fig. 6). Two facts emerge from this figure. The first is that as the diol chain length is increased, the concentration required to inhibit microbial growth decreases. Also, the position of the hydroxyl groups affects antimicrobial activity. The 1,2 diols are more inhibitory than the 1,3 diols in a given series.

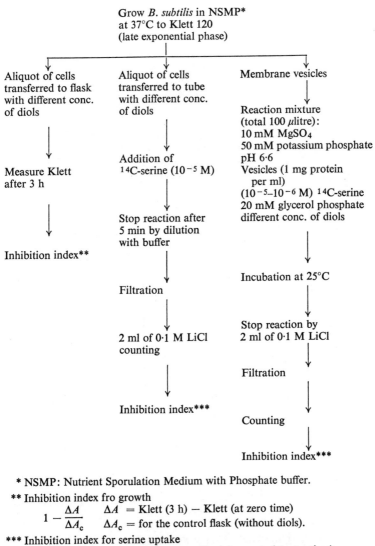

* NSMP: Nutrient Sporulation Medium with Phosphate buffer.
** Inhibition index fro growth

$$1 - \frac{\Delta A}{\Delta A_c} \qquad \Delta A = \text{Klett (3 h)} - \text{Klett (at zero time)}$$
$$\Delta A_c = \text{for the control flask (without diols).}$$

*** Inhibition index for serine uptake

$$1 - \frac{\Delta \text{cpm}}{\Delta \text{cpm}_c} \qquad \Delta \text{cpm} = \text{cpm (5 min)} - \text{cpm (at zero time)}$$
$$\Delta \text{cpm}_c = \text{for the control (without diols).}$$

FIG. 5.   Flow sheet for experimental procedure.

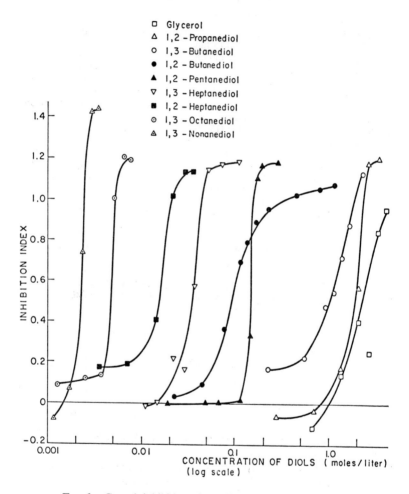

FIG. 6. Growth inhibition of *Bacillus subtilis* 60015 by diols.

When the diols are esterified the growth inhibitory properties also change (Fig. 7). The most dramatic effect is that esterification decreases the concentration required to inhibit growth. Also, the longer the side chain, the greater the antimicrobial effect. Note that esterification of both hydroxyl groups tends to decrease the growth inhibitory properties.

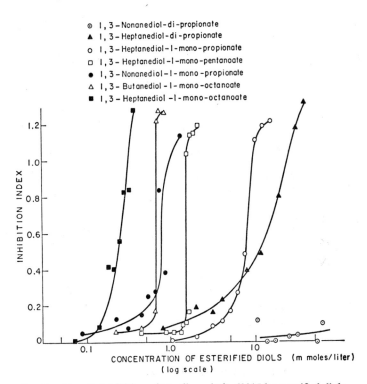

FIG. 7.   Growth inhibition of *Bacillus subtilis* 60015 by esterified diols.

IN VITRO EFFECTS OF DIOLS

In vitro studies were then conducted with membrane vesicles prepared as described by Freese *et al.*[23] and as outlined in Fig. 5. As a measure of the amino acid transport capabilities of membrane vesicles uptake of ^{14}C-serine was employed and α-glycerol-phosphate served as the energy source. The results as presented in Fig. 8

indicate similar concentration and positional effects as described for the growth inhibition studies. This is best seen when Fig. 9 is examined. The concentration required to inhibit the microbial growth by 50% or serine uptake *in vitro* by 50% for a given diol is remarkably similar. When serine uptake is determined on whole cells

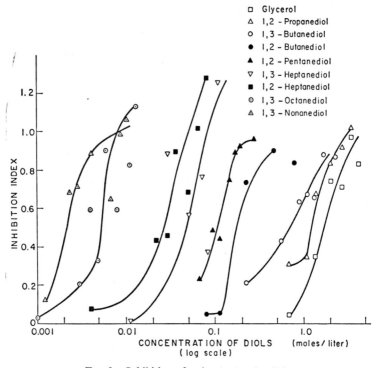

Fig. 8.   Inhibition of serine *in vitro* by diols.

i.e. in vivo, a like correlation is established (Fig. 10). Thus, the antimicrobial effects of humectants (glycerol and/or aliphatic diols) result from the inhibition of substrate transport into bacteria.

SUMMARY AND CONCLUSIONS

Humectants employed in foods may have different biological effects as described above. Considerable more fundamental as well as applied research is required. Attention should be given to methods that may increase the antimicrobial properties of humectants. An obvious avenue open for research is to explore how pH and temperature control the antimicrobial properties of humectants with both Gram-positive and Gram-negative organisms.

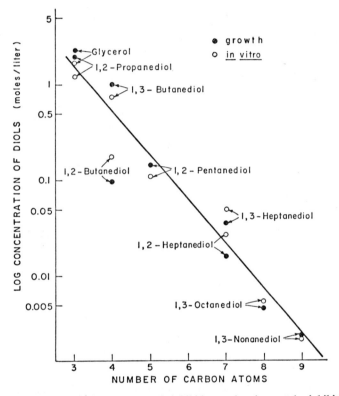

FIG. 9. Relationship between growth inhibition and serine uptake inhibition *in vitro*. 50% inhibitory concentration (inhibition index 0·5) *v*. chain length of diols.

A recent example of the importance of temperature on the bactericidal action of fatty acids on *E. coli* is to be found in the report by Fay and Farias.[25] 'Cold shocked' bacteria were observed to be more sensitive to fatty acids. The application of chilling to improve the bactericidal action of fatty acids in foods is proposed and discussed.

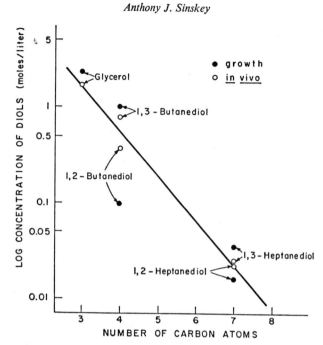

Fig. 10. Relationship between growth inhibition and serine uptake inhibition *in vivo*. 50% inhibitory concentration (inhibition index 0·5) *v.* chain length of diols.

ACKNOWLEDGEMENTS

This research was supported part by Research Grant No. FD-00149 and FD-00530 from the Food and Drug Administration, USPHS and by a grant (NIH 5 PO/ESO D 597) from the NIH.

The research on the antimicrobial properties of diols was obtained by M. Akedo, a Ph.D. candidate at MIT. Discussions with Dr Gomez of MIT are also appreciated.

REFERENCES

1. Karel, M. (1976). 'Technology and application of new intermediate moisture foods', this volume, p. 4.
2. Scott, W. J. (1957). *Adv. Fd. Res.*, **7**, p. 83.

3. Christian, J. H. B. (1963). 'Water activity and growth of microorganisms', in: *Recent Advances in Food Science*, ed. J. Hawthorn and J. M. Leitch, Butterworths, London, Vol. 3, p. 248.
4. Mossel, D. A. A. and Ingram, M. (1955). *J. Appl. Bact.*, **18**, p. 232.
5. Mossel, D. A. A. (1975). 'Water and Microorganisms in Foods—a Synthesis', in: *Water Relations of Foods*, ed. R. B. Duckworth, Academic Press, London, p. 347.
6. Leistner, L. and Rödel, W. (1975). 'The significance of water activity for microorganisms', in: *Water Relations of Foods*, ed. R. B. Duckworth, Academic Press, London, p. 309.
7. Kushner, D. J. (1971). 'Influence of solutes and ions on microorganisms', in: *Inhibition and Destruction of the Microbial Cell*, ed. W. B. Hugo, Academic Press, London.
8. Troller, J. A. (1973). *J. Milk Food Technol.*, **36**, p. 276.
9. Baird-Parker, A. C. and Freame, B. (1967). *J. Appl. Bact.*, **30**, p. 420.
10. Calhoun, C. L. and Frazier, W. C. (1966). *Appl. Microbiol.*, **14**, p. 416.
11. Marshall, B. J., Ohye, D. F. and Christian, J. H. B. (1971). *Appl. Microbiol.*, **21**, p. 363.
12. Hollis, F., Kaplow, M., Klose, R. and Halik, J. (1968). 'Parameters of moisture content for stabilization of food products', Tech. Report 69-26-F2, Natick, US Army Natick Lab.
13. Hollis, F., Kaplow, M., Halik, J. and Nordstrom, H. (1969). 'Parameters of moisture content for stabilization of food products (Phase II)', Tech. Report. 70-12-FL. Natick, US Army Natick Lab.
14. Sahoo, B. N. (1971). Ph.D. Thesis. University of Missouri, Columbia, Missouri.
15. Chordash, R. A. and Potter, N. N. (1972). *J. Milk Fd Technol.*, **35**, p. 395.
16. Collins, J. L., Chen, C. C., Park, H. R., Mundt, J. D., McCarthy, I. E. and Johnston, M. R. (1972). *J. Food Sci.*, **37**, p. 160.
17. Labuza, T. P., Cassil, S. and Sinskey, A. J. (1972). *J. Food Sci.*, **37**, p. 160.
18. Plitman, M., Park, Y., Gomez, R. and Sinskey, A. J. (1973). *J. Food Sci.*, **38**, p. 1004.
19. Haas, G. J., Bennett, D., Herman, E. B. and Collette, D. (1975). *Food Product Dev.*, **9**, p. 86.
20. Robertson, O. H., Appel, E. M., Puck, T. T., Lemon, H. M. and Ritter, M. H. (1948). *J. Inf. Dis.*, **83**, p. 124.
21. Olitzky, J. and Mattyl, K. G. (1967). *Appl. Microbiol.*, **15**, p. 205.
22. Labuza, T. P. (1975). 'Storage stability and improvement of intermediate moisture foods', Final Report on Contract NAS9-12560. Phase III with the National Aeronautics and Space Administration, Houston. Published by University of Minnesota, St Paul, Minnesota.
23. Freese, E., Sheu, C. W. and Galliers, E. (1973). *Nature*, **241**, p. 321.
24. Frankenfeld, J. W., Karel, M., Labuza, T. P. and Sinskey, A. J. (1974). US Patent 3,806,615.
25. Fay, J. P. and Farias, R. N. (1976). *Applied and Environ. Microbiol.*, **31**, p. 153.

DISCUSSION

Measures: Are you saying that you think the inhibition of amino-acid transport is responsible for the inhibition of growth, or that something else is the cause?

Sinskey: What I think happens is that these lipophilic agents go into the membrane, and they uncouple the ability of the membrane to energise and to carry things across. It is interesting, too, that what this system represents is a system to which a cell can adjust very readily, at low concentrations, but when it gets up to higher concentrations, the cell loses its battle for the control of its regulatory mechanism, and it dies.

Mann: While this is very interesting from a microbiological point of view, and perhaps even to petfood manufacturers, from the point of view of human foodstuffs I have great doubts about the value of using glycols. First, would they be acceptable from a toxicity point of view, and secondly, and more important, would they be acceptable from an organoleptic point of view?

Sinskey: For one thing, I am not a promoter of diols and glycols. I agree with you, they smell and taste terrible. I think the next logical step would be to take membrane materials from human cell systems, and try to find those humectant compounds that don't interact with the human membranes. The regulatory people now look at this as a system to screen food additives. So for human foods, maybe the glycol itself would not be important, but I think the concept is very important.

Leistner: How do the desorption and adsorption processes compare as far as costs are concerned in the preparation of intermediate moisture foods, and for which products is the adsorption process economically feasible?

Sinskey: I'm afraid I have no idea. I don't think it's very easy. I'm not enough of a processor or a technologist to be able to give you an answer. I could refer you to a paper in Food Product Development, 1975, where it is shown that one can have a much higher water content at a given water activity, and describes the processes concerned.

Karel: I don't think that an adsorption process would be nearly as economical as a blending process. But I think the difference in the behaviour of the adsorption and desorption hysteresis loops may be more important in setting reference values. Many people have performed experiments in adsorption, because it's easy to do it this way, but actually in practice we deal with desorption. The adsorptive approach may be more important as a way of knowing what to expect than as a design for a process.

I am very interested in this particular subject because I have prepared a paper on protein lipid interactions which I have to present in May. Professor Sinskey—since you have worked with vesicles, I suggest that it would be interesting to take a look at whether the compounds which modify membrane permeability act on the inside or the outside of the membrane, because there is now evidence of asymmetry both in proteins and in phospholipids. What one would want to know is—are the compounds that are getting into the cell the ones that are doing the most damage?

Sinskey: Another comment I didn't have time to make was that we have done these experiments also with esters of these diols and the results show that the ester becomes more effective as you increase the acid group. If you put the ester on both the OH groups for all practical purposes it loses biological effect.

I personally think that, in microbiology anyway, the future fundamental mechanistic research is going to come out of an understanding of how the membrane behaves in this type of system.

Barker: It seems that as the compounds you have mentioned become more lipid soluble, they become more effective as antimicrobics.

Sinskey: That's possibly the case; I don't show any data on lipid solubility. If you calculate the partition coefficient in numbers, you will find that it relates very nicely to the inhibition index, until these longer chain compounds invert and form micelles, and their effectiveness then decreases. You have to understand that for butane diol and most of the experimental compounds that we obtain there is no solubility data provided in the literature.

Barker: What I am trying to do, as a food manufacturer, is to translate what you have told us into food terms. Some of these compounds look to be very effective, but perhaps some of their effectiveness may be lost in food with, say, 10% fat.

Karel: Professor Sinskey is a co-inventor of a patent we have, and some of the work we did was in fact done in foods. So at least there is a level in such things as a pork slurry, and a pork-based baby food, where this doesn't happen.

Sinskey: One thing that might be pointed out is the fact that the anti-microbial activity of butane diol was first observed when Professor Miller of MIT was feeding rats. The diet of control animals was getting mouldy and the other diet, with butane diol, wasn't. That's actually how this study evolved.

19

Interactions of Micro-organisms with the Environment of Intermediate Moisture Foods

J. C. MEASURES and G. W. GOULD

Unilever Research Laboratory,
Colworth House, Sharnbrook, Bedfordshire, England

ABSTRACT

The concept of water activity has come into common use in microbiology since 1957 when Scott, in his excellent review, pointed out its advantages in relating the general effects of several commonly used food preservation techniques and processes on microbial growth and survival. Unfortunately the term is currently used rather more loosely than either it was used by Scott or its definition warrants. Though micro-organisms evidently do detect and react to a low water activity in their environment that is to say in biological terms a low local concentration of free water molecules, other changed properties in a low water activity environment are often just as important.

An obvious example of such a changed local environment is the increased number of molecules of a specific solute that may be present. Thus, in a 1 M solution of a non-ionic solute, one in every 54 molecules is a solute molecule, and in solutions of ionic solutes there will be even more. This number should be compared to the concentration of nutrient molecules that biological systems have evolved to react to, which are often a few micromolar, or about 100 000 times more disperse. One must consider also the effects of such solute concentrations on processes which are occurring at cell surfaces, such as transport phenomena, which are necessarily exposed to the environment. Effects on both vegetative growth and spore generation are likely to be at least partially due to specific solute effects. A further example is the effect of osmotic stress which may often, but not always, be related to water activity. In some cases one can see specific adaptive mechanisms, for example in vegetative micro-organisms, and in others only passive results, for example in altered heat resistance of vegetative micro-organisms. There are effects which are not strictly related to water activity at all. For example, the non-equilibrium or hysteresis effect described mainly by Labuza's group, in which water content seems to be important.

Finally there are effects due to water activity per se, but these are much less defined. Thus, some moulds tend to be more tolerant of low water activity, irrespective of solute, than bacteria. And spore heat resistance, in the absence of any environmental solutes, can be shown to be dependent on water activity alone when spores are equilibrated in atmospheres of differing equilibrium relative humidity.

Although water activity is a convenient term for microbiologists to employ because it can be easily measured, it is misguided and some-times misleading to assume that it is also necessarily what micro-organisms react to or recognise.

INTRODUCTION

In seeking a reason for the effectiveness of many traditional preserva-tion systems, attention has been focused on the concept of water activity to any great extent only since 1957 when Scott's excellent review was published.[1] Prior to this date such factors as drying, salting and sugaring were largely regarded as having separate and unrelated effects on the growth of micro-organisms.

Historically, sun drying of fruits and strips of meat was probably the earliest use of lowered a_w as a preservation aid, although salting was known to the Ancient Greeks. The most frequently quoted example of salting is that of meat on sailing ships, while sugaring was later used for fruit. After the discovery of micro-organisms, the effects of salt and sugar on microbial growth was found to correlate well with the use of these compounds to preserve foods. Probably the first hint of the general underlying concept was the conclusion by Rockwell and Ebertz[2] that solutes like salt and sugar dehydrate any biological material with which they come into contact. And later, the water requirements of microbial cells and the effects of relative humidity on spoilage were considered as parts of general treatises on preservation.[3-6] It is not unfair however to credit Scott[1] as the first reviewer who stressed the importance of water relations and introduced the concept of water activity to micro-biologists.

Scott was most particular and exact in his review in the way he described the use and applications of water activity to food preservation, and it is only more recently that various inconsistencies and irregularities have been recognised. It is hoped that in this review the reasons for some of the inconsistencies will become clear. It is reasonable to begin by asking how a micro-organism recognises that its environment has a low water activity. What is the factor a micro-organism 'sees'?

SOLUTE CONCENTRATION AS AN EFFECTER

First of all, the most studied effects of water activity in microbiology, with the notable exception of some spore heat resistance studies which we shall return to later, are concerned with increased concentration of solutes in the environment of the microbial cell. It is worth reminding ourselves at this point that a major effect of drying as a food process is to increase the concentration of solutes already dissolved in the aqueous phase. A food almost always includes various low molecular weight dissolved solutes and concentration of these has much the same effect as the addition of large amounts of exogenous solute. Therefore determination of growth limits, for example, by equilibration methods[7] is not intrinsically better than by addition of a *range* of solutes.

Most microbial cells react to concentrations of nutrients as low as micromolar, in that transport of such nutrients into the cell occurs at these concentrations. And because most transport is an active process, and exhibits saturation kinetics, concentrations of such nutrients of about 100 micromolar and above will saturate the system. For this reason even the addition of large amounts of a compound like proline, which at lower concentration aids growth of many bacterial species at lowered water activity, can inhibit growth.

Further, since microbial transport systems in general show kinetics with Michaelis constants (*i.e.* concentration of substrate giving half maximal rate) between 0·1 and 100 micromolar, the ratio of transport substrate molecules to solvent water molecules is usually between 1–5·5 × 10^8 and 1–5·5 × 10^5. Comparing this to the ratio of solute molecules to solvent molecules in a one molar solution shows the magnitude of the difference between what the cell has evolved to recognise and what is imposed on it. A molar solution of a non-ionic solute like sucrose contains one sucrose molecule for every 54·5 water molecules. In other words the cell encounters at least 10 000 molecules of sucrose for each desirable substrate molecule. One molar sucrose will, in fact, lower the water activity only to about 0·98, which is hardly even close to the top of the intermediate moisture food range. Obviously, as the water activity is lowered further the magnitude of the difference becomes greater. What is most important to remember is that, whatever steps the microbial cell takes to counteract an alteration in its water activity, any process, enzyme activity, etc., occurring on the outside surface of the microbial cell will be exposed to this huge increase in numbers of solute molecules. The most obvious examples are the transport processes, and one of the remarkable features of microbial growth at low water activity is that transport of substrate into the cell continues in the presence of, for example, sodium chloride concentrations which would completely inhibit enzymic processes within the cell were these to be exposed to the solute.

EFFECTS OF SOLUTE TYPE ON MICROBIAL GROWTH

Although Scott[1] considered that water activity effects were independent of solute, it has since been shown many times that the nature of the solute molecule is most important in determining the effects of a given water activity on microbial growth. For instance Scott[8] had compared the growth of 14 food-poisoning strains of *Staphylococcus aureus*, on media in which a_w was adjusted by adding sugar or salts, or in media prepared from different concentrations of dried soup, milk or meat. In general, the limiting a_w for growth was independent of the solute used but some specific effects of solutes were noted on growth rate and lag period. The limiting a_w for growth after 30 days was 0·88 in nutrient broth adjusted with sucrose or with glucose plus a mixture of salts. Some strains grew down to a_w 0·86 in media adjusted with salt alone or with sucrose plus salts. Scott[1] himself reported that growth rates of *Aspergillus amstelodami* were greater in sucrose and glucose than in magnesium chloride, sodium chloride or glycerol at the same a_w. Onishi[9] found that osmotolerant yeasts, particularly those isolated from high-sugar sources, could grow at lower a_w when sucrose or glucose was used as regulator than when sodium chloride was used.

Viability studies may show great differences between solutes. Thus Onishi[10] found that cells of *Saccharomyces rouxii* grown in the presence of 18% NaCl, but not those grown in the presence of 50% glucose, lost K^+ rapidly when washed with water. Non-growing cells suspended in 18% NaCl in buffer died rapidly unless glucose, a source of energy, was present. Onishi interpreted these results to show that NaCl had a specific effect on cell permeability.

Similarly, Anand and Brown[11] found that yeasts were more tolerant of low a_w in the presence of sugars than in polyethylene glycol (average molecular weight 200). Kang *et al.*[12] found that glycerol allowed germination and growth of *Clostridium welchii* spores at lower a_w than sucrose or NaCl, while with the same organisms, Strong *et al.*[13] found that NaCl and KCl gave higher a_w limits than glucose. An extensive study by Marshall *et al.*[14] of a large variety of bacteria showed that at similar a_w levels, glycerol was more inhibitory than sodium chloride to relatively salt-tolerant bacteria (*e.g.* Micrococcaceae and *Vibrio metchnickoovii*), but less inhibitory than sodium chloride to salt-sensitive species (*e.g.* most spore-formers, Enterobacteriaceae and *Pseudomonas fluorescens*).

In Table 1 are presented the growth limits of various organisms in some commonly used solutes. It is evident that wide variation occurs; notably between sodium chloride and glycerol. Equilibration is equivalent to the effects of high concentrations of a number of low molecular weight solutes such as amino acids, sugars and nucleotides, and this also gives a different value.

In general the solutes can be divided into two groups; those to which cells are impermeable in large amounts, or more strictly whose uptake exhibits saturation kinetics, which usually includes most salts and sugars, and those which are able to pass freely across the membrane and whose concentration distribution between the inside and the outside of the cell is passively determined, such as glycerol and urea. But even these classifications vary from organism to organism. Thus yeasts may be permeable to some sugars[15] and sometimes impermeable to glycerol.[16] The dependency of the effects of polyethylene glycol on molecular weight also varies between organisms, apparently in relation to the maximum molecular size which can enter the cell.[17]

TABLE 1

Water activity limits for growth of micro-organisms

| Organism | Solute | | | | Ref. |
	NaCl	Glucose	Glycerol	Equilibration[a]	
Pseudomonas fluorescens	0·970	0·970	0·950	—	24
Escherichia coli	0·950	—	0·935	0·932	14
Salmonella newport	0·950	—	0·935	—	14
Clostridium botulinum A	0·945	—	0·930	—	14
Bacillus cereus	0·925	—	0·920	—	14
Staphylococcus aureus	0·830	—	0·890	0·860	14, 25, 26
Saccharomyces cerevisiae	0·940	0·919	—	0·895	7, 9
Saccharomyces rouxii	0·860	0·845[b]	—	0·902	7, 9
Aspergillus flavus	—	—	—	0·780	27
Aspergillus chevalieri	—	—	—	0·710	27
Aspergillus amstelodami	—	—	—	0·710	1
Aspergillus echinulatus	—	—	—	0·640	28
Monascus bisporus	—	—	—	0·605	1, 29

[a] Growth on agar of standard media equilibrated over salt solutions in a desiccator.

[b] One strain reported to grow at a_w 0·62 in fructose syrup.[30]

It can now be asked to what extent it is possible to explain the limit on growth determined by low water activity; or how different is the response of the cell to what one would anticipate judged on the effect of low water activity on isolated cell processes? Thus Fig. 1 shows the effects of sodium chloride on the respiration of *Bacillus subtilis*, on the enzyme aldolase from the same species in cell-free extract, and on growth. Figure 2 shows a similar comparison for glycerol. It is clear that whereas sodium chloride inhibits individual cell processes *in vitro* more than it does growth, glycerol has the opposite property. In neither case is it immediately clear what determines the growth limit. An examination of a number of isolated metabolic processes shows that there is no correlation between the inhibition of growth and any one key process. In Fig. 2 it appears that the closest correlation is between inhibition of the enzyme aldolase and growth of *Bacillus subtilis*. Although for this species the correlation is quite good, for other species it is not. The enzyme is inhibited to much the same extent by glycerol for all species tested. However, the inhibition of growth varies widely between species.

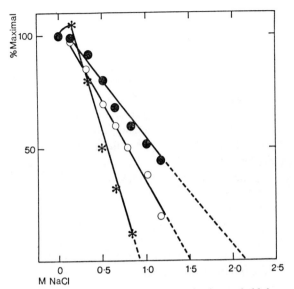

FIG. 1. Effect of sodium chloride on growth, respiration and aldolase activity of *Bacillus subtilis.* ●, growth; ○, aldolase;, * respiration.

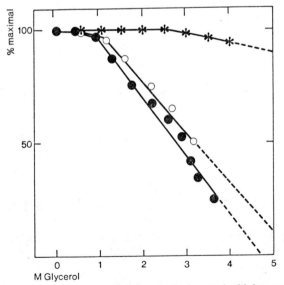

FIG. 2. Effect of glycerol on growth, respiration and aldolase activity of *Bacillus subtilis.* ●, growth; ○, aldolase; *, respiration.

Perhaps the clearest evidence that micro-organisms 'see' different environments with different solutes, is shown by the different metabolic changes that are induced. Thus intracellular accumulation of K^+ ions occurs in halophilic bacteria,[18] of polyols in osmophilic yeasts[16] and of amino acids in non-halophilic bacteria[19] during growth in solutes to which the cell is impermeable. Further, changes in membrane lipid composition have been observed for one species under these conditions.[20] No evidence has been found for any of these biochemical changes during growth in solutes to which the cell is permeable, such as glycerol. Indeed the accumulation of amino acids in non-halophilic bacteria may well be controlled by the imposition of an osmotic stress, which removes water from the cell and increases the effective K^+ ion concentration.[19] No such mechanism is possible with a solute which passes freely into the cell.

The main purpose of such adaptive mechanisms seems to be the maintenance of the intracellular water content at a relatively constant level, which enables cellular metabolism to proceed despite the externally adverse conditions.

What then inhibits microbial growth at lowered water activities? The possibilities include:

(1) The accumulated solute itself is inhibitory at high concentrations.
(2) The external solute is imperfectly excluded, and is inhibitory.
(3) The energy required to maintain the adapted state may be more than the cell can provide.
(4) Metabolic processes at the surface, unprotected by adaptation, may be inhibited.

All of these may operate to varying degrees in different circumstances.

EFFECTS OF SORPTION HYSTERESIS

Among effects on microbial growth and survival which may occur in intermediate moisture foods, in addition to those due to water activity itself, one of the most remarkable recently has been that due to sorption hysteresis. However, without detracting from the great usefulness of this effect, it serves to illustrate one more hazard in the use of the water activity concept to describe a situation in which it does not really apply.

It was shown that the method of attaining a given water activity made a substantial difference to the subsequent growth of micro-organisms.[21-23]

For example, a pork product formed by addition of solutes, or by partial dehydration (*i.e.* on the desorption loop of the hysteresis curve) allowed growth of *Staphylococcus aureus* at a_w 0·880, while a product formed by total dehydration and subsequent rehydration (*i.e.* adsorption loop of the curve), showed a decrease in viable count at the same a_w.[22] The total water content was lower in the adsorption samples, and the authors concluded that this was the important controlling parameter. The problem with these results is that in both cases a water activity is quoted for the samples. It is evident that both loops of the curve *cannot* be at equilibrium, and hence water activity, which is only applicable at equilibrium cannot be used. The authors measure relative humidity to obtain an estimate of water activity and not *equilibrium* relative humidity. That said, the microbiological results obtained are valid. Growth does depend in these non-equilibrium systems on water content or on the method of preparation. If products can be created with non-equilibrium water distribution, and the rate of equilibration made slow, then there may be new preservation opportunities. It would be unfortunate if the opportunities were to be missed simply because water activity does not explain results obtained in situations in which it is used, but does not really apply.

EFFECTS OF SOLUTES ON GERMINATION OF BACTERIAL SPORES

The initiation of germination of bacterial spores involves a number of changes that occur in rapid sequence, *i.e.* loss of heat resistance, loss of refractility, leakage of calcium and dipicolinic acid, increase in volume due to imbibition of water and increase in metabolic activity. Spores may undergo these changes in environments that are unsuitable for subsequent outgrowth and for growth of vegetative cells, and such environments include those with lowered water activities. Consequently, it is generally true to say that germination of spores of a particular organism will occur (though perhaps at a much reduced rate) at a_w values below those that will arrest growth of the vegetative cells.[31,32]

In intermediate moisture foods at particular water activities one might therefore expect the heat resistant spore count to slowly fall as spores germinate and then, being unable to grow, slowly die.

The rate at which spores germinate will depend to some extent on the a_w, but much more so on the nature of the solute. In general, three classes of solute may be recognised that have quantitatively very different effects.[33] First, the ionic solutes, salts like NaCl, KCl, $MgCl_2$ and $CaCl_2$, are generally the most inhibitory, and the salts of multivalent cations are more inhibitory than those of monovalent ones. Second, the non-ionic solutes that are unable to easily permeate cell membranes, like sucrose and glucose, are less inhibitory than the salts. Third, the non-ionic solutes that can rapidly permeate cell membranes, like glycerol, dimethyl sulphoxide and urea, are only weakly inhibitory.

The effectiveness of these classes of solutes can differ very greatly so that, for example, germination of *B. cereus* spores was inhibited at a_w 0·85 by glycerol, 0·90 by dimethyl sulphoxide, 0·95 by NaCl[33] and 0·98 by $CaCl_2$.[34] Germination of *Cl. botulinum* spores at pH 7·0 was hardly inhibited at a_w 0·89 by glycerol but was strongly inhibited at a_w 0·93 by NaCl.[31]

These studies of germination in the presence of single solutes show differences that cannot be explained in terms of water activity alone. Even more revealing are experiments carried out in our laboratory in which the effects of mixed solutes were tested. In general any effects of mixed solutes on *vegetative growth* are completely additive. However, in the case of spore germination this is not necessarily the case. Figure 3 shows the extent of germination of *B. subtilis* after 30 min as a percentage of the control, in the presence of a range of sodium chloride concentrations, and in the presence or absence of glycerol. It is clear that the presence of both glycerol and sodium chloride is antagonistic in some combinations. Thus, in the presence of 3·2M glycerol alone germination is 32% of control, but in the presence of 3·2M glycerol plus 0·2M sodium chloride, which has a lower water activity, germination is 40% of control. This is more remarkable when one considers that 0·2M sodium chloride alone causes 35% inhibition of germination. The antagonism is interesting because it occurs not only with glycerol, which is classically used as a

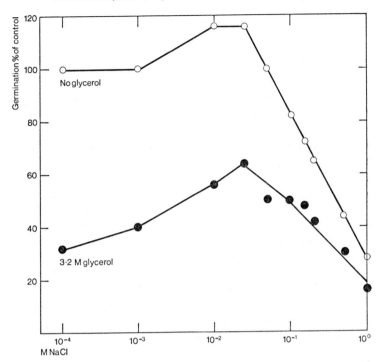

FIG. 3.   Germination of spores of *Bacillus subtilis*. Effect of sodium chloride in the presence and absence of glycerol. The figure shows the amount of germination after 30 min incubation as a percentage of that occurring in salt and glycerol-free controls.

humectant, but also with other glycols some of which are tradition-ally regarded as bactericides, for example ethane diol, trimethylene glycol, 1,6 hexane-diol.[35] In these cases the amounts of glycol required to inhibit germination may only be a few millimoles, but the inhibition is still antagonised by sodium chloride. The role of depressed water activity in this inhibition is therefore very unclear even with a compound such as glycerol which probably exhibits antimicrobial properties most nearly approximated to those expected to a substance with purely humectant properties.

HEAT RESISTANCE OF SPORES

It is generally agreed that the heat resistance of bacterial spores depends, at least partly, upon maintenance of a low concentration of water in the central protoplast of the cell. It has been proposed that the low water content is brought about by compressive contraction of the surrounding cortex[36] or, alternatively, by expansion of material within the cortex[37] during spore formation. Gould and Dring[38] presented evidence that supported the latter hypothesis and suggested that it was the osmotic activity of electronegative peptido-glycan in the cortex, and positively charged counterions associated with it, that was responsible for the expansion. The central protoplast was envisaged as being osmotically dehydrated by, and in osmotic equilibrium with, the surrounding cortex. It is, therefore, not surprising that procedures capable of changing the osmotic environ-ment of spores also influence their heat resistance.

Reduction in water activity usually causes an increase in the heat resistance of bacterial spores, but the magnitude of the increase is very dependent on the means by which a_w is reduced.

Table 2 summarises data that illustrate the principal trends that have been reported. Equilibration of spores in atmospheres at different equilibrium relative humidities may result in very great increases in heat resistance, *i.e.* even about 10^5-fold (*Cl. botulinum* type E in Table 2). This effect is much greater with spores that are normally relatively heat-sensitive at a_w values near 1·0 (*e.g. Cl. botulinum* type E) than with spores that are amongst the most heat resistant at a_w values near 1·0 (*e.g. B. stearothermophilus*,[39] Table 2). Heat resistance in such equilibrated systems is generally maximal at a_w values near 0·3 whether the spores are normal, acid-treated ('H-form') or treated with calcium acetate ('Ca-form') as described by Alderton and Snell.[40]

Reduction of a_w by addition of solutes to suspensions of spores also tends to increase the heat resistance of spores and these systems more closely represent the situation in intermediate moisture foods than do the solute-free systems referred to above. The increases in heat resistance, however, seldom match the large increases in resistance that occur in the absence of added solutes. For example, an examina-tion of the data in Table 2 shows that, in the intermediate moisture food range from about a_w 0·7 to 0·9, and in the presence of commonly used food humectants, increases in heat resistance by factors of more than about ten-fold are uncommon, even though the extent of resistance will vary with the nature of the organism and the solute and even with the history of the spores (*e.g.* whether they were wet or dry prior to suspension in the solutions and heating[41]).

TABLE 2

Increased heat resistance of bacterial spores at low water activities

Procedure used to lower a_w	Organism	Heat resistance of spores at the indicated a_w values (figures listed are D-values[a] relative to those at a_w approx. 1·0)								Ref.
		0·98	0·95	0·9	0·8	0·7	0·5	0·3	0	
Equilibration in the absence of added solutes	B.stearothermophilus			3·0	6·2	3·5	17·5	22·5	0·6	39
	B.megaterium			13·3	67	2 700	1 340	270	100	39
	Cl.botulinum type E			400	1 000	8 000	100 000	10 000		39
Glycerol	B.subtilis			1·0					0·08	41
	B.subtilis		1·1	6·5	2·1	66	1·5	0·5	3·7	45
Glucose	B.subtilis		0·4	0·25	2·0					45
	B.coagulans		1·3	0·6	2·2					46
Sucrose	B.cereus T	1·7	4·0			5·5	19	71		42
	B.coagulans		2·4							46
	B.stearothermophilus	0·4	0·3	0·3						47
NaCl	B.subtilis		0·65		0·85	1·4				45
	B.subtilis v. niger	1·0	0·9	1·2						47
	B.coagulans		0·62							46
LiCl	B.subtilis		0·5	0·46	0·36		1·5	3·9	4·6	45

[a] Heat resistance of all species was assumed to be unity at approx. 1·0. A z value of 10°C was used to compare values obtained at different temperatures.

Much greater increases in heat resistance are likely to occur to germinated spores and to vegetative cells in intermediate moisture foods than to spores. Protection against inactivation by heat seems to result (as in the dormant spore) from withdrawal of water from the cell's protoplast by osmosis. Consequently, cells are most effectively protected by solutes like sucrose which cannot readily permeate the cell membrane, whereas protection by permeant solutes like glycerol is weak because they set up no osmotic gradient and are therefore relatively ineffective in dehydrating the protoplast. For example, the heat resistance of just-germinated spores of *B. cereus* was increased more than 30 000-fold by suspension in just 1·5M sucrose (but not glycerol),[42] *i.e.* at a_w approximately 0·98. During outgrowth, as the cell's content of low molecular weight 'pool' components increased, the protection afforded by sucrose decreased greatly, and experiments with *B. subtilis* vegetative cells in which pools had been artificially raised or depleted suggested that (as one might expect) sucrose afforded most protection to pool-depleted cells, *i.e.* to those cells that it would most effectively dehydrate by osmosis.[43]

The extent of protection of vegetative cells in intermediate moisture foods may not allow them to exceed the heat resistance of spores; however, suspension in solutions of sucrose and other impermeant solutes may raise the heat resistance of some vegetative cells as much as nearly 1000-fold (*e.g. Salmonella senftenberg*[44] and *see* Corry, this volume).

CONCLUSIONS

The effect of the environment within an intermediate moisture food on the growth of particular micro-organisms will depend largely on the effectiveness of the adaptation mechanisms possessed by those micro-organisms. It is likely that these mechanisms have evolved principally in response to osmotic stress, and they operate in such a way that the cell maintains a high water content over wide ranges of environmental osmolality. It is useful, for the food technologist, that the osmolality in the aqueous phase of intermediate foods generally correlates with the measured a_w. However, there are sufficient exceptions and specific effects, dependent upon permeability of cells to different solutes, etc., to indicate caution in the too-liberal use of

a_w as a meaningful parameter in food preservation. At the same time, it is unfortunately not yet possible to suggest a more meaningful and yet readily usable parameter.

As with growth, the modification of heat resistance of spores, germinated spores and vegetative cells at the a_w values typical of intermediate moisture foods, probably results largely from osmotic dehydration of the cells. These effects again, therefore, may generally correlate with the measured a_w, but depend more specifically on the solute permeability of the microbial cells and on other chemical and physical properties of the solute molecules.

REFERENCES

1. Scott, W. J. (1957). *Adv. Food Res.*, **7**, p. 83.
2. Rockwell, G. E. and Ebertz, E. G. (1924). *J. Infect. Dis.*, **35**, p. 573.
3. Mossel, D. A. A. and Westerdijk, J. (1949). *Leeuwenhoek ned. Tijdschr.*, **15**, p. 190.
4. Schelhorn, M. von (1951). *Adv. Food Res.*, **3**, p. 429.
5. Mossel, D. A. A. and Ingram, M. (1955). *J. Appl. Microbiol.*, **18**, p. 232.
6. Clayson, D. H. F. (1955). *J. Sci. Food Agric.*, **6**, p. 565.
7. Burcik, E. (1950). *Arch. Mikrobiol.*, **15**, p. 203.
8. Scott, W. J. (1953). *Aust. J. Biol. Sci.*, **6**, p. 549.
9. Onishi, N. (1957). *Bull. Agric. Chem. Soc., Japan*, **21**, p. 137.
10. Onishi, N. (1963). *Adv. Food Res.*, **12**, p. 53.
11. Anand, J. C. and Brown, A. D. (1968). *J. Gen. Microbiol.*, **52**, p. 205.
12. Kang, C. K., Woodburn, M., Pagenkopf, A. and Cheney, R. (1969). *Applied Microbiol.*, **18**, p. 798.
13. Strong, D. H., Foster, E. F. and Duncan, C. L. (1970). *Appl. Microbiol.*, **19**, p. 980.
14. Marshall, B. J., Ohye, D. F. and Christian, J. H. B. (1971). *Appl. Microbiol.*, **21**, p. 363.
15. Conway, E. J. and Downey, M. (1950). *Biochem. J.*, **47**, p. 347.
16. Brown, A. D. (1974). *J. Bacteriol.*, **118**, p. 769.
17. Cox, C. S. (1966). *J. Gen. Microbiol.*, **43**, p. 303.
18. Christian, J. H. B. and Waltho, J. A. (1961). *J. Gen. Microbiol.*, **25**, p. 97.
19. Measures, J. C. (1975). *Nature*, **257**, p. 398.
20. Kanemasa, Y., Yoshioka, T. and Hayashi, H. (1972). *Biochim. Biophys. Acta*, **280**, p. 444.
21. Labuza, T. P., Cassil, S. and Sinskey, A. J. (1972). *J. Food Sci.*, **37**, p. 160.
22. Plitman, M., Park, Y., Gomez, R. and Sinskey, A. J. (1973). *J. Food Sci.*, **38**, p. 1004.
23. Acott, K. M. and Labuza, T. P. (1975). *J. Food Technol.*, **10**, p. 603.

24. Limsong, S. and Frazier, W. C. (1966). *Appl. Microbiol.*, **14,** p. 899.
25. Tatini, S. R. (1973). *J. Milk Food Technol.*, **36,** p. 559.
26. Clayson, D. H. F. and Blood, R. M. (1957). *J. Sci. Food Agric.*, **8,** p. 404.
27. Ayerst, G. (1969). *J. Stored Prod. Res.*, **5,** p. 127.
28. Snow, D. (1949). *Annals. Appl. Biol.*, **31,** p. 102.
29. Pitt, J. I. and Christian, J. H. B. (1968). *Appl. Micribiol.*, **16,** p. 1853.
30. Schelhorn, M. von (1950). *Z. Lebenzm.-untersuch. u. Forsch.*, **91,** p. 117.
31. Baird-Parker, A. C. and Freame, B. (1967). *J. Appl. Bact.*, **30,** p. 420.
32. Jakobsen, M., Filtenborg, D. and Bramsnaes, F. (1972). *Lebensmit.-w. Technol.*, **5,** p. 159.
33. Jakobsen, M. and Murrell, W. G. (1976). In: *Spore Research* 1976, ed. A. N. Barker, J. Wolf, D. J. Ellar, G. J. Dring and G. W. Gould, Academic Press, London, in press.
34. Hashimoto, T., Frieben, W. R. and Conti, S. F. (1969). *J. Bact.*, **100,** p. 1385.
35. Robertson, O. H., Appel, E. M., Puck, T. T., Lemon, H. M. and Ritter, M. H. (1948). *J. Infect. Dis.*, **83,** p. 124.
36. Lewis, J. C., Snell, N. S. and Burr, H. K. (1960). *Science N.Y.*, **132,** p. 544.
37. Alderton, G. and Snell, N. (1963). *Biochem. Biophys. Res. Commun.*, **10,** p. 139.
38. Gould, G. W. and Dring, G. J. (1975). *Nature*, **258,** p. 402.
39. Murrell, W. G. and Scott, W. J. (1966). *J. Gen. Microbiol.*, **43,** p. 411.
40. Alderton, G. and Snell, N. (1970). *Appl. Microbiol.*, **19,** p. 565.
41. Kooiman, W. J. and Jacobs, R. P. W. M. (1976). In: *Spore Research* 1976, ed. A. N. Barker, J. Wolf, D. J. Ellar, G. J. Dring and G. W. Gould, Academic Press, London, in press.
42. Dring, G. J. and Gould, G. W. (1975). *Biochim. Biophys. Res. Commun.*, **66,** p. 202.
43. Gould, G. W. and Dring, G. J. (1976). In: *Spore Research* 1976, ed. A. N. Barker, J. Wolf, D. J. Ellar, G. J. Dring and G. W. Gould, Academic Press, London, in press.
44. Corry, J. E. L. (1974). *J. Appl. Bact.*, **37,** p. 31.
45. Harnulv, B. G. and Snygg, G. B. (1972). *J. Appl. Bact.*, **35,** p. 615.
46. Anderson, E. S., Esselen, W. B. Jr. and Fellers, C. R. (1949). *Fd. Res.*, **14,** p. 499.
47. Briggs, A. and Yazdany, S. (1970). *J. Appl. Bact.*, **33,** p. 621.

DISCUSSION

Sinskey: How is potassium activating these enzymes? Are you sure it is on the enzyme and not on the gene level?

Measures: Activation of the enzyme certainly occurs, and it occurs unidirectionally. I am not sure which way round it is, but I think it may be something to do with the dissociation of the enzyme where one form of the enzyme operates in one direction better than the other.

Gould: You mentioned that potassium may be the intracellular substance the increase in concentration of which stimulates the rise in amino-acid level during osmoregulation. What happens if you add large amounts of potassium exogenously? Is it possible to trick a cell into beginning to accumulate amino acids?

Measures: I have not tested the effect of adding excess potassium. The only thing I have done with potassium is to consider the effect of potassium chloride, in parallel experiments to sodium chloride, on growth rates. They follow one another down to about a_w 0·94, and then below that potassium is lethal to the cells. I am not quite sure what that means, but I suspect there is some kind of barrier that fails.

Karel: There has been quite a bit of work on the resistance of micro-organisms to other low water activity conditions and low temperatures. One of the theories is that there is a critical reduction in cell volume, at which the water activity and the temperature become lethal. Have you looked at any of the low-temperature resistant micro-organisms to see if they are producers of similar osmotic effects?

Measures: No, I haven't looked, but it wouldn't surprise me at all. Frost resistance in plants, certainly, is due to amino acids.

Sinskey: Have you tried to see how membrane vesicles would regulate in this type of situation?

Measures: I haven't thought really about transport or its kinetics at all. The kinetics of vesicles are a little strange. The vesicles prepared from cells grown during the absence of salt have a salt optimum of about 3 % for the uptake of proline. Adapted cells have an optimum for the uptake of proline 3 % above the salt concentration they were grown at. This is a sort of self-adaptive mechanism.

Sinskey: So the vesicle can tolerate transport.

Index